THEN
SINGS
MY SOUL

THEN
SINGS
MY SOUL

ROBERT J. MORGAN

THOMAS NELSON
Since 1798

NASHVILLE DALLAS MEXICO CITY RIO DE JANEIRO

Published in Nashville, Tennessee, by Thomas Nelson. Thomas Nelson is a registered trademark of Thomas Nelson, Inc.

Thomas Nelson, Inc., titles may be purchased in bulk for educational, business, fund-raising, or sales promotional use. For information, please e-mail SpecialMarkets@ThomasNelson.com.

ISBN 978-0-7852-3182-0 (SE)

Library of Congress Cataloging-in-Publication Data is available.

ISBN 0-7852-4939-7

Printed in the United States of America

10 11 12 13 14 LB 5 4 3 2

TO
Audrey Claire

Contents

EASTER

THANKSGIVING

PATRIOTIC

OTHER FAVORITES

INDICES

From Heaven Above to Earth I Come

Martin Luther, translated by Catherine Windworth

Attr. to Martin Luther

1. From heav'n a - bove to earth I come, to bear good news to ev - ery home; glad tid - ings of great joy I bring, Where - of I now will say and sing.

2. To you, this night, is born a Child Of Mar - y, chos - en moth - er mild; This ten - der Child of low - ly birth, Shall be the joy of all your earth.

3. 'Tis Christ our God, who far on high Had heard your sad and bit - ter cry; Him - self will your Sal - va - tion be, Him - self from sin will make you free.

4. These are the to - kens ye shall mark, The swad - dling clothes and man - ger dark; There shall ye find the young Child laid, By Whom the heav'ns and earth were made.

From Heaven Above to Earth I Come

1531

Then God blessed them, and God said to them, "Be fruitful and multiply; fill the earth and subdue it." Genesis 1:28

Martin Luther never expected to marry, for he had taken a vow of celibacy as an Augustinian monk. Even after discovering the great Reformation truths of *Scripture Alone, Faith Alone*, he still intended to keep his vow. As the Reformation picked up steam and other monks began to marry, he exclaimed, "Good heavens! They won't give me a wife."

It wasn't just monks who were renouncing their celibacy, however; it was nuns too. When Luther heard that a group of nuns from a nearby cloister wanted to escape their situation (which amounted to virtual captivity), he agreed to help them, though doing so was a serious violation of the law. Enlisting the aid of a local merchant named Leonard Kopp, Luther arranged for the nuns to be smuggled out in the empty barrels used to deliver herring to the nunnery. It was a fishy plan if ever there was one, but it worked.

Having liberated these women, Luther now felt responsible for placing them in homes. He managed to find husbands for all but one—Katharina Von Bora. Two years passed, and Luther was deeply troubled by his failure to find her a husband. She was now twenty-six years old, brilliant and effervescent, but still unclaimed.

In a visit to his parents, Luther, then forty-two, joked that he might have to marry Katharina himself. His dad heartily endorsed the idea, and, to make a long story short, the two were married on June 27, 1525.

By autumn, Katharina informed Martin that she was pregnant, and Luther cheerfully announced, "My Katharina is fulfilling Genesis 1:28."

"There's about to be born a child of a monk and a nun," he bragged to friends. Accordingly, little Hans was born on June 7, 1526.

Luther was devoted to his son, and five years later he wrote this Christmas carol for him. Luther called it "a Christmas child's song concerning the child Jesus," and it was sung each year during the Christmas Eve festivities at Luther's massive home—a former Augustinian monastery—on the upper end of Wittenberg's main street.

For more than five hundred years it has been one of Lutheranism's greatest carols, delighting children today just as it thrilled little Hans in the sixteenth century.

We Sing, Emmanuel, Thy Praise

Paul Gerhardt

Nikolaus Hermann

1. We sing, Em - man - u - el, Thy praise, Thou Prince of Life and Fount of grace, Thou Flow'r of heav'n and Star of morn, Thou Lord of lords, Thou vir - gin born. Hal - le - lu - jah!

2. For Thee, since first the world was made, So ma - ny hearts have watched and prayed; The pa - tri - archs' and proph - ets' throng For Thee have hoped and wait - ed long. Hal - le - lu - jah!

3. Now art Thou here, Thou ev - er blest! In low - ly man - ger dost Thou rest. Thou, mak - ing all things great, art small; So poor art Thou, yet cloth - est all. Hal - le - lu - jah!

4. But I, Thy ser - vant, Lord, to - day Con - fess my love and free - ly say, I love Thee tru - ly, but I would That I might love Thee as I should. Hal - le - lu - jah!

We Sing, Emmanuel, Thy Praise

1654

I will be glad and rejoice in You; I will sing praise to Your name, O Most High.
Psalm 9:2

Paul Gerhardt might be called the "Charles Wesley of Germany," for he was a prolific hymnist who gave Lutheranism some of its warmest hymns. Paul grew up in Grafenhaynichen, Germany, where his father was mayor. This village near Wittenberg was devastated by the Thirty Years' War, and Paul's childhood was marked by scenes of bloodshed and death. But he had a good mind and heart, and he enrolled at the University of Wittenberg at age twenty-one.

After graduation, Paul found a job in Berlin tutoring children. During this time, encouraged by Johann Crüger, choirmaster at Berlin's St. Nicholas Church, he began writing hymns. When Crüger published a hymnbook in 1648, Paul was delighted to find his hymns in it. Others were added to later editions. In all, Gerhardt wrote 123 hymns. His hymnody reflects the shift from the rugged theological hymns of Luther to the more subjective, devotional songs of German Pietistic revival. Best known are "Give to the Winds Your Fears," "Jesus, Thy Boundless Love to Me," and "O Sacred Head, Now Wounded" (which he translated).

Paul was ordained into the ministry at age forty-four and began preaching in and around Berlin. In 1651, he became chief pastor at Mittenwalde, just outside Berlin, and later he returned to Berlin to labor at St. Nicholas Church alongside his mentor, Johann Crüger.

At that point, however, Paul became embroiled in a conflict with the Elector Friedrich Wilhelm, who wanted Lutheran clergymen to sign an edict limiting their freedom of speech on theological matters. Refusing, Paul was deposed from his pulpit in February of 1666. He was even forbidden to lead private worship in his home. During this time, four of his five children died, and in 1668, his wife also passed away.

Late that year, 1668, Paul assumed the pastorate of the Lutheran church in Lübben an der Spree, where he ministered faithfully until his death on May 27, 1676. He was buried in the crypt beneath the altar of the church where he preached. Today the church is known locally as the "Paul Gerhardt Church," and a monument at the entrance reminds visitors of the church's famous pastor-poet.

This Christmas carol, "We Sing, Emmanuel, Thy Praise," has a hauntingly beautiful melody that seems to express the sorrows through which Gerhardt passed. But the words are full of praise, every verse ending in an exuberant "Hallelujah!"

Just like Paul Gerhardt's life.

While Shepherds Watched Their Flocks

Nahum Tate

George Frideric Handel

1. While shep - herds watched their flocks by night, All seat - ed on the ground, The an - gel of the Lord came down, And glo - ry shone a - round, And glo - ry shone a - round.

2. "Fear not!" said he, for might - y dread Had seized their trou - bled mind; "Glad ti - dings of great joy I bring To you and all man - kind, To you and all man - kind.

3. "To you in Da - vid's town this day Is born, of Da - vid's line, The Sav - ior, who is Christ the Lord, And this shall be the sign— And this shall be the sign:

4. "The heaven - ly Babe you there shall find To hu - man view dis - played, All mean - ly wrapt in swath - ing - bands And in a man - ger laid, And in a man - ger laid.

While Shepherds Watched Their Flocks

1700

He will feed His flock like a shepherd; He will gather the lambs with His arm, and carry them in His bosom, and gently lead those who are with young.
Isaiah 40:11

T his popular carol owes its endurance to two men with dark financial woes. The first, Nahum Tate, was born in Dublin in 1652 to a preacher who was literally named Faithful—Rev. Faithful Teate (original spelling). After attending Trinity College in Dublin, young Nahum migrated to London to be a writer. His success was slow in coming, but he dabbled with plays, adapted the prose of others, and eventually was named poet laureate in 1692 and appointed royal historiographer ten years later. Unfortunately, Nahum was intemperate and careless in handling money, and he lived in perpetual financial distress. He died in an institution for debtors in 1715.

His chief claim to fame was his collaboration with Nicholas Brady in compiling a hymnbook entitled *The New Version of the Psalms of David*, published in 1696. It was reissued in 1700 with a supplement in which this carol first appeared. The words to "While Shepherds Watched Their Flocks" represent a very literal paraphrase of Luke 2:8–14, making this one of our most biblically accurate Christmas carols.

The second man instrumental in the song's success was George Frideric Handel, composer of the music to which this carol is sung. Handel was born in Germany with the inborn talent of a musical genius. His father pressured the young man to enter law school, but George would not be denied, writing his first composition by age twelve and amazing choirmasters with his artistry. He eventually moved to London, where he enjoyed great success for a season. Then his popularity waned, his income dwindled, and he went bankrupt. It was the remarkable success of *Messiah* that salvaged Handel's career—and bank account. Through it all, Handel's powerful personality pressed on.

How ironic! These two men never met; they both struggled with poverty, faced bankruptcy, and worried about making ends meet—yet they enriched the world beyond measure, providing millions of people for scores of generations with the gift of song every Advent season.

Joy to the World!

Isaac Watts

George Frideric Handel
Arranged by Lowell Mason

1. Joy to the world! the Lord is come; Let earth re - ceive her
2. Joy to the world! the Sav - ior reigns; Let men their songs em -
3. No more let sin and sor - row grow, Nor thorns in - fest the
4. He rules the world with truth and grace And makes the na - tions

King. Let ev - ery heart pre - pare Him room,
ploy, While fields and floods, Rocks, hills and plains
ground. He comes to make His bless - ings flow
prove The glo - ries of His righ - teous - ness

And heav'n and na - ture sing, And heav'n and na - ture
Re - peat the sound - ing joy, Re - peat the sound - ing
Far as the curse is found, Far as the curse is
And won - ders of His love, And won - ders of His

1. And heav'n and na - ture sing, And

sing, And heav'n, and heav'n and na - ture sing.
joy, Re - peat, re - peat the sound - ing joy.
found, Far as, far as the curse is found.
love, And won - ders, and won - ders of His love.

heav'n and na - ture sing,

Joy to the World!

1719

Shout joyfully to the LORD, all the earth; break forth in song, rejoice, and sing praises. Psalm 98:4

*U*ntil Isaac Watts came along, most of the singing in British churches was from the Psalms of David. The church—especially the Church of Scotland—had labored over the Psalms with great effort and scholarship, translating them into poems with rhyme and rhythm suitable for singing. As a young man in Southampton, Isaac had become dissatisfied with the quality of singing, and he keenly felt the limitations of being able to only sing these psalms. So he "invented" the English hymn.

He did not, however, neglect the Psalms. In 1719, he published a unique hymnal—one in which he had translated, interpreted, and paraphrased the Old Testament Psalms through the eyes of New Testament faith. He called it simply *The Psalms of David Imitated in the Language of the New Testament*. Taking various psalms, he studied them from the perspective of Jesus and the New Testament, and then formed them into verses for singing.

"I have rather expressed myself as I may suppose David would have done if he lived in the days of Christianity," Watts explained, "and by this means, perhaps, I have sometimes hit upon the true intent of the Spirit of God in those verses farther and clearer than David himself could ever discover."

Watts's archenemy, Thomas Bradbury, was greatly critical of Watts's songs, which he called *whims* instead of *hymns*. He accused Watts of thinking he was King David. Watts replied in a letter, "You tell me that I rival it with David, whether he or I be the sweet psalmist of Israel. I abhor the thought; while yet, at the same time, I am fully persuaded that the Jewish psalm book was never designed to be the only Psalter for the Christian church."

"Joy to the World!" is Isaac Watts's interpretation of Psalm 98, which says, "Shout joyfully to the Lord, all the earth" (verse 4). As he read Psalm 98, Isaac pondered the real reason for shouting joyfully to the Lord—the Messiah has come to redeem us. The result, despite the now-forgotten criticisms of men like Bradbury, has been a timeless carol that has brightened our Christmases for nearly three hundred years.

Hark! The Herald Angels Sing

Charles Wesley

Felix Mendelssohn

1. Hark! the her - ald an - gels sing, "Glo - ry to the new - born King;
2. Christ, by high - est heav'n a - dored, Christ, the ev - er - last - ing Lord;
3. Hail the heav'n born Prince of Peace! Hail the Sun of Right-teous-ness!

Peace on earth and mer - cy mild, God and sin - ners rec - on - ciled."
Late in time be - hold Him come, Off - spring of a vir - gin's womb.
Light and life to all He brings, Ris'n with heal - ing in His wings.

Joy - ful, all ye na - tions, rise, Join the tri - umph of the skies;
Veiled in flesh the God-head see, Hail, th'in - car - nate De - i - ty!
Mild He lays His glo - ry by, Born that man no more may die;

With an - gel - ic hosts pro-claim, "Christ is born in Beth - le - hem."
Pleased as man with men to dwell, Je - sus our Em - man - u - el.
Born to raise the sons of earth, Born to give them sec - ond birth.

Hark! The Herald Angels Sing

<u>1739</u>

Then the angel said to them, "Do not be afraid, for behold, I bring you good tidings of great joy which will be to all people." Luke 2:10

Upon his conversion, Charles Wesley immediately began writing hymns, each one packed with doctrine, all of them exhibiting strength and sensitivity, both beauty and theological brawn. He wrote constantly, and even on horseback his mind was flooded with new songs. He often stopped at houses along the road and ran in asking for "pen and ink."

He wrote more than six thousand hymns during his life, and he didn't like people tinkering with the words. In one of his hymnals, he wrote, "I beg leave to mention a thought which has been long upon my mind, and which I should long ago have inserted in the public papers, had I not been unwilling to stir up a nest of hornets. Many gentlemen have done my brother and me (though without naming us) the honor to reprint many of our hymns. Now they are perfectly welcome to do so, provided they print them just as they are. But I desire they would not attempt to mend them, for they are really not able. None of them is able to mend either the sense or the verse. Therefore, I must beg of them these two favors: either to let them stand just as they are, to take things for better or worse, or to add the true reading in the margin, or at the bottom of the page, that we may no longer be accountable either for the nonsense or for the doggerel of other men."

But one man did the church a great favor by polishing up one of Charles's best-loved hymns. When Charles was thirty-two, he wrote a Christmas hymn that began:

> *Hark, how all the welkin rings,*
> *"Glory to the King of kings;*
> *Peace on earth, and mercy mild,*
> *God and sinners reconciled!"*
> *Joyful, all ye nations, rise,*
> *Join the triumph of the skies;*
> *Universal nature say,*
> *"Christ the Lord is born to-day!"*

The word *welkin* was an old English term for "the vault of heaven." It was Charles's friend, evangelist George Whitefield, who, when he published this carol in his collection of hymns in 1753, changed the words to the now beloved "Hark! The Herald Angels Sing."

Hallelujah Chorus

from *Messiah*

George Frideric Handel

George Frideric Handel

Hal - le - lu-jah! Hal - le - lu-jah! Hal-le - lu-jah! Hal-le-lu-jah! Hal-

le - lu-jah! Hal - le - lu-jah! Hal - le - lu-jah! Hal-le-

lu- jah! Hal-le - lu - jah! Hal - le - lu - jah! For the Lord

God om-nip - o - tent reign - eth. Hal - le - lu - jah!

Hallelujah Chorus
(from *Messiah*)

1741

Let the heavens rejoice, and let the earth be glad; and let them say among the nations, "The LORD reigns." 1 Chronicles 16:31

His father tried to discourage his musical interests, preferring that he enter the legal profession. But it was the organ, harpsichord, and violin that captured the heart of young George Frideric Handel. Once, accompanying his father to the court of Duke Johann Adolf, George wandered into the chapel, found the organ, and started improvising. The startled Duke exclaimed, "Who is this remarkable child?"

This "remarkable child" soon began composing operas, first in Italy, then in London. By his twenties, he was the talk of England and the best-paid composer on earth. He opened the Royal Academy of Music. Londoners fought for seats at his every performance, and his fame soared around the world.

But the glory passed. Audiences dwindled. His music became outdated, and he was thought of as an old fogey. Newer artists eclipsed the aging composer. One project after another failed, and Handel, now bankrupt, grew depressed. The stress brought on a case of palsy that crippled some of his fingers. "Handel's great days are over," wrote Frederick the Great. "His inspiration is exhausted."

Yet his troubles also matured him, softening his sharp tongue. His temper mellowed, and his music became more heartfelt. One morning Handel received by post a manuscript from Charles Jennens. It was a word-for-word collection of various biblical texts about Christ. The opening words from Isaiah 40 moved Handel: "Comfort ye, comfort ye my people . . ."

On August 22, 1741, he shut the door of his London home and started composing music for the words. Twenty-three days later, the world had *Messiah*. "Whether I was in the body or out of the body when I wrote it, I know not," Handel later said, trying to describe the experience. *Messiah* opened in London to enormous crowds on March 23, 1743, with Handel leading from his harpsichord. King George II, who was present that night, surprised everyone by leaping to his feet during the "Hallelujah Chorus." No one knows why. Some believe the king, being hard of hearing, thought it was the national anthem.

No matter—from that day audiences everywhere have stood in reverence during the stirring words: "Hallelujah! For He shall reign forever and ever."

Handel's fame was rekindled, and even after he lost his eyesight, he continued playing the organ for performances of his oratorios until his death in London, April 14, 1759.

O Come, All Ye Faithful

Ascribed to John Francis Wade
Translated by Frederick Oakeley

John Francis Wade

1. O come all ye faith - ful, Joy - ful and tri - um - phant, O come ye, O come ye to Beth - le - hem. Come and be - hold Him, Born the King of an - gels.
2. Sing choirs of an - gels, Sing in ex - ul - ta - tion, O sing all ye bright Hosts of heav'n a - bove. Glo - ry to God, All glo - ry in the high - est.
3. Yea, Lord, we greet Thee, Born this hap - py morn - ing; Je - sus to Thee be all glo - ry giv'n. Word of the Fa - ther Now in flesh ap - pear - ing.

Refrain

O come let us a - dore Him, O come let us a - dore Him, O come let us a - dore Him, Christ the Lord.

O Come, All Ye Faithful
1743

And when they had come into the house, they saw the young Child with Mary His mother, and fell down and worshiped Him. And when they had opened their treasures, they presented gifts to Him: gold, frankincense, and myrrh. Matthew 2:11

J ohn Francis Wade, author of this hymn, was hounded out of England in 1745. He was a Roman Catholic layman in Lancashire; but because of persecution arising from the Jacobite rebellion, streams of Catholics fled to France and Portugal, where communities of English-speaking Catholics appeared.

But how could he, a refugee, support himself? In those days, the printing of musical scores was cumbersome, and copying them by hand was an art. In the famous Roman Catholic College and Ministry Center in Douay, France, Wade taught music and became renowned as a copyist of musical scores. His work was exquisite.

In 1743, Wade, thirty-two, had produced a copy of a Latin Christmas carol beginning with the phrase *Adeste Fidelis, Laeti triumphantes.* At one time historians believed he had simply discovered an ancient hymn by an unknown author, but most scholars now believe Wade himself composed the lyrics. Seven original hand-copied manuscripts of this Latin hymn have been found, all of them bearing Wade's signature.

John Wade passed away on August 16, 1786, at age seventy-five. His obituary honored him for his "beautiful manuscripts" that adorned chapels and homes.

As time passed, English Catholics began returning to Britain, and they carried Wade's Christmas carol with them. More time passed, and one day an Anglican minister named Rev. Frederick Oakeley, who preached at Margaret Street Chapel in London, came across Wade's Latin Christmas carol. Being deeply moved, he translated it into English for Margaret Street Chapel. The first line of Oakeley's translation said, "Ye Faithful, Approach Ye."

Somehow "Ye Faithful, Approach Ye" didn't catch on, and several years later Oakeley tried again. By this time, Oakeley, too, was a Roman Catholic priest, having converted to Catholicism in 1845. Perhaps his grasp of Latin had improved because as he repeated over and over the Latin phrase *Adeste Fidelis, Laeti triumphantes,* he finally came up with the simpler, more vigorous "O Come, All Ye Faithful, Joyful and Triumphant!"

So two brave Englishmen, Catholics, lovers of Christmas and lovers of hymns, living a hundred years apart, writing in two different nations, combined their talents to bid us come, joyful and triumphant, and adore Him born the King of angels.

O come, let us adore Him, Christ the Lord

Come, Thou Long-Expected Jesus

Charles Wesley

Rowland H. Prichard

1. Come, Thou long ex - pect - ed Je - sus,
From our fears and sins re - lease us,
2. Born Thy peo - ple to de - liv - er,
Born to reign in us for - ev - er,

Born to set Thy peo - ple free;
Let us find our rest in Thee.
Born a Child and yet a King;
Now Thy gra - cious king - dom bring.

Is - rael's strength and con - so - la - tion, Hope of all the
By Thine own e - ter - nal Spir - it, Rule in all our

earth Thou art; Dear de - sire of ev - ery
hearts a - lone; By Thine all - suf - fi - cient

na - tion, Joy of ev - ery long - ing heart.
mer - it, Raise us to Thy glo - rious throne.

Come, Thou Long-Expected Jesus

1744

You therefore must endure hardship as a good soldier of Jesus Christ.
2 Timothy 2:3

t's hard to imagine the difficulties faced by John and Charles Wesley and their fellow evangelists as they traveled by horseback from town to town, facing mobs, enduring harsh conditions and severe weather. Here is a sampling from Charles's journal as he pressed into Wales in March of 1748.

Wed., March 23rd. I was . . . not to set out till past seven. The continual rain and sharp wind were full in my teeth. I rode all day in great misery, and had a restless, painful night at Tan-y-bwlch.

Thur., March 24th. I resolved to push for Garth, finding my strength would never hold out for three more days riding. At five (a.m.), I set out in hard rain, which continued all day. We went through perils of water. I was quite gone when we came at night to a little village. There was no fire in the poor hut. A brother supplied us with some, nailed up our window, and helped us to bed. I had no more rest than the night before.

Fri., March 25th. I took horse again at five, the rain attending us still . . . The weather grew more severe. The violent wind drove the hard rain full in our faces. I rode till I could ride no more; walked the last hour; and by five dropped down at Garth.

Charles's primary purpose in going to Garth was to preach, but he had another motive as well. It was also to see Miss Sally Gwynee, whom he wanted to marry. Marriage required a regular income, however, and Sally's parents were concerned about Charles's ability to sustain a family with no regular source of finances. Charles agreed to publish two volumes of his *Hymns and Sacred Poems*.

The income from royalties more than satisfied Sally's parents, and the two were married on Saturday, April 8, 1749.

"Come, Thou Long-Expected Jesus" wasn't introduced in this two-volume set of *Hymns and Sacred Songs* containing a total of 455 hymns. It had been published earlier, in a 1745 edition of Christmas hymns entitled *Hymns for the Nativity of Our Lord*. This little hymnal contained eighteen Christmas carols Charles had written, of which "Come, Thou Long-Expected Jesus" is the best known.

Angels, from the Realms of Glory

James Montgomery

Henry T. Smart

1. An - gels from the realms of glo - ry, Wing your flight o'er
2. Shep - herds in the fields a - bi - ding, Watch - ing o'er your
3. Sag - es, leave your con - tem - pla - tions, Bright - er vi - sions
4. Saints, be - fore the al - tar bend - ing, Watch - ing long in
5. All cre - a - tion, join in prais - ing, God, the Fath - er,

all the earth; Ye who sang cre - a - tion's sto - ry,
flocks by night; God with man is now re - sid - ing,
beam a - far; Seek the great De - sire of na - tions,
hope and fear; Sud - den - ly the Lord, de - scend - ing,
Spir - it, Son; Ev - er - more your voic - es rais - ing,

Now pro - claim Mes - si - ah's birth.
Yon - der shines the in - fant Light.
Ye have seen His na - tal star.
In His tem - ple shall ap - pear.
To th'et - er - nal Three in One.

Come and wor-ship, come and wor-ship; Wor-ship Christ, the new-born King!

Angels, from the Realms of Glory

1816

Praise Him, all His angels; Praise Him, all His hosts! Psalm 148:2

Like all Moravians, John Montgomery had a burden for world evangelism. He was the only Moravian pastor in Scotland, but he and his wife felt God's call to be missionaries to the island of Barbados. Tearfully placing their six-year-old son, James, in a Moravian settlement in Bracehill near Ballymena, County Antrim, Ireland, they sailed away. James never saw them again, for they perished in Barbados.

Left with nothing, James was enrolled in a school in England. When he didn't do well, he was apprenticed by school authorities to a baker. Baking wasn't for James. He ran away and spent his teenage years drifting from pillar to post, writing poetry and trying his hand at one thing then another. He eventually settled down in Sheffield, England.

In his early twenties, James began working for the local newspaper, the *Sheffield Register*, and there he found his niche. He loved writing. It was a politically active newspaper, and when its owner had to suddenly flee the country to avoid persecution and imprisonment, James purchased the paper and renamed it the *Sheffield Iris*. His editorials, too, proved unpopular with local officials. On two separate occasions he was thrown into jail. But he emerged from prison a celebrity, and he used his newly acquired fame to promote his favorite issues.

Chief among them was the gospel. Despite the loss of his parents, James Montgomery remained devoted to Christ and to the Scriptures, and he championed the cause of foreign missions and the British Bible Society.

As the years passed, he became the most respected leader in Sheffield, and his writings were eagerly read by its citizens. Early on Christmas Eve, 1816, James, forty-five, opened his Bible to Luke 2, and was deeply impressed by verse 13. Pondering the story of the heralding angels, he took his pen and started writing. By the end of the day, his new Christmas poem was being read in the pages of his newspaper. It was later set to music and was first sung on Christmas Day, 1821, in a Moravian Church in England: "Angels, from the Realms of Glory."

His parents would have been proud.

Silent Night

Joseph Mohr — Franz Gruber

1. Si - lent night, ho - ly night, All is calm, all is bright. Round yon vir - gin moth - er and child; Ho - ly in - fant, so ten - der and mild, Sleep in heav - en - ly peace; Sleep in heav - en - ly peace.

2. Si - lent night, ho - ly night, Shep - herds quake at the sight. Glo - ries stream from heav - en a - far, Heaven-ly hosts sing "Al - le - lu - ia. Christ the Sa - vior is born; Christ the Sav - ior is born."

3. Si - lent night, ho - ly night, Won - drous star, lend thy light. With the an - gels, let us sing, Al - le - lu - ia to our King. Christ the Sa - vior is born; Christ the Sav - ior is born.

4. Si - lent night, ho - ly night, Son of God, love's pure light. Ra - diant beams from Thy ho - ly face, With the dawn of re - deem - ing grace. Je - sus, Lord, at Thy birth; Je - sus, Lord, at Thy birth.

Silent Night

1818

Therefore the Lord Himself will give you a sign: Behold, the virgin shall conceive and bear a Son, and shall call His name Immanuel. Isaiah 7:14

I t was Christmas Eve in the Austrian Alps. At the newly constructed Church of St. Nicholas in Oberndorf, a Tyrol village near Salzburg, Father Joseph Mohr prepared for the midnight service. He was distraught because the church organ was broken, ruining prospects for that evening's carefully planned music. But Father Joseph was about to learn that our problems are God's opportunities, that the Lord causes all things to work together for good to those who love Him. It came into Father Joseph's mind to write a new song, one that could be sung organless. Hastily, he wrote the words, "Silent night, holy night, all is calm, all is bright . . ." Taking the text to his organist, Franz Gruber, he explained the situation and asked Franz to compose a simple tune.

That night, December 24, 1818, "Silent Night" was sung for the first time as a duet accompanied by a guitar at the aptly named Church of St. Nicholas in Oberndorf.

Shortly afterward, as Karl Mauracher came to repair the organ, he heard about the near disaster on Christmas Eve. Acquiring a copy of the text and tune, he spread it throughout the Alpine region of Austria, referring to it as *Tiroler Volkslied*.

The song came to the attention of the Strasser Family, makers of fine chamois-skin gloves. To drum up business at various fairs and festivals, the four Strasser children would sing in front of their parents' booth. Like the Von Trapp children a century later, they became popular folk singers throughout the Alps.

When the children—Caroline, Joseph, Andreas, and Amalie—began singing *"Tiroler Volkslied"* at their performances, audiences were charmed. It seemed perfect for the snow-clad region, and perfect for the Christian heart. "Silent Night" even came to the attention of the king and queen, and the Strasser children were asked to give a royal performance, assuring the carol's fame.

"Silent Night" was first published for congregational singing in 1838 in the German hymnbook *Katholisches Gesang—und Gebetbuch für den öffentlichen und häuslichen Gottesdienst zunächst zum Gebrauche der katholischen Gereinden im Königreiche Sachsen*. It was used in America by German-speaking congregations, then appeared in its current English form in a book of Sunday school songs in 1863.

Were it not for a broken organ, there would never have been a "Silent Night."

The First Noel

Traditional English Carol

Traditional English Melody

1. The first No - el, the an - gel did say, Was to cer - tain poor
2. They look - ed up and saw a star Shin - ing in the
3. And by the light of that same star, Three Wise Men
4. Then en - tered in those Wise Men three, Full rev - erent -

shep - herds, in fields as they lay; In fields where they lay
east, be - yond them far, And to the earth it
came from coun - try far; To seek for a King was
ly up - on their knee, And of - fered there, in

keep-ing their sheep, On a cold win-ter's night that was so deep.
gave great light, And so it con - tin - ued both day and night.
their in - tent, And to fol - low the star, wher - ev - er it went.
His pres - ence, Their gold, and myrrh, and frank - in - cense.

No - el, No - el, No - el, No - el, Born is the King of Is - ra - el.

The First Noel

1823

And there were shepherds living out in the fields nearby, keeping watch over their flocks at night. Luke 2:8 NIV

o other carol casts such a spell. The sweet, plaintive strains of "The First Noel," quietly sung on a snow-clad Christmas Eve, bring tears to the eyes and gentle peace to the heart. "Noel, Noel, Noel, Noel. Born is the King of Israel."

If only we knew who wrote it! It first appeared anonymously in *Some Ancient Christmas Carols*, published by Davis Gilbert in 1823, and the traditional music evidently came from an unknown source in the west of England.

The poetry itself is plain. If we were to recite this rather lengthy piece, we'd get only a garbled sense of the Christmas story. There's no indication in Scripture, for example, that the shepherds saw the Magi's star. And the final verse of the original carol seems anticlimactic. But when combined with its wistful music, the words glow and our hearts are strangely warmed.

The word *noel* seems to be a French word with Latin roots: *natalis*, meaning "birthday." Modern hymns omit several of the verses. Here is the complete version:

The first Noel the angels did say was to certain poor shepherds in fields as they lay;
In fields where they lay keeping their sheep on a cold winter's night that was so deep.
Noel, Noel, Noel, Noel; Born is the King of Israel.

They looked up and saw a star shining in the East, beyond them far,
And to the earth it gave great light, and so it continued, both day and night.

And by the light of that same star three wise men came from country far,
To seek for a King was their intent, and to follow the star wherever it went.

This star drew nigh to the northwest; o'er Bethlehem it took its rest.
And there it did both stop and stay, right over the place where Jesus lay.

Then they did know assuredly within that house, the King did lie
One entered in then for to see and found the babe in poverty.

Then entered in those wise men three, full reverently, upon bended knee,
And offered there, in His presence, their gold and myrrh and frankincense.

If we in our time do well we shall be free from death and hell
For God hath prepared for us all a resting place in general.
Noel, Noel, Noel, Noel; Born is the King of Israel.

O Holy Night

O Holy Night

1847

The star which they had seen in the East went before them, till it came and stood over where the young Child was. Matthew 2:9

 he words of "O Holy Night" were written in 1847 by a French wine merchant named Placide Clappeau, the mayor of Roquemaure, a town in the south of France. We know little about him except that he wrote poems as a hobby.

We know more about the man who composed the music, a Parisian named Adolphe Charles Adam. The son of a concert pianist, Adams was trained almost from infancy in music and piano. In his midtwenties, he wrote his first opera and thereafter wrote two operas a year until his death at age fifty-two. Near the end of his life, he lost his savings in a failed business venture involving the French national opera, but the Paris Conservatory rescued him by appointing him professor of music.

It was John Dwight, son of Yale's president, Timothy Dwight ("I Love Thy Kingdom, Lord"), who discovered this French Carol, "Christian Midnight," and translated it into the English hymn "O Holy Night."

After graduating from Harvard and Cambridge, John was ordained as minister of the Unitarian church in Northampton, but his pastoring experience wasn't happy. In 1841, George and Sophia Ripley founded a commune named Brook Farm "to prepare a society of liberal, intelligent, and cultivated persons, whose relations with each other would permit a more simple and wholesome life." John was hired as director of the Brook Farm School and began writing a regular column on music for the commune's publication.

Greatly influenced by the liberal views of Ralph Waldo Emerson, he became fascinated by the German culture, especially the symphonic music of Ludwig van Beethoven, and it was largely his influence that introduced Americans to Beethoven's genius.

When Brook Farm collapsed in 1847, John Dwight moved into a cooperative house in Boston and established a career in music journalism. He penned articles on music for major publications, and in 1852 he launched his own publication, *Dwight's Journal of Music.* He became America's first influential classical music critic. He was opinionated, sometimes difficult, a great promoter of European classical music, and an early advocate of Transcendentalism.

How odd that a wine merchant, a penniless Parisian, and a liberal clergyman should give Christianity one of its holiest hymns about the birth of Jesus Christ, Savior of the world.

Once in Royal David's City

Cecil F. Alexander

Henry J. Gauntlett

1. Once in roy - al Da - vid's cit - y Stood a
2. He came down to earth from Heav - en, Who is
3. For He is our child - hood's pat - tern; Day by
4. And our eyes at last shall see Him, Through His

low - ly cat - tle shed, Where a moth - er laid her
God and Lord of all, And His shel - ter was a
day, like us He grew; He was lit - tle, weak and
own re - deem - ing love, For that Child so dear and

Ba - by In a man - ger for His bed: Mar - y
sta - ble, And His cra - dle was a stall; With the
help - less, Tears and smiles like us He knew; And He
gen - tle Is our Lord in Heav'n a - bove, And He

was that moth - er mild, Je - sus Christ her lit - tle Child.
poor, and mean, and low - ly, Lived on earth our Sav - ior ho - ly.
feel - eth for our sad - ness, And He shar - eth in our glad - ness.
leads His chil - dren on To the place where He is gone.

Once in Royal David's City

1848

Joseph also went up from Galilee, out of the city of Nazareth, into Judea, to the city of David, which is called Bethlehem, because he was of the house and lineage of David, to be registered with Mary, his betrothed wife, who was with child.
Luke 2:4–5

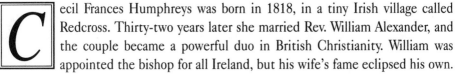

Cecil Frances Humphreys was born in 1818, in a tiny Irish village called Redcross. Thirty-two years later she married Rev. William Alexander, and the couple became a powerful duo in British Christianity. William was appointed the bishop for all Ireland, but his wife's fame eclipsed his own.

Mrs. Alexander had a deep heart for children, devoting much time to teaching Sunday school and writing songs for youngsters. She helped establish a school for the deaf and founded a Girl's Friendly Society in Londonderry. She worked tirelessly to provide food for the hungry and comfort to the sick.

One of her Sunday school pupils—a little boy who happened to be her godson—was struggling to understand the Apostles' Creed and certain portions of the Catechism. Mrs. Alexander began to mull the possibility of converting the Apostles' Creed into songs for children.

The Apostles' Creed begins: "I believe in God, the Father Almighty, Maker of heaven and earth, and in Jesus Christ, His only Son, our Lord." For the phrase "Maker of heaven and earth," the creative teacher wrote the famous song "All Things Bright and Beautiful."

The Creed goes on to say about Jesus Christ: "who was conceived of the Holy Spirit, born of the Virgin Mary." That spurred the writing of the great Christmas carol "Once in Royal David's City."

The next phrase, "suffered under Pontius Pilate, was crucified, died, and was buried," became the basis for the hymn "There Is a Green Hill Far Away."

The Creed goes on to speak of the second coming of Christ, prompting Mrs. Alexander to write a lesser-known, beautiful hymn entitled "He Is Coming! He Is Coming!"

These hymns were published in 1848 in Mrs. Alexander's book *Hymns for Little Children.* It became one of the most successful hymn publishing projects in history, going through more than one hundred editions and telling children the world over what happened "once in royal David's city."

It Came upon the Midnight Clear

Edmund H. Sears

Richard Storrs Willis

1. It came up-on the mid-night clear, That glo - rious song of old;
2. Still thro' the clo - ven skies they come, With peace - ful wings un-furled;
3. For lo, the days are has-tening on, By proph - et bards fore-told;

From an - gels bend - ing near the earth To touch their harps of gold.
And still their heaven - ly mu - sic floats, O'er all the wear - y world.
When with the ev - er - cir - cling years, Comes round the age of gold.

"Peace on the earth good will to men, From heaven's all gra - cious King!"
A - bove its sad and low - ly plains, They bend on hov - ering wing;
When peace shall o - ver all the earth, Its an - cient splen - dors fling;

The world in sol - emn still-ness lay To hear the an - gels sing.
And ev - er o'er its Ba - bel sounds The bless-ed an - gels sing.
And the whole world give back the song Which now the an - gels sing.

It Came upon the Midnight Clear

1849

And suddenly there was with the angel a multitude of the heavenly host praising God and saying: "Glory to God in the highest, and on earth peace, goodwill toward men!" Luke 2:13–14

E dmund Hamilton Sears is the author of two Christmas carols that are mirror images of each other, written fifteen years apart.

He was born in Sandisfield, Massachusetts, on April 6, 1819, and attended Union College in Schenectady, then Harvard Divinity School. He was ordained in the Unitarian ministry and chose to devote himself to small towns in Massachusetts, where he had time to study, think, and write.

At twenty-four, he wrote "Calm on the Listening Ear," a Christmas carol based on the song of the angels in Luke 2. It proved very similar to the more-famous carol he would later write. Having the same meter and theme, and it can be sung to the same tune:

> *Calm on the listening ear of night | Come heaven's melodious strains,*
> *Where wild Judea stretches far | Her silver-mantled plains.*
> *Celestial choirs, from courts above, | Shed sacred glories there,*
> *And angels, with their sparkling lyres, | Make music on the air.*

Fifteen years later, he wrote its more famous twin. "It Came upon the Midnight Clear" is an unusual carol in that there is no mention of Christ, of the newborn Babe, or of the Savior's mission. Sears, after all, was Unitarian. The author's only focus is the angelic request for peace on earth.

Notice again the date of the hymn. It was written as the clouds of civil strife were darkening the United States, setting the stage for the War Between the States. We can grasp the concern that drove Edmund to write this hymn by reading a stanza now usually omitted from most hymnals:

> *Yet with the woes of sin and strife | The world hath suffered long;*
> *Beneath the angel-strain have rolled | Two thousand years of wrong;*
> *And man, at war with man, hears not | The love song which they bring:*
> *O hush the noise, ye men of strife, | And hear the angels sing!*

Edmund Sears became well-known because of his hymns and books. He was awarded a doctor of divinity degree in 1871, and took a preaching tour of England, where he was met by large congregations. He died in Weston, Massachusetts, on January 16, 1876.

O Come, O Come, Emmanuel

Latin Hymn, 9th Century
Translated by John M. Neale

Thomas Helmore

1. O come, O come, Em - man - u - el, And ran - som cap - tive
2. O come, thou Wis - dom from on high, Who or - derest all things
3. O come, De - sire of na - tions, bind All peo - ples in one
4. O come, thou Day - spring, come and cheer Our spir - its by Thine

Is - ra - el, That mourns in lone - ly ex - ile here
might - i - ly; To us the path of knowl - edge show
heart and mind. From dust Thou brought us forth to life;
ad - vent here; Dis - perse the gloom - y clouds of night,

Un - til the Son of God ap - pear.
And teach us in her ways to go. Re - joice! Re - joice! Em-
De - liv - er us from earth - ly strife.
And death's dark shad - ows put to flight.

man - u - el Shall come to thee, O Is - ra - el!

O Come, O Come, Emmanuel

1851

Behold, the virgin shall be with child, and bear a Son, and they shall call His name Immanuel. Matthew 1:23

*T*he origins of this plaintive carol date to medieval times. In the 800s, a series of Latin hymns were sung each day during Christmas Vespers from December 17 to 23. Each of these hymns began with the word *O* and were called the "Great" or "O" Antiphons (the word *antiphon* means "psalm" or "anthem"). These hymns were apparently restructured into verse form in the 1100s, and finally published in Latin in 1710. In the mid-1800s, they were discovered by an English minister named John Mason Neale, who wove together segments of them to produce the first draft of "O Come, O Come, Emmanuel," which was published in 1851. Neale's original version said, "Draw nigh, draw nigh, Emmanuel."

Neale is a man worth knowing. He was born in London on January 24, 1818, the son of an evangelical Anglican clergyman. He attended Cambridge University and proved to be a brilliant student and prize-winning poet. While there, Neale was influenced by the Oxford Movement and became attracted to Roman Catholicism. In 1841, he was ordained into the Anglican ministry, but his poor health and Catholic leanings prevented him from gaining a parish ministry.

He was appointed instead as the director of Sackville College, a home for old men. (Sackville College, started by Robert Sackville, Earl of Dorset, in the early 1600s as a home for the elderly, is still going strong today in East Grinstead, Sussex.) This was the perfect job for Neale, for he was a compassionate man with a great heart for the needy, but he was also a scholar needing time for research and writing.

As a high church traditionalist, Neale disliked the hymns of Isaac Watts and longed to return Christianity to the liturgical dignity of church history. He was an outspoken advocate of returning church buildings to their former glory. He campaigned, for example, against certain types of stoves that spoiled the tastefulness and charm of English churches. He also worked hard to translate ancient Greek and Latin hymns into English.

In today's hymnals, we find Neale and Watts side by side, the old differences having been forgotten. We owe a debt of gratitude to John Mason Neale every time we sing one of his Christmas carols: "Good King Wenceslas," "O Come, O Come, Emmanuel," "Good Christian Men, Rejoice," and his Palm Sunday hymn, "All Glory, Laud, and Honor."

Good King Wenceslas

John M. Neale

Swedish Carol

1. Good King Wen-ces - las looked out on the Feast of Ste - phen,
2. "Hith - er, page, and stand by me, if you know it, tell - ing,
3. "Bring me food and bring me wine, bring me pine logs hith - er,
4. "Sire, the night is dark - er now, and the wind blows stron - ger,
5. In his mas-ter's steps he trod, where the snow lay dint - ed;

When the snow lay round a - bout, deep and crisp and e - ven.
Yon - der peas - ant, who is he? Where and what his dwell - ing?"
You and I will see him dine, when we bear them thith - er."
Fails my heart, I know not how; I can go no long - er."
Heat was in the ver - y sod which the saint had print - ed.

Bright - ly shone the moon that night, though the frost was cru - el,
"Sire, he lives a good league hence, un - der-neath the moun - tain,
Page and mon-arch, forth they went, forth they went to - geth - er,
"Mark my foot-steps, my good page, tread now in them bold - ly,
There-fore, Chris-tian men, be sure, wealth or rank pos - sess - ing,

When a poor man came in sight, gath-ering win - ter fu - el.
Right a-gainst the for - est fence, by Saint Ag - nes' foun - tain."
Through the cold wind's wild la-ment and the bit - ter weath - er.
You shall find the win-ter's rage freeze your blood less cold - ly."
You who now will bless the poor shall your-selves find bless - ing.

Good King Wenceslas

1854

But when you give a feast, invite the poor, the maimed, the lame, the blind. And you will be blessed, because they cannot repay you; for you shall be repaid at the resurrection of the just. Luke 14:13–14

T his story is about two men—a Bohemian duke and an Anglican minister—who lived nearly a thousand years apart.

Wenceslas was born in Bohemia, in modern Czechoslovakia, in the early 900s. His father, the Czech ruler, Duke Ratislav, gave him a good education supervised by his godly grandmother. When his father died, Wenceslas, seeing his mother mishandle affairs of state, stepped in at age eighteen, seizing the reins of government. From the beginning, he proved a different sort of king. He sought good relations with surrounding nations, particularly with Germany. He took steps to reform the judicial system, reducing the number of death sentences and the arbitrary power of judges. He encouraged the building of churches and showed heart-felt concern for the poor. He reportedly cut firewood for orphans and widows, often carrying the provisions on his own shoulders through the snow.

Wenceslas's brief reign ended suddenly. His pagan and rebellious brother, Boles-lav, murdered him on September 28, 929, as he left for church. His people venerated him as a martyr, and today Wenceslas is the patron saint of Czechoslovakia.

He would be hardly remembered, however, but for John Mason Neale, an Anglican minister with a passion for returning church architecture and music to their ancient grandeur. Neale helped establish a committee to investigate and restore dilapidated church buildings in Great Britain. He was particularly upset at the ugly stoves in-stalled to heat churches in Victorian times.

Disliking the hymns of Isaac Watts, he also sought to return church music to its medieval roots. Neale worked hard to translate ancient Greek, Latin, and Syrian hymns into English. In so doing, he gave us the Christmas carols "Good Christian Men Rejoice" (a fourteenth-century text set to a fourteenth-century tune) and "O Come, O Come Emmanuel" (a ninth-century text set to a fifteenth-century tune). He also translated the Palm Sunday hymn "All Glory, Laud, and Honor."

"Good King Wenceslas" is not a translation, but an original poem written by Neale to honor a godly monarch's concern for the poor. Neale himself worked with the needy, serving as warden of a charitable residence for indigent old men.

John Neale's antiquated opinions were widely scorned in his own day, but we're still singing his songs.

Now Praise We Christ the Holy One

Caelius Sedulius

from *Eyn Enchyridion*

1. Now praise we Christ, the Ho - ly One,
2. He Who Him - self all things did make
3. The no - ble moth - er bore a Son—
4. Up - on a man - ger filled with hay
5. The heav - enly choirs re - joice and raise

The bless - ed vir - gin Mar - y's Son,
A ser - vant's form vouch - safed to take
For so did Ga - briel's prom - ise run—
In pov - er - ty con - tent He lay;
Their voice to God in songs of praise.

Far as the glo - rious sun doth shine,
That He as man man - kind might win
Whom John con - fessed and leaped with joy
With milk was fed the Lord of all,
To hum - ble shep - herds is pro - claimed

1.2.3.4.

E'en to the world's re - mote con - fine.
And save His crea - tures from their sin.
Ere yet the moth - er knew her Boy.
Who feeds the rav - ens when they call.
The Shep - herd Who the

5.

world hath framed.

Now Praise We Christ the Holy One

1854

Let them praise the name of the LORD, for His name alone is exalted; His glory is above the earth and heaven. Psalm 148:13

eneath the merriment of Christmas, a melancholy stream flows like an underground river. It isn't simply feelings of nostalgia or the holiday blues; it's the pathos of the imponderable—the unsearchable sorrow of God-in-flesh coming to die for the sins of the world.

If we miss this feeling, somehow we've missed Christmas.

I think the very oldest hymns of Christmas best open our hearts to these bittersweet feelings of wonder. Few experiences are more powerful, for example, than attending a Christmas Eve worship service and hearing the somber strains of the ancient canticle "Now Praise We Christ the Holy One."

Hearing it, one has the sense of attending midnight Mass in an ancient torch-lit cathedral on Christmas Eve or of being present in the halls of a medieval monastery as brown-robed monks shuffle through the cloisters, their haunting chants echoing through the shadowed corridors. Consider how this simple verse cuts to the heart of the mysterious wonder of Christmas:

> *Upon a manger filled with hay*
> *In poverty content He lay;*
> *With milk was fed the Lord of all,*
> *Who feeds the ravens when they call.*

Caelius Sedulius was a Latin Christian who lived in the 400s, probably in Rome. We know little about him except that he seems to have been an expert in pagan literature who, following his conversion, devoted himself to writing Christian poetry and became one of the most influential hymnists in the early church.

"Now Praise We Christ," originally part of a longer Latin hymn entitled *"A Solis Ortus Cardine,"* was excerpted and translated into German by Martin Luther in the 1520s and rendered into English in 1854 by Richard Massie, an Anglican rector in Eccleston, England.

We don't want to live in dark moods of imponderable mystery, but neither do we want to miss them altogether. They allow us to emerge from the tender sadness of the manger to sing with the angels in the skies above the shepherds' field.

Of the Father's Love Begotten

Aurelius Prudentius

Sanctus Trope, 11th Century

1. Of the Fa - ther's love be - got - ten, ere the worlds be - gan to be, He is Al - pha and O - me - ga, He the source, the End - ing He, Of the things that are, that have been, And that fu - ture years shall see, ev - er - more and ev - er - more!

2. At His Word the worlds were fram - èd; He com - mand - ed; it was done: Heav'n and earth and depths of o - cean in their three - fold or - der one; All that grows be - neath the shin - ing Of the moon and burn - ing sun, ev - er - more and ev - er - more!

3. O ye heights of heav'n a - dore Him; an - gel hosts, His prais - es sing; Powers, do - min - ions, bow be - fore Him, and ex - tol our God and King! Let no tongue on earth be si - lent, Ev - ery voice in con - cert sing, ev - er - more and ev - er - more!

4. Christ, to Thee with God the Fa - ther, and, O Ho - ly Ghost, to Thee, Hymn and chant with high thanks-giv - ing, and un - wea - ried prais - es be: Hon - or, glo - ry, and do - min - ion, And e - ter - nal vic - to - ry, ev - er - more and ev - er - more!

36

Of the Father's Love Begotten

1854

For God so loved the world that He gave His only begotten Son, that whoever believes in Him should not perish but have everlasting life. John 3:16

ast year a college student sauntered into my office to tell me about a new song he'd discovered, one with a haunting melody and pensive words, and pulling out a CD, he played it for me. I smiled when I realized his "new" song was one of our oldest hymns, "Of the Father's Love Begotten."

This ancient Latin hymn is by Aurelius Clemens Prudentius, who was born in northern Spain in AD 348, not long after Christianity was legalized in the Roman Empire following three centuries of persecution. Prudentius became a lawyer and provincial governor in Spain, where his leadership skills attracted the attention of Emperor Theodosius I. He was then appointed to an imperial military post.

It may have been shortly afterward that Prudentius gave his life to Christ and began writing Christian poetry. At age fifty-seven, he retired from government service and entered a monastery, where he devoted himself exclusively to worship and writing. Today we have nearly four hundred poems from his hand. His *"Psychomachia"* ("The Contest of the Soul") was the first completely allegorical poem in European literature and cast a long shadow over medieval times.

Prudentius has been called "the prince of early Christian poets." Although he and Ambrose ("Come, Thou Redeemer of the Earth") both were writing hymns about the same time, the ones by Prudentius are more reflective, displaying greater warmth and glow. Perhaps it was his warm Spanish blood.

"Of the Father's Love Begotten" is among the greatest Christmas carols in Western history, and thankfully its popularity is on the increase, partly owing to the tender beauty of its probing score, DIVINUM MYSTERIUM, composed nearly a thousand years ago. John Mason Neale translated the poem from Latin into English in 1854.

My young collegian would say that if you've never heard "Of the Father's Love Begotten," throw down this book and run—don't walk—to your nearest music store and find a quality recording of it. I agree. It's worth learning.

We Three Kings of Orient Are

John H. Hopkins, Jr.   John H. Hopkins, Jr.

1. We three kings of O - ri - ent are, Bear-ing gifts we trav - erse a - far;
2. Born a King on Beth-le-hem's plain, Gold I bring to crown Him a - gain;
3. Frank-in - cense to of - fer have I, In-cense owns a De - i - ty nigh;
4. Myrrh is mine, its bit - ter per - fume, Breathes a life of gath - er-ing gloom;
5. Glo - rious now be-hold Him a - rise, King and God and Sac - ri - fice;

Field and foun - tain, moor and moun - tain, Fol - low-ing yon - der star.
King for - ev - er, ceas - ing nev - er, O - ver us all to reign.
Prayer and prais - ing, all men rais - ing, Wor-ship Him, God on high.
Sor - rowing, sigh - ing, bleed-ing, dy - ing, Sealed in the stone cold tomb.
Al - le - lu - ia, al - le - lu - ia! Earth to heav'n re - plies.

O star of won-der, star of night, Star with roy - al beau-ty bright;

West-ward lead-ing, still pro - ceed-ing, Guide us to Thy per - fect light.

We Three Kings
of Orient Are
1857

Now after Jesus was born in Bethlehem of Judea in the days of Herod the king, behold, wise men from the East came to Jerusalem . . . Matthew 2:1

Strange but true: a visit from St. Nicholas paved the way for "We Three Kings." It happened like this. After the War of 1812, Anglicans in America decided to establish their own seminary for training Episcopalian ministers. The proposal was first made in 1814; and in 1817, the Episcopalian General Convention voted to locate the school in New York City. But where in New York?

Clement Clarke Moore, son of New York's Episcopalian bishop, was an up-and-coming land developer. He had recently become well-known because of a poem he had written, which began:

> *'Twas the night before Christmas, when all through the house*
> *not a creature was stirring, not even a mouse . . .*

The popularity of his poem (reportedly written following a sleigh ride home from Greenwich Village) made his name a household word. The fame and increased income made him a more generous and sought-after layman.

Moore owned a large estate in the undeveloped northern regions of Manhattan. He referred to it as "a quiet, rural retreat on the picturesque banks of the Hudson." Hearing that the Episcopalians needed land for their seminary, he offered a portion of his estate, and thus was born General Theological Seminary. Moore, also a linguist and Hebrew scholar, became one of General's first professors, teaching biblical languages.

Some years later a reporter named John H. Hopkins Jr. enrolled in this seminary. Born in Pittsburgh, Hopkins had matriculated at the University of Vermont before moving to New York to pursue legal studies. But he fell in love with the Lord's work, enrolled in General, and graduated from the seminary in 1850. In 1855, he was hired as the school's first instructor of church music.

Hopkins wrote "We Three Kings" as part of a Christmas pageant produced by General Theological Seminary in 1857. In 1863, it was published in his *Carols, Hymns, and Songs*. This hymnal went through three editions by 1882, establishing Hopkins as a leader in Episcopalian hymnody. He wrote other hymns, but most have fallen into obscurity. "We Three Kings" was his crowning achievement, made possible, in a way, through the generosity of another poet whose most famous work ends:

> *But I heard him exclaim, 'ere he drove out of sight,*
> *Merry Christmas to all, and to all a good night!*

Come, Thou Redeemer of the Earth

Ambrose of Milan
Translated by John M. Neale

15th Century
Adapted by Michael Praetorius

1. Come, Thou Redeemer of the earth,
And manifest Thy virgin birth:
Let every age adoring fall;
Such birth befits the God of all.

2. Begotten of no human will,
But of the Spirit, Thou art still
The Word of God in flesh arrayed,
The promised Fruit to man displayed.

3. The virgin womb that burden gained
With virgin honor all unstained;
The banners there of virtue glow;
God in His temple dwells below.

4. Thy cradle here shall glitter bright,
And darkness breathe a newer light,
Where endless faith shall shine serene,
And twilight never intervene.

Come, Thou Redeemer of the Earth

1862

I know that my Redeemer lives, and He shall stand at last on the earth. Job 19:25

This carol stretches back into the early, misty centuries of Christian history. It was written by the mighty Ambrose, bishop of Milan, whose personal story is as remarkable as his carol is wonderful.

Ambrose was born about AD 340 in Gaul (modern France), where his father was governor before moving his family to Rome. In the empire's capital, Ambrose became a noted poet, a skilled orator, and a respected lawyer. At age thirty-four, he was named governor of an Italian province and headquartered in Milan.

A crisis arose in Milan after the death of popular Bishop Auxentius as the city argued about his replacement. Tensions ran high. Assembling the people, Ambrose used his oratorical powers to appeal for unity; but while he was speaking, a child reportedly cried out, "Let Ambrose be bishop!" The crowd took up the chant, and the young governor, to his dismay, was elected the city's pastor.

Taking the call seriously, Ambrose became a great preacher and a deft defender of true doctrine. He wrote books and treatises, sermons, hymns, and letters. He tended Milan as a shepherd would. Under his preaching a young, hot-blooded infidel named Aurelius Augustine was converted to Christ, and St. Augustine went on to become one of the greatest heroes in the history of Christian theology.

Ambrose continued preaching until he fell sick in AD 397. When distressed friends prayed for his healing, he replied, "I have so lived among you that I cannot be ashamed to live longer, but neither do I fear to die; for we have a good Lord." On Good Friday, April 3, Ambrose lay with his hands extended in the form of the cross, moving his lips in prayer. His friends huddled in sadness and watched. Sometime past midnight, their beloved bishop passed to his good Lord.

Sixteen centuries have come and gone, and today the hymns of Ambrose are better known than his sermons. His beloved Christmas carol, "*Veni, Redemptor gentium,*" was translated from Latin by John Mason Neale in 1862 and set to a lovely, lilting fifteenth-century melody named PUER NOBIS NASCITUR.

Angels We Have Heard on High

French Carol

French Melody

1. An - gels we have heard on high Sweet - ly sing-ing o'er the plains,
2. Shep-herds, why this ju - bi - lee? Why your joy - ous strains pro - long?
3. Come to Beth - le - hem and see Him whose birth the an - gels sing;

And the moun-tains in re - ply Ech - o - ing their joy - ous strains.
What the glad-some tid - ings be, Which in - spire your heav'n - ly song?
Come a - dore on bend - ed knee, Christ the Lord, the new - born King.

Glo - - - - - - - - - - ri - a

in ex - cel - sis De - o! Glo - - - - - - - -

ri - a in ex - cel - sis De - o!

Angels We Have Heard on High

1855

And suddenly there was with the angel a multitude of the heavenly host praising God and saying: "Glory to God in the highest, and on earth peace, goodwill toward men!" Luke 2:13–14

*L*es Anges dans nos Campagnes" was a French carol dating from the 1700s, which appeared in several different versions. It was published in English in 1862, the words saying:

> *Angels we have heard on high | Sweetly singing o'er the plains,*
> *And the mountains in reply | Echoing their joyous strains.*
> Gloria, in excelsis Deo!

An older version had the title "Harken All! What Holy Singing!" The words, translated into English, said:

> *Hearken, all! What holy singing | Now is sounding from the sky!*
> *'Tis a hymn with grandeur ringing, | Sung by voices clear and high.*
> Gloria, in excelsis Deo!

Still another primitive version speaks from the shepherds' vantage point, saying:

> *Shepherds in the field abiding, | Tell us when the seraph bright*
> *Greeted you with wondrous tiding, | What you saw and heard that night.*
> Gloria, in excelsis Deo!

Hymns are usually authored by human beings like us, but in this case obscure verses by unknown French poets were coupled with a refrain that was literally composed by angels in heaven: *Gloria, in excelsis Deo.* That's the Latin wording for the angelic anthem "Glory to God in the highest!" It comes from Luke 2:14 in the Vulgate, the Latin version of the Bible. The Latin word *Gloria* means "glory," and *in excelsis* is the phrase for "in the highest." Our English words *excel* and *excellent* come from the same root, meaning "to rise" or "to ascend" or "to be high." The Latin word *Deo* means "God."

This was the song proclaimed by the angels over Shepherds' Field the night Christ was born. The musical score stretches out and emphasizes the words in a way that is uniquely fun to sing and deeply stirring, as we lift our voices to proclaim: Jesus has come! Hope has arrived on earth! A Savior is born! Glory to God on High! *Gloria, in excelsis Deo!*

Thou Didst Leave Thy Throne

Emily E. S. Elliott

Timothy R. Matthews

1. Thou didst leave Thy throne and Thy king-ly crown When Thou cam-est to earth for me, But in Beth-le-hem's home was there found no room For Thy ho-ly na-tiv-i-ty. O come to my heart, Lord Je-sus: There is room in my heart for Thee!

2. Heav-en's arch-es rang when the an-gels sang, Pro-claim-ing Thy roy-al de-cree, But of low-ly birth didst Thou come to earth And in great hu-mil-i-ty. O come to my heart, Lord Je-sus. There is room in my heart for Thee!

3. The fox-es found rest, and the birds their nest In the shade of the for-est tree; But Thy couch was the sod, O Thou Son of God, In the des-erts of Gal-i-lee. O come to my heart, Lord Je-sus. There is room in my heart for Thee!

4. Thou cam-est, O Lord, with the liv-ing word That should set Thy peo-ple free; But with mock-ing scorn and with crown of thorn They bore Thee to Cal-va-ry. O come to my heart, Lord Je-sus. There is room in my heart for Thee!

5. When the heavens shall ring and the an-gels sing At Thy com-ing to vic-tor-y, Let Thy voice call me home, say-ing, "Yet there is room, There is room at My side for thee." And my heart shall re-joice, Lord Je-sus, When Thou com-est and call-est me.

Thou Didst Leave Thy Throne

1864

And she brought forth her firstborn Son, and wrapped Him in swaddling cloths, and laid Him in a manger, because there was no room for them in the inn.
Luke 2:7

 Emily Elliott was born south of London, in the little holiday town of Brighton on the English Channel, in 1836. Her father, Edward Elliott, was pastor of St. Mark's Church there. His invalid aunt—Charlotte Elliott, well-known hymnist and the author of the invitational hymn "Just as I Am"—lived nearby.

While working with children in the church choir and the local parish school, Emily, then in her late twenties, wanted to use the Christmas season to teach them about the entire life and mission of the Savior. As she studied Luke 2:7, she wrote this hymn. The first and second verses speak of our Lord's birth, but the third verse describes His life as an itinerate preacher. The next stanza describes His death on Calvary, and the last verse proclaims His Second Coming.

Emily had her hymn privately printed, and it was first performed in her father's church during the Christmas season of 1864. Six years later, she included it in a magazine she edited called *Church Missionary Juvenile Instructor.*

Several years later, Emily inserted this carol into her book of poems and hymns entitled *Chimes for Daily Service.* "Thou Didst Leave Thy Throne" first appeared in the United States in *The Sunday School Hymnal,* published in Boston in 1871.

Emily devoted her life to Sunday school work, to ministering to the down-and-out in Brighton's rescue missions, and to sharing the message of Christ through poems, hymns, and the printed page. Another of her carols was widely used for many years during the Christmas season, though it isn't well-known today. The words are ideally suited for the children Emily so loved. This carol, too, encompasses our Lord's entire life and mission:

There came a little Child to earth long ago;
And the angels of God proclaimed His birth, high and low.

Out on the night, so calm and still, their song was heard;
For they knew that the Child on Bethlehem's hill was Christ the Lord.

In mortal weakness, want and pain, He came to die,
That the children of earth might in glory reign with Him on high.

And evermore in robes so fair and undefiled,
Those ransomed children His praise declare, who was a Child.

I Heard the Bells on Christmas Day

Henry Wadsworth Longfellow

Jean Baptiste Calkin

1. I heard the bells on Christ - mas day Their
2. And thought how, as the day had come, The
3. And in de - spair I bowed my head: "There
4. Then pealed the bells more loud and deep: "God
5. Till ring - ing, sing - ing on its way, The

old fa - mil - iar car - ols play, And wild and sweet the
bel - fries of all Chris - ten - dom Had rolled a - long th'un -
is no peace on earth," I said, "For hate is strong, and
is not dead, nor doth He sleep; The wrong shall fail, the
world re - volved from night to day, A voice, a chime, a

words re - peat, Of peace on earth, good - will to men.
bro - ken song Of peace on earth, good - will to men.
mocks the song Of peace on earth, good - will to men."
right pre - vail, With peace on earth, good - will to men."
chant sub - lime, Of peace on earth, good - will to men!

I Heard the Bells on
Christmas Day

1864

Behold, He who keeps Israel shall neither slumber nor sleep. Psalm 121:4

The famous Longfellow brothers were born and raised in Portland, Maine, in the 1800s. Henry Wadsworth was born in 1807, and younger brother Samuel arrived in 1819. Henry became a Harvard professor of literature and one of America's greatest writers, and Samuel became a Unitarian minister and a hymnist.

While Henry was publishing his books, however, dark clouds were gathering over his life and over all America. In 1861, his wife tragically died when her dress caught fire in their home in Cambridge, Massachusetts. That same year, the Civil War broke out, tearing the nation apart. Two years later, during the fiercest days of the conflict, Henry's son, Charley, seventeen, ran away from home and hopped aboard a train to join President Lincoln's army.

Charley proved a brave and popular soldier. He saw action at the Battle of Chancellorsville in 1863, but in early June he contracted typhoid fever and malaria and was sent home to recover. He missed the Battle of Gettysburg, but by August, Charley was well enough to return to the field. On November 27, during the battle of New Hope Church in Virginia, he was shot through the left shoulder. The bullet nicked his spine and came close to paralyzing him. He was carried into the church and later taken to Washington to recuperate.

Receiving the news on December 1, 1863, Henry left immediately for Washington. He found his son well enough to travel, and they headed back to Cambridge, arriving home on December 8. For weeks Henry sat by his son's bedside, slowly nursing his boy back to health.

On Christmas Day, December 25, 1863, Henry gave vent to his feelings in this plaintive carol that can only be understood against the backdrop of war. Two stanzas, now omitted from most hymnals, speak of the cannons thundering in the South and of hatred tearing apart "the hearth-stones of a continent." The poet feels like dropping his head in despair, but then he hears the Christmas bells. Their triumphant pealing reminds him that "God is not dead, nor doth He sleep."

The Sunday school children of the Unitarian Church of the Disciples in Boston first sang this song during that year's Christmas celebration. How wonderful that such a song should emerge from the bloody clouds of the War Between the States.

What Child Is This?

William C. Dix

English Melody

1. What child is this, who laid to rest, on Mar-y's lap is sleep-ing?
2. Why lies He in such mean es-tate, where ox and ass are feed-ing?
3. So bring Him in-cense, gold, and myrrh; come peas-ant, king to own Him.

Whom an-gels greet with an-thems sweet, while shep-herds watch are keep-ing?
Good Chris-tian, fear; for sin-ners here the si-lent Word is plead-ing.
The King of kings, sal-va-tion brings, let lov-ing hearts en-throne Him.

This, this is Christ the King, whom shep-herds guard and an-gels sing;
Nails, spear, shall pierce Him thro', the cross be borne, for me, for you.
Raise, raise the song on high, The vir-gin sings her lul-la-by.

Haste, haste to bring Him laud, the Babe, the Son of Mar-y.
Hail, hail the Word made flesh, the Babe, the Son of Mar-y.
Joy, joy for Christ is born, the Babe, the Son of Mar-y.

What Child Is This?

<u>1865</u>

So it was, when the angels had gone away from them into heaven, that the shepherds said to one another, "Let us now go to Bethlehem . . ." Luke 2:15

Feelings of sadness come over me whenever I hear this deeply moving carol. It is, after all, set in the key of E minor, the "saddest of all keys." Yet triumphant joy dispels the sadness as we exclaim, "This, this is Christ the King, whom shepherds guard and angels sing."

The melancholic melody is a famous old British tune called "Greensleeves," originally a ballad about a man pining for his lost love, the fair Lady Greensleeves. Tradition says it was composed by King Henry VIII for Anne Boleyn. That's unlikely, but we do know that Henry's daughter, Queen Elizabeth I, danced to the tune.

Shakespeare referred to it twice in his play *The Merry Wives of Windsor.* In Act V, for example, Falstaff says, "Let the sky rain potatoes; let it thunder to the tune of 'Green Sleeves.'"

It was licensed to two different printers in 1580, and soon thereafter was being used with religious texts. Its first association with Christmas came in 1642, in a book titled *New Christmas Carols,* in which it was used with the poem "The Old Year Now Away Has Fled." The last verse says, "Come, give's more liquor when I doe call, / I'll drink to each one in this hall . . . And God send us a happy new yeare!"

For nearly 150 years, however, "Greensleeves" has been most identified with "What Child Is This?" The words of this carol are taken from a longer poem written by an insurance agent named William Chatterton Dix, born in Bristol, England, in 1837. His father was a surgeon who wanted his son to follow his footsteps. But having no interest in medicine, William left Bristol Grammar School, moved to Glasgow, and sold insurance.

His greatest love was his prose and poetry for Christ. He wrote two devotional books, a book for children, and scores of hymns, two of which remain popular Christmas carols: "What Child Is This?" and "As with Gladness Men of Old."

All of Dix's hymns should be more widely sung today, for they are masterpieces of poetry, filled with rich scriptural truth. His exultant hymn "Alleluia!" begins:

Alleluia! Sing to Jesus! His the scepter, His the throne.
Alleluia! His the triumph, His the victory alone.

Who Is He in Yonder Stall?

Benjamin R. Hanby

Benjamin R. Hanby

1. Who is He in yon-der stall, At whose feet the shep-herds fall?
2. Who is He the peo-ple bless For His words of gen-tle-ness?
3. Who is He that stands and weeps At the grave where Laz-arus sleeps?
4. Lo! at mid-night, who is He Prays in dark Geth-sem-a-ne?
5. Who is He that from the grave Comes to heal and help and save?

Who is He in deep dis-tress, Fast-ing in the wil-der-ness?
Who is He to whom they bring All the sick and sor-row-ing?
Who is He the gath-ering throng Greet with loud tri-um-phant song?
Who is He on yon-der tree Dies in grief and ag-o-ny?
Who is He that from His throne Rules through all the world a-lone?

'Tis the Lord! O won-drous stor-ry! 'Tis the Lord! the King of

glo-ry! At His feet we hum-bly fall, Crown Him! crown Him, Lord of all!

Who Is He in Yonder Stall?

1866

For the LORD takes pleasure in His people; He will beautify the humble with salvation. Psalm 149:4

Would you believe it? This beautiful Christmas carol about the birth of Jesus Christ was written by the same American who composed "Up on the Housetop," arguably the first popular Christmas song emphasizing the role of Santa Claus: "Up on the housetop, click, click, click, / Down thru' the chimney with good Saint Nick."

Benjamin Russell Hanby was born in Rushville, Ohio, in 1833, to a United Brethren minister. As a young man, Benjamin attended Oberlin University in Westerville, Ohio. Those were the days leading up to the Civil War, and young Benjamin became a passionate and outspoken abolitionist. His home in Westerville became a secret stop on the famous Underground Railroad.

According to reports, a freed slave named Joe Selby stopped at Hanby's home one day, looking for work and wanting to earn enough money to purchase the freedom of his girlfriend, Nellie Gray. Joe fell ill, however, and died of pneumonia before he could free her, and Benjamin deeply grieved as he watched Joe die. It was reportedly from this experience that Hanby wrote his most famous song, "Darling Nellie Gray."

Hanby sent the song to the Oliver Ditson Company, a Boston publishing firm, but heard nothing back. One day he learned that "Darling Nellie Gray" was a hit. As it turned out, the executives at Oliver Ditson had filed for the song's copyright in their own names, though still listing him as the author. When he wrote asking for his share of the profits, the company sent him a dozen copies of the sheet music along with a note saying, "We have the money and you have the fame. That balances the account."

Hanby went on to become a college employee, a school principal, a pastor, and a songwriter before dying in his early thirties just after the conclusion of the Civil War. "Up on the Housetop" was published in about 1860, and "Who Is He in Yonder Stall?" was published in 1866, the year before Hanby's death. Today his home, located a block from Otterbein College, is owned by the Ohio Historical Society and in his memory is managed by the Westerville Historical Society.

O Little Town of Bethlehem

Phillips Brooks

Lewis H. Redner

1. O lit-tle town of Beth-le-hem, How still we see thee lie;
2. For Christ is born of Ma-ry And gath-ered all a-bove;
3. How si-lent-ly, how si-lent-ly, The won-drous gift is giv'n;
4. O, ho-ly child of Beth-le-hem, De-scend to us we pray;

A-bove thy deep and dream-less sleep, The si-lent stars go by.
While mor-tals sleep the an-gels keep Their watch of won-dering love.
So God im-parts to hu-man hearts, The bless-ings of His heaven.
Cast out our sin and en-ter in, Be born in us to-day.

Yet in thy dark streets shin-eth The ev-er-last-ing Light;
O, morn-ing stars to-geth-er Pro-claim the ho-ly birth;
No ear may hear His com-ing, But in this world of sin;
We hear the Christ-mas an-gels, The great glad tid-ings tell;

The hopes and fears of all the years, Are met in thee to-night.
And prais-es sing to God the King And peace to men on earth.
Where meek souls will Re-ceive Him still, The dear Christ en-ters in.
O, come to us a-bide with us, Our Lord, Em-man-u-el.

O Little Town of Bethlehem
1868

Bethlehem . . . though you are little among the thousands of Judah, yet out of you shall come forth to Me the One to be Ruler in Israel. Micah 5:2

At nearly six feet six, weighing three hundred pounds, Phillips Brooks cast a long shadow. He was a native Bostonian, the ninth generation of distinguished Puritan stock, who entered the Episcopalian ministry and pastored with great power in Philadelphia and in Boston. His sermons were topical rather than expositional, and he's been criticized for thinness of doctrine. Nonetheless he's considered one of America's greatest preachers. His delivery came in lightning bursts; he felt he had more to say than time in which to say it.

While at Philadelphia's Holy Trinity Church, Phillips, thirty, visited the Holy Land. On December 24, 1865, traveling by horseback from Jerusalem, he attended a five-hour Christmas Eve service at the Church of the Nativity in Bethlehem. He was deeply moved. "I remember standing in the old church in Bethlehem," he later said, "close to the spot where Jesus was born, when the whole church was ringing hour after hour with splendid hymns of praise to God, how again and again it seemed as if I could hear voices I knew well, telling each other of the *Wonderful Night* of the Savior's birth."

Three years later, as he prepared for the Christmas season of 1867, he wanted to compose an original Christmas hymn for the children to sing during their annual program. Recalling his magical night in Bethlehem, he wrote a little hymn of five stanzas and handed the words to his organist, Lewis Redner, saying, "Lewis, why not write a new tune for my poem. If it is a good tune, I will name it 'St. Lewis' after you."

Lewis struggled with his assignment, complaining of no inspiration. Finally, on the night before the Christmas program, he awoke with the music ringing in his soul. He jotted down the melody, then went back to sleep. The next day, a group of six Sunday school teachers and thirty-six children sang "O Little Town of Bethlehem."

Brooks was so pleased with the tune that he did indeed name it for his organist, changing the spelling to ST. LOUIS, so as not to embarrass him. The fourth stanza, usually omitted from our hymnbooks, says:

Where children pure and happy pray to the blessèd Child,
Where misery cries out to Thee, Son of the mother mild;
Where charity stands watching and faith holds wide the door,
The dark night wakes, the glory breaks, and Christmas comes once more.

There's a Song in the Air

Josiah G. Holland

Karl P. Harrington

1. There's a song in the air! There's a star in the sky!
2. There's a tu-mult of joy O'er the won-der-ful birth,
3. In the light of that star Lie the a-ges im-pearled;
4. We re-joice in the light, And we ech-o the song

There's a moth-er's deep prayer, And a ba-by's low cry!
For a Vir-gin's sweet Boy, Is the Lord of the earth.
And that song from a-far Has swept o-ver the world.
That comes down thro' the night From the heav-en-ly throng.

And the star rains its fire while the beau-ti-ful sing,
Lo, the star rains its fire while the beau-ti-ful sing,
Ev-ery hearth is a-flame, and the beau-ti-ful sing
Ay! we shout to the love-ly E-van-gel they bring,

For the man-ger of Beth-le-hem, cra-dles a King!
For the man-ger of Beth-le-hem, cra-dles a King!
In the homes of the na-tions that Je-sus is King!
As we greet in His cra-dle our Sav-ior and King!

There's a Song in the Air
1872

Praise the LORD! Sing to the LORD a new song, and His praise in the assembly of saints. Psalm 149:1

For a long time, Josiah Gilbert Holland was known to his friends as a failure at just about everything he tried. Dropping out of high school, he tried his hand at photography, then calligraphy. When those professions didn't pan out, Josiah, twenty-one, enrolled in Berkshire Medical College. After graduation, he practiced medicine in Springfield, Massachusetts, for a while before quitting to start a newspaper. The paper folded after six months. At length, he joined the editorial staff of another newspaper, the *Springfield Republican,* and there he finally found his niche in writing.

In 1865, the world was stunned by the tragic assassination of Abraham Lincoln. The next year it was Josiah Holland who published the first major biography of Lincoln. In it, he presented Lincoln as a "true-hearted Christian" and provided a number of stories to reinforce the point. When Lincoln's free-thinking law partner, William Herndon, read the book, he refuted it. Lincoln was an "infidel," declared Herndon, and he died as an "unbeliever." To this day, historians argue about Lincoln's religious faith, or lack of it. But the notoriety put Josiah Holland on the literary map of his day.

In 1870, he became a founder and the senior editor of *Scribner's Magazine.* He continued publishing books and was quite prolific. In 1872, he published *The Marble Prophecy and Other Poems.* In it were the four stanzas of "There's a Song in the Air." It was an unusual poem, in that the first four lines of each stanza contained six syllables each, but the fifth and sixth lines were twice as long. Two years later, it was set to music in a collection of Sunday school songs, but didn't achieve widespread popularity.

Several years after Josiah's death in 1881, a Latin professor named Karl Pomeroy Harrington read "There's a Song in the Air." Harrington was an amateur musician who had begun writing melodies as a youngster on the small organ in his childhood home. Harrington later inherited that old Estey organ and moved it to his vacation cottage in North Woodstock, New Hampshire. While spending the summer there in 1904, he sat down at the old instrument, pumping the bellows with the foot pedals, and hammered out the lovely melodic tune to which "There's a Song in the Air" is now widely sung.

Away in a Manger

Anonymous

James R. Murray

1. A - way in a man - ger, no crib for a bed,
2. The cat - tle are low - ing, the ba - by a - wakes,
3. Be near me, Lord Je - sus; I ask Thee to stay

The lit - tle Lord Je - sus laid down His sweet head.
But lit - tle Lord Je - sus, no cry - ing He makes.
Close by me for - ev - er, and love me, I pray.

The stars in the sky look down where He lay,
I love Thee, Lord Je - sus, look down from the sky,
Bless all the dear chil - dren in Thy ten - der care,

The lit - tle Lord Je - sus, a - sleep on the hay.
And stay by my cra - dle till morn - ing is nigh.
And take us to heav - en to live with Thee there.

Away in a Manger

1887

And she brought forth her firstborn Son, and wrapped Him in swaddling cloths, and laid Him in a manger, because there was no room for them in the inn.
Luke 2:7

*T*his is commonly known as "Luther's Cradle Hymn." But did the great German reformer, Martin Luther, really write the words? Did he sing them by the cradle of his little son, Hans? This is a great mystery in hymnology.

In 1887, "Away in a Manger" appeared in a little book of songs entitled *Dainty Songs for Little Lads and Lasses,* published in Cincinnati by the John Church Company. The songbook was compiled by James R. Murray. A notation beneath "Away in a Manger" said, "Luther's Cradle Hymn (Composed by Martin Luther for his children and still sung by German mothers to their little ones). Only stanzas 1 and 2 were given.

"Away in a Manger" quickly became America's favorite children's carol, the words being sung to forty-one different tunes! Everyone assumed the poem had been written by the great reformer, Martin Luther.

Then in 1945, Richard Hill published a fascinating article entitled "Not So Far Away in a Manger" in which he announced he had discovered the first two stanzas of "Away in a Manger" in an 1885 songbook entitled *Little Children's Book,* published by German Lutherans in Pennsylvania. No authorship was given. Nor could Hill find any appearance of this carol in German church history or in Luther's works.

After extensive research, Hill concluded, "It seems essential to lay [aside] once for all the legend that Luther wrote a carol for his children, which no one else knew anything about, until it suddenly turned up in English dress four hundred years later in Philadelphia. Luther can well afford to spare the honor." But he adds, "Although Luther himself had nothing to do with the carol, the colonies of German Lutherans in Pennsylvania almost certainly did."

So the mystery endures. Who wrote "Away in a Manger"? There were apparently two unknown writers: a German Lutheran in Pennsylvania who wrote the first two stanzas, with another unknown author adding a third verse that first appeared in an 1892 songbook published by Charles H. Gabriel.

Well, who cares? Certainly not the generations of children around the world who have come to love and know the little Jesus through this sweet carol, and who have gone to sleep praying:

I love Thee, Lord Jesus; look down from the sky
And stay by my cradle till morning is nigh.

Go, Tell It on the Mountain

John W. Work, Jr.

American Folk Song

Go, tell it on the moun-tain, O-ver the hills and ev-ery-where;

Go, tell it on the moun-tain, That Je-sus Christ is born!

1. While shep-herds kept their watch-ing O'er si-lent flocks by night, Be-
2. The shep-herds feared and trem-bled When lo! A-bove the earth Rang
3. Down in a low-ly man-ger The hum-ble Christ was born, And

hold through-out the heav-ens There shone a ho-ly light.
out the an-gel cho-rus That hailed our Sav-ior's birth.
brought us God's sal-va-tion That bless-ed Christ-mas morn.

Go, Tell It on the Mountain

1907

Then the shepherds returned, glorifying and praising God for all the things that they had heard and seen, as it was told them. Luke 2:20

During the bitter days of slavery, black workers on American plantations solaced themselves with song and created a unique form of American hymnology—the Negro spiritual. It was the Jubilee Singers of Fisk University in Nashville, Tennessee, that took the plantation songs of the Negro slaves to the entire world. One of the last "spirituals" to be uncovered and published was this unique Christmas carol, "Go, Tell It on the Mountain."

How did it come about?

John Wesley Work Jr. was born in Nashville on or about August 6, 1871. His father was choir director for a Nashville church, and he often wrote his own arrangements. John grew up singing in his dad's choirs, and when he enrolled in Fisk University, he became active in its music program, though his primary subjects were history and Latin. Returning to Fisk to work on his master's degree, John was eventually hired as professor of Latin and Greek. But his greatest love was the preservation and performance of the Negro spiritual.

Many of the spirituals had been published, but "Go, Tell It on the Mountain" was largely unknown, though it had been performed by the Jubilee Singers since 1879. Some of the original stanzas were obscure, for spirituals, by definition, were unwritten songs passed from plantation to plantation and from generation to generation. The chorus, however, was crystal clear and highlighted the theme for the whole: "Go, tell it on the mountain, / That Jesus Christ is born."

Intrigued by the chorus and melody, John wrote two new stanzas for this song, and it became his custom before sunrise on Christmas morning to take students caroling from building to building, singing "Go, Tell It on the Mountain." It was first published in 1907 in *Work's Folk Songs of the Negro as Sung on the Plantations*.

John Work has been called the first black collector of Negro folk songs, a pursuit continued by his two sons, John Wesley Work II and Frederick J. Work. Both young men served on the faculty of Fisk University, working with the Jubilee Singers and collecting and publishing African-American spirituals and folk music.

"Go Tell It on the Mountain" is classic in that genre. To black slaves in antebellum America, the birth of a liberating Savior was a message to be heralded from the highest mountains.

It still is, for us all.

Jesus Christ Is Born Today!

Robert J. Morgan

from *Lyra Davidica*

1. Je - sus Christ is born to - day! Al - le - lu - ia!
2. Heav - enly choirs an - nounce His birth! Al - le - lu - ia!
3. Born to die and rise a - gain! Al - le - lu - ia!

See Him in the man - ger lay! Al - le - lu - ia!
Shep - herd boys pro - claim His worth! Al - le - lu - ia!
Con - quering death and hell and sin! Al - le - lu - ia!

Ten - der Babe, yet God Most High. Al - le - lu - ia!
Sheep and ox - en gath - er round! Al - le - lu - ia!
Now a - bove the clouds He lives! Al - le - lu - ia!

Ma - ker of the earth and sea and sky. Al - le - lu - ia!
Beth - le - hem's shed is ho - ly ground! Al - le - lu - ia!
Ev - er - last - ing love and life He gives! Al - le - lu - ia!

Jesus Christ Is Born Today!

2005

While I live I will praise the LORD; I will sing praises to my God while I have my being. Psalm 146:2

A dolf Hitler rose to power in Germany, determined to take over the German church and dictate the nation's religion. He falsely accused many of the clergymen of treason, theft, or sexual malpractice; and priests, nuns, and church leaders were arrested on trumped-up charges. Religious publications were suspended. Hitler encouraged couples to be married by state officials rather than by priests and pastors. In 1935, he outlawed prayer in the schools, and he did all he could to replace Bible reading with Nazi propaganda.

He had greater difficulty with the holidays because Germans had faithfully observed Easter and Christmas for centuries. He sought instead to keep the holidays but to reinterpret their meaning. Easter became a celebration heralding the arrival of spring, and Christmas was turned into a totally pagan festival. Carols and nativity plays were banned from the schools in 1938, and even the name *Christmas* was changed to *Yuletide.*

Holy days became holidays, and the sacred was secularized.

Today we're amazed to observe the same thing happening in America as social libertarians, aided by the media and the courts, seem determined to drain Christmas of its religious significance and make it a purely secular, pagan holiday.

Let's do whatever it takes to remind our society that one can't even spell the word *Christmas* without Christ. We need to stay focused on Him during the season; to proclaim His birth, life, death, and resurrection; to worship Him; and to follow the example of the shepherds—"When they had seen Him, they made widely known the saying which was told them concerning this Child" (Luke 2:17).

Every generation of Christians needs to write its own songs of Christmas. Here is my modest contribution, a new carol set to an old melody, one usually reserved for Easter, when we join voices in Charles Wesley's jubilant anthem "Christ the Lord Is Risen Today." The melody, EASTER HYMN, is perhaps our most triumphant hymn setting, written in the early 1700s by an unknown composer.

Why use it only once a year? We can sing the Allelujahs at Christmas too!

Joyful, Joyful, We Adore Thee

Henry van Dyke

Ludwig van Beethoven

1. Joy - ful, joy - ful, we a - dore Thee, God of glo - ry Lord of love;
2. All Thy works with joy sur-round Thee, Earth and heaven re - flect Thy rays;
3. Thou art giv - ing and for - giv - ing. Ev - er bless - ing, ev - er blest,
4. Mor - tals join the might - y cho - rus, Which the Morn - ing Stars be - gan.

Hearts un - fold like flow'rs be - fore Thee, Open-ing to the sun a - bove.
Stars and an - gels sing a - round Thee, Cen - ter of un - bro - ken praise.
Well - spring of the joy of liv - ing, O - cean depth of hap - py rest!
Fa - ther love is reign-ing o'er us, Broth - er love binds man to man.

Melt the clouds of sin and sad - ness; Drive the dark of doubt a - way;
Field and for - est, vale and moun-tain, Flow - ery mea-dow, flash - ing sea,
Thou our Fa - ther, Christ our Broth - er, All who live in love are Thine.
Ev - er sing - ing, march we on - ward, Vic - tors in the midst of strife;

Giv - er of im - mor - tal glad-ness, Fill us with the light of day!
Chant - ing bird and flow - ing foun-tain, Call us to re - joice in Thee.
Teach us how to love each oth - er; Lift us to the joy di - vine.
Joy - ful mu - sic lifts us sun-ward, In the tri - umph song of life.

Joyful, Joyful, We Adore Thee

1907

For I know the thoughts that I think toward you, says the LORD, thoughts of peace and not of evil, to give you a future and a hope. Jeremiah 29:11

O nce, when recovering from a bout of depression, I found this hymn very therapeutic. "Melt the clouds of sin and sadness, drive the dark of doubt away," it says. "Giver of immortal gladness, fill us [me] with the light of day." Notice how every phrase of this prayer is bursting with exuberance: the Lord is our "wellspring of the joy of living," our "ocean depth of happy rest," and we ask Him to "lift us to the joy divine."

The author of the hymn, Henry Jackson van Dyke, was born in Pennsylvania in 1852 and became pastor of the Brick Presbyterian Church in New York City.* Henry later became professor of English literature at Princeton and the author of a number of books, including the still-popular *The Other Wise Man.* He went on to occupy a number of eminent positions, including:

- American ambassador to the Netherlands and Luxembourg (appointed by his friend, Woodrow Wilson)
- Lieutenant commander in the United States Navy Chaplains Corps during World War I
- Moderator of the General Assembly of the Presbyterian Church
- Commander of the Legion of Honor
- President of the National Institute of Arts and Letters
- Chairman of the committee that compiled the Presbyterian *Book of Common Worship*

In 1907, Henry van Dyke was invited to preach at Williams College in Massachusetts. At breakfast one morning, he handed the college president a piece of paper, saying, "Here is a hymn for you. Your mountains [the Berkshires] were my inspiration. It must be sung to the music of Beethoven's 'Hymn of Joy.'"

When he was later asked about his hymn, van Dyke replied, "These verses are simple expressions of common Christian feelings and desires in this present time—hymns of today that may be sung together by people who know the thought of the age, and are not afraid that any truth of science will destroy religion, or any revolution on earth overthrow the kingdom of heaven. Therefore this is a hymn of trust and joy and hope."

---

*Henry Jackson van Dyke's resignation from Brick Church in 1899 paved the way for Maltbie Babcock to be called as its pastor. See the story behind "This Is My Father's World."

Alas! and Did My Savior Bleed

Isaac Watts

Hugh Wilson

1. A - las! and did my Sav - ior bleed And did my Sov - ereign die? Would He de - vote that sa - cred head, For such a worm as I?

2. Was it for crimes that I have done, He suf - fered on the tree? A - maz - ing pi - ty, grace un - known, And love be - yond de - gree!

3. Well might the sun in dark - ness hide And shut His glo - ries in; When Christ the might - y Ma - ker died For man, the crea - ture's sin.

4. Thus might I hide my blush - ing face While His dear cross ap - pears; Dis - solve my heart in thank - ful - ness And melt mine eyes to tears.

5. But drops of grief can ne'er re - pay, The debt of love I owe; Here, Lord, I give my - self a - way, 'Tis all that I can do.

Alas! and Did My Savior Bleed

1707

But God forbid that I should boast except in the cross of our Lord Jesus Christ.
Galatians 6:14

After his graduation from college, Isaac Watts returned to Southampton, England, and spent two years writing hymns for Above Bar Congregational Church. He then moved to London to tutor children in a wealthy family of Dissenters. While there he joined Mark Lane Independent Chapel. Soon he was asked to be a teacher in the church, and in 1698, he was hired as associate pastor. There, on his twenty-fourth birthday, he preached his first sermon. In 1702, he became senior pastor of the church, a position he retained the rest of his life. He was a brilliant Bible student, and his sermons brought the church to life.

In 1707, his *Hymns and Spiritual Songs* was published. Isaac had written most of these hymns in Southampton while in his late teens and early twenties. Included was a hymn now considered the finest hymn ever written in the English language. It was based on Galatians 6:14: "But God forbid that I should boast except in the cross of our Lord Jesus Christ." Originally the first stanza said, "When I survey the wondrous cross / Where the young Prince of Glory died . . ." In an enlarged 1709 edition, Watts rewrote the lines to say:

> *When I survey the wondrous cross*
> *On which the Prince of glory died,*
> *My richest gain I count but loss,*
> *And pour contempt on all my pride.*

Also included in the 1707 hymnbook was "Heavenly Joy on Earth," better known today as "Come, We That Love the Lord," or "We're Marching to Zion."

Another hymn was "Godly Sorrow Arising from the Sufferings of Christ," better known as "Alas! and Did My Savior Bleed." This hymn later played a major role in the conversion of a great American hymnist. In 1851, Fanny Crosby, thirty-one, attended a revival service at John Street Methodist Church in New York. "After a prayer was offered," she recalled, "they began to sing the grand old consecration hymn, 'Alas! and Did My Savior Bleed' and when they reached the third line of the fifth stanza, 'Here, Lord, I give myself away,' my very soul was flooded with celestial light."

How right that Watts should, long after his death, play a part in winning to Christ the author of a new generation of hymns and gospel songs!

Christ the Lord Is Risen Today

Charles Wesley

from *Lyra Davidica*

1. Christ the Lord is risen to - day, Al - - le - lu - ia!
2. Lives a - gain our glo - rious King, Al - - le - lu - ia!
3. Love's re - deem - ing work is done, Al - - le - lu - ia!
4. Soar we now where Christ has led, Al - - le - lu - ia!

Sons of men and an - gels say: Al - - - le - lu - ia!
Where, O death, is now thy sting? Al - - - le - lu - ia!
Fought the fight, the bat - tle won, Al - - - le - lu - ia!
Fol - lowing our ex - alt - ed Head, Al - - - le - lu - ia!

Raise your joys and tri - umphs high, Al - - - le - lu - ia!
Dy - ing once He all doth save, Al - - - le - lu - ia!
Death in vain for - bids Him rise, Al - - - le - lu - ia!
Made like Him, like Him we rise, Al - - - le - lu - ia!

Sing, ye heavens, and earth, re - ply: Al - - - le - lu - ia!
Where thy vic - tor - y, O grave? Al - - - le - lu - ia!
Christ hath o - pened par - a - dise, Al - - - le - lu - ia!
Ours the cross, the grave, the skies, Al - - - le - lu - ia!

Christ the Lord Is Risen Today

1739

And if Christ is not risen, then our preaching is empty and your faith is also empty.
1 Corinthians 15:14

J ohn and Charles Wesley found themselves out of favor with many fellow Anglican ministers who spurned their fiery evangelistic preaching. Many pulpits were closed to them.

A friend from his Oxford days, George Whitefield, twenty-two, who was having the same trouble, began preaching in the open air. In London, he asked Charles to stand with him as he preached to thousands in the open air at Blackheath, and Charles, too, got a vision for reaching the multitudes.

He made his first attempt in the outskirts of London. "Franklyn, a farmer, invited me to preach in his field," he wrote. "I did so to about 500. I returned to the house rejoicing." Soon he was preaching to thousands. "My load was gone, and all my doubts and scruples. God shone upon my path; and I knew this was his will concerning me."

A man named Joseph Williams heard Charles in Bristol: "I found him standing on a table-board, in an erect posture . . . surrounded by, I guess, more than a thousand people, some of them fashionable persons, but most of the lower rank of mankind. He prayed with uncommon fervency . . . He then preached about half an hour in such a manner as I have scarce ever heard any man preach . . . I think I never heard any man labor so earnestly to convince his hearers they were all by nature in a sinful, lost, undone, damnable state; that notwithstanding, there was a possibility of their salvation, through faith in Christ . . . All this he backed up with many texts of Scripture, which he explained and illustrated, and then by a variety of the most forcible motives, arguments, and expostulation, did he invite, allure, quicken, and labor, if it were possible, to compel all, and every of his hearers, to believe in Christ for salvation."

Charles Wesley still preaches today in much the same way, through his ageless hymns that are sung around the world each week. Perhaps his most exuberant anthem is the one he simply called "Hymn for Easter Day," published in 1739. It originally consisted of eleven stanzas. The "Alleluias" were added later, but appropriately, for this is a hymn one never gets tired of singing:

Christ, the Lord, is risen today, Alleluia!
Sons of men and angels say, Alleluia!
Raise your joys and triumphs high, Alleluia!
Sing, ye heavens, and earth, reply, Alleluia!

Crown Him with Many Crowns

Matthew Bridges/Godfrey Thring

George J. Elvey

1. Crown Him with man-y crowns, The Lamb up-on His throne. Hark! how the heaven-ly an-them drowns All mu-sic but its own! A-wake, my soul and sing Of Him who died for Thee; And hail Him as thy match-less King Through all e-ter-ni-ty.

2. Crown Him the Lord of love: Be-hold His hands and side, Rich wounds, yet vi-si-ble a-bove, In beaut-y glo-ri-fied; No an-gel in the sky Can ful-ly bear that sight, But down-ward bends His won-der-ing eye At mys-ter-ies so bright.

3. Crown Him the Lord of life, Who tri-umphed o'er the grave, Who rose vic-tor-ious to the strife, For those He came to save. His glo-ries now we sing, Who died and rose on high, Who died e-ter-nal life to bring, And lives that death may die.

4. Crown Him the Lord of heaven: One with the Fath-er known, One with the Spir-it Through Him given From yon-der glor-ious throne. All hail, Re-deem-er, hail! For Thou hast died for me; Thy praise and glo-ry shall not fail Through-out e-ter-ni-ty.

Crown Him with Many Crowns

1851

. . . and on His head were many crowns . . . Revelation 19:12

T he original form of this hymn was written by Matthew Bridges and consisted of six eight-line stanzas. He thought of his hymn as a sermon in song, based on Revelation 19:12: ". . . and on His head were many crowns." He called his hymn "The Song of the Seraphs." Bridges, who once wrote a book condemning Roman Catholics, ended up converting to Catholicism in 1848. He followed John Henry Newman out of the Church of England.

In 1874, Godfrey Thring, a staunch Anglican clergyman, feared that some of Bridges's verses smacked too much of Catholic doctrine. Verse 2, for example, said:

Crown Him the virgin's Son, the God incarnate born,
Whose arm those crimson trophies won which now His brow adorn;
Fruit of the mystic rose, as of that rose the stem;
The root whence mercy ever flows, the Babe of Bethlehem.

It seems odd to us now that such a verse would cause controversy, but in the end Thring wrote six new verses for the same song. "Crown Him with Many Crowns," therefore, became a six-verse hymn that was written twice!

Over the years these twelve stanzas have become intermingled in the hymnbooks, with editors mixing and matching the verses. Here are the first lines of all twelve verses, the first six by Bridges, the last six by Thring:

- Stanza 1: *Crown Him with many crowns, the Lamb upon His throne . . .*
- Stanza 2: *Crown Him the virgin's Son, the God incarnate born . . .*
- Stanza 3: *Crown Him the Lord of love, behold His hands and side . . .*
- Stanza 4: *Crown Him the Lord of peace, Whose power a scepter sways . . .*
- Stanza 5: *Crown Him the Lord of years, the Potentate of time . . .*
- Stanza 6: *Crown Him the Lord of Heaven, one with the Father known . . .*
- Stanza 7: *Crown Him with crowns of gold . . .*
- Stanza 8: *Crown Him the Son of God, before the worlds began . . .*
- Stanza 9: *Crown Him the Lord of light . . .*
- Stanza 10: *Crown Him the Lord of life, who triumphed over the grave . . .*
- Stanza 11: *Crown Him the Lord of lords, who over all doth reign . . .*
- Stanza 12: *Crown Him the Lord of heaven, enthroned in worlds above . . .*

My Jesus, I Love Thee

William R. Featherston

Adoniram J. Gordon

1. My Jesus I love Thee; I know Thou art mine.
2. I love Thee, Be - cause Thou hast first lov - ed me,
3. I'll love Thee in life, I will love Thee in death,
4. In man - sions of glo - ry And end - less de - light,

For Thee all the fol - lies Of sin I re - sign.
And pur - chased my par - don On Cal - va - ry's tree.
And praise Thee As long as Thou lend - est me breath;
I'll ev - er a - dore Thee In heav - en so bright.

My gra - cious Re - deem - er, My Sa - vior art Thou.
I love Thee For wear - ing the thorns On Thy brow,
And say when the death dew Lies cold on my brow,
I'll sing with the glit - ter - ing crown On my brow,

If ev - er I loved Thee, My Je - sus, 'tis now.
If ev - er I loved Thee, My Je - sus, 'tis now.
"If ev - er I loved Thee, My Je - sus 'tis now."
"If ev - er I loved Thee, My Je - sus, 'tis now."

My Jesus, I Love Thee

1864

We love Him because He first loved us. 1 John 4:19

T he young people of today are utterly dissolute and disorderly," fumed grumpy old Martin Luther in the sixteenth century. The philosopher Plato agreed. "The youth are rebellious, pleasure-seeking, and irresponsible," he wrote. "They have no respect for their elders." Socrates complained, "Children now love luxury. They have bad manners, contempt for authority. They show disrespect for elders, and love chatter."

A six-thousand-year-old Egyptian tomb bears this inscription: "We live in a decadent age. Young people no longer respect their parents. They are rude and impatient. They inhabit taverns and have no self-control."

The next time you think the "modern generation" is going from bad to worse, remember that God always has a rich handful of teenage heroes ready to change the world. In Bible times, we read of Joseph the dreamer, Daniel in Babylon, David the giant-killer, and the virgin Mary (likely still a teen).

As a teenager, Charles Spurgeon preached to great crowds, but when they referred to his youthfulness, he replied, "Never mind my age. Think of the Lord Jesus Christ and His preciousness."

In our own day, we've been deeply moved by young people like seventeen-year old Cassie Bernall of Littleton, Colorado, who was shot for her faith during the Columbine tragedy.

Some of our greatest hymns were also written by young adults. Isaac Watts wrote most of his most memorable hymns at about the age of nineteen. When poet John Milton was fifteen, he wrote the well-known "Let Us with a Gladsome Mind." The hymn "Work for the Night Is Coming" was written by an eighteen-year-old. And this hymn of deep devotion, "My Jesus, I Love Thee," was written by William Ralph Featherston at age sixteen. Sixteen!

Featherston was born July 23, 1846, in Montreal. He died in the same city twenty-six years later. His family attended the Wesleyan Methodist Church, and it seems likely that William wrote this hymn as a poem celebrating his conversion to Christ. Reportedly, he sent it to an aunt living in California, and somehow it was published as an anonymous hymn in a British hymnal in 1864.

Little else is known about the origin of the hymn or its author, but that's all right. It's enough just to know that God can change the world through anyone—regardless of age—who will say, "My Jesus, I love Thee, I know Thou art mine. For Thee, all the follies of sin I resign."

Jesus Paid It All

Elvina M. Hall

John T. Grape

1. I hear the Sav-ior say, "Thy strength in-deed is small;
2. Lord, now in-deed I find, Thy power and Thine a-lone,
3. For noth-ing good have I, Where-by Thy grace to claim;
4. And when be-fore the throne, I stand in Him com-plete;

Child of weak-ness watch and pray, Find in Me thine all in all."
Can change the lep-er's spots And melt the heart of stone.
I'll wash my gar-ments white, In the blood of Cal-vary's Lamb.
"Je-sus died my soul to save," My lips shall still re-peat.

Je - sus paid it all, all to Him I owe;

Sin had left a crim-son stain, He washed it white as snow.

Jesus Paid It All

1865

Not with the blood of goats and calves, but with His own blood He entered the Most Holy Place once for all, having obtained eternal redemption. Hebrews 9:12

I t was Sunday morning at Monument Street Methodist Church in Baltimore. Rev. George Schrick was droning on in a lengthy prayer while, up in the choir loft, Elvina Hall's mind was wandering. She thumbed quietly through the hymnbook, then began doodling on the flyleaf. By and by these words came to her, which she scribbled on the front flap of her hymnal:

I hear my Savior say / Thy strength indeed is small,
Thou hast naught My debt to pay, / Find in Me thy all in all.

Yea, nothing good have I, / Whereby Thy grace to claim;
I'll wash my garments white / In the blood of Calvary's Lamb.

And now complete in Him, / My robe His righteousness,
Close sheltered 'neath His side, / I am divinely blest,

When from my dying bed / My ransomed soul shall rise,
Jesus paid it all / Shall rend the vaulted skies.

Elvina's poem fell into the hands of John T. Grape, a coal merchant and the church organist at Monument Street Methodist Church. As it happened, the church was being renovated, and the small organ had been taken to Grape's house for safekeeping. There he composed the music to "Jesus Paid It All."

Through the years, the words of this hymn have been edited and altered, but its great theme of redemption has remained untouched.

⌐⊃

The colorful preacher Rowland Hill was once preaching to a crowd of people when wealthy aristocrat Lady Ann Erskine drove up in her coach. Seeing her, Rev. Hill changed his sermon.

"I have something for sale," he suddenly declared. "Yes, I have something for sale. It is the soul of Lady Ann Erskine. Is there anyone here that will bid for her soul? Ah, do I hear a bid? Who bids? Satan bids. Satan, what will you give for her soul? 'I will give riches, honor, and pleasure.' But stop, do I hear another bid? Yes, Jesus Christ bids. Jesus, what will You give for her soul? 'I will give eternal life.' Lady Ann Erskine, you have heard the two bids—which will you take?"

Lady Erskine, realizing Christ had purchased her soul with His life's blood on the Cross, took Him.

I Will Sing of My Redeemer

Philip P. Bliss

James McGranahan

1. I will sing of my Re - deem-er, And His won - drous love to me.
2. I will tell the won-drous sto - ry, How my lost es - tate to save,
3. I will praise my dear Re - deem-er; His tri - um - phant power I'll tell,

On the cru - el cross He suffered, From the curse to set me free.
In His boundless love and mer-cy He the ran - som free - ly gave.
How the vic - to - ry He giv-eth O - ver sin and death and hell.

Sing, oh sing, of my Re - deem-er. With His blood He pur - chased

me. On the cross He sealed my par-don, Paid the debt and made me free.

I Will Sing of My Redeemer

1874

For you were bought at a price; therefore glorify God in your body and in your spirit, which are God's. 1 Corinthians 6:20

As a ten-year-old boy, when Philip Paul Bliss heard the sounds of a piano for the first time, his imagination was deeply stirred. Later, riding his horse Old Fanny, he became a traveling musician. In 1870, he joined the staff of a Chicago church as music director and Sunday school superinten-dent. In March 1874, he became the song leader and children's director for the evangelistic campaigns of Major Daniel W. Whittle. All the while, Philip was penning some of America's favorite gospel songs.

By the end of 1876, Philip needed a break. He had just written the music to "It Is Well with My Soul" and finished a whirlwind tour of meetings with Major Whittle. While he and his wife, Lucy, were spending the Christmas holidays with his family in Pennsylvania, a telegram arrived requesting they come to Chicago to sing at Moody's Tabernacle on the last Sunday of the year.

On December 29, 1876, leaving their two small children with Philip's mother, they boarded the *Pacific Express*. The snow was blinding, and the eleven-coach train was run-ning about three hours late. About eight o'clock that night as the train creaked over a chasm near Ashtabula, Ohio, the trestle bridge collapsed. The engine reached solid ground on the other side of the bridge, but the other cars plunged seventy-five feet into the ravine.

Philip survived the crash and crawled out through a window. But within moments, fire broke out, and Lucy was still inside, pinned under the twisted metal of the iron seats. The other survivors urged Philip not to crawl back into the flaming wreckage. "If I cannot save her, I will perish with her," he shouted, plunging into the fiery car. Both Philip and Lucy died. He was thirty-eight.

Philip's trunk finally arrived in Chicago safely. In it were found the words to the last hymns he had written, one of which was:

I will sing of my Redeemer,
And His wondrous love to me;
On the cruel cross He suffered,
From the curse to set me free.

Sing, oh sing, of my Redeemer,
With His blood, He purchased me.
On the cross, He sealed my pardon,
Paid the debt, and made me free.

At Calvary

William R. Newell

Daniel B. Towner

1. Years I spent in van-i-ty and pride, Car-ing not my Lord was cru-ci-fied, Know-ing not it was for me He died On Cal-va-ry.
2. By God's Word at last my sin I learned; Then I trem-bled at the law I'd spurned, Till my guilt-y soul im-plor-ing turned To Cal-va-ry.
3. Now I've giv'n to Je-sus ev-'ry-thing; Now I glad-ly own Him as my King; Now my rap-tured soul can on-ly sing Of Cal-va-ry.
4. O the love that drew sal-va-tion's plan! O the grace that brought it down to man! O the might-y gulf that God did span At Cal-va-ry!

Mer-cy there was great and grace was free; Par-don there was mul-ti-plied to me; There my bur-dened soul found lib-er-ty, At Cal-va-ry.

At Calvary

1895

But God demonstrates His own love toward us, in that while we were still sinners, Christ died for us. Romans 5:8

W hen Dr. R. A. Torrey was president of the Moody Bible Institute of Chicago, he received a letter from a distressed father. The man, a pastor, had a prodigal son named Bill who was breaking his heart. Would Dr. Torrey let the boy enroll at Moody? Dr. Torrey replied that while he sympathized with the man, it wasn't possible to admit the boy. Moody was a Bible school, not a reformatory. The man wrote back, doubling his entreaties. Finally Dr. Torrey agreed, provided the boy meet with him daily and abide by the rules.

The arrangement didn't go well at first, and Dr. Torrey thought the experiment was hopeless. The boy had serious problems and seemed torn apart by turbulence. But he did keep the rules, and day by day he ventilated his frustrations to Dr. Torrey and—as it turned out—was more attentive to Torrey's answers than it appeared.

To make a long story short, several years later that boy, William R. Newell, was a beloved professor at Moody Bible Institute.

In 1895, William began thinking of putting his testimony into verse form. The idea rolled around in the back of his mind for several weeks, then one day on his way to lecture, the lines came to him. Ducking into an empty classroom, he jotted down the words on the back of an envelope. As he hurried on to class, he happened to meet Dr. Daniel Towner, director of music at the Institute. Handing him the verses, William gently suggested they could use a good melody. By the time Dr. Newell finished his lecture, the completed tune was ready.

"Bill," said Dr. Towner, "I was so taken with the poem you gave me that I went immediately to my studio and composed a tune. I feel that it could be the best song that either of us will ever write in our lifetime."

The two men sang it together, and it was published shortly after.

Bill Newell went on to become a well-known Bible teacher throughout the Midwest and the author of a popular series of Bible commentaries. He once said that had he not gone through his troubled years, he might never have fully understood the importance of Calvary's grace.

Mercy there was great, and grace was free;
Pardon there was multiplied to me;
There my burdened soul found liberty at Calvary.

There Is Power in the Blood

Lewis E. Jones

Lewis E. Jones

1. Would you be free From your bur-den of sin? There's pow'r in the blood,
2. Would you be free, From your pas-sion and pride? There's pow'r in the blood,
3. Would you be whit-er, Much whit-er than snow? There's pow'r in the blood,
4. Would you do ser-vice For Je-sus your King? There's pow'r in the blood,

Pow'r in the blood; Would you o'er ev-il a vic-tor-y win? There's
Pow'r in the blood; Come for a cleans-ing To Cal-va-ry's tide; There's
Pow'r in the blood; Sin stains are lost In its life giv-ing flow; There's
Pow'r in the blood; Would you live dai-ly, His prais-es to sing? There's

won-der-ful pow'r in the blood. There is pow'r, pow'r, Won-der work-ing pow'r,
There is pow'r, there is pow'r, Won-der work-ing pow'r,

In the blood of the Lamb; There is pow'r, pow'r,
In the blood of the Lamb. There is pow'r, there is pow'r,

Won-der work-ing pow'r, In the pre-cious blood of the Lamb.

There Is Power in the Blood

1899

Inasmuch as there is none like You, O LORD (You are great, and Your name is great in might). Jeremiah 10:6

Both the words and music of this old hymn were written during a camp meeting at Mountain Lake Park, Maryland, by Lewis Jones. Jones, a California native, graduated from Moody Bible Institute and spent his vocational life with the Young Men's Christian Association (YMCA). On the side, he wrote hymns. This, his best known, is particularly effective in resisting the "wiles of the devil."

One day, as missionary Dick Hillis preached in a Chinese village, his sermon was suddenly interrupted by a piercing cry. Everyone rushed toward the scream, and Dick's coworker, Mr. Kong, whispered that an evil spirit had seized a man. Dick, having not previously encountered demon possession, didn't believe him.

Just then, a woman rushed toward them. "I beg you help me!" she cried. "An evil spirit has again possessed the father of my children and is trying to kill him."

The two evangelists entered the house, stepping over a filthy old dog lying in the doorway. The room was charged with a sense of evil. "An evil spirit has possessed Farmer Ho," Kong told the onlookers. "Our God, the 'Nothing-He-Cannot-Do One' is more powerful than any spirit, and He can deliver this man. First, you must promise you will burn your idols and trust in Jesus, son of the Supreme Emperor."

The people nodded. Kong asked Dick to begin singing the hymn "There Is Power in the Blood." With great hesitation, Dick began to sing, "Would you be free from your burden of sin . . ."

"Now," continued Kong, "in the name of Jesus we will command the evil spirit to leave this man." Kong began praying fervently. Suddenly the old dog in the doorway vaulted into the air, screeching, yelping, whirling in circles, and snapping wildly at his tail. Kong continued praying, and the dog abruptly dropped over dead.

Instantly Dick remembered Luke 8, the demons of the Gadarenes who invisibly flew into the herd of swine. As Kong finished praying, Farmer Ho seemed quiet and relaxed, and soon he was strong enough to burn his idols. At his baptism shortly afterward, he testified, "I was possessed by an evil spirit who boasted he had already killed five people and was going to kill me. But God sent Mr. Kong at just the right moment, and in Jesus I am free."*

---

*This story is related in *Steel in His Soul: The Dick Hillis Story* by Jan Winebrenner (Chicago: Moody Press, 1985), chapter 6, "The Day the Dog Died."

In the Garden

C. Austin Miles

C. Austin Miles

1. I come to the gar-den a-lone, While the dew is still on the
2. He speaks, and the sound of His voice is so sweet, the birds hush their
3. I'd stay in the gar-den with Him, Though the night a-round me be

ros - es; And the voice I hear, fall-ing on my ear, The
sing - ing, And the mel-o-dy that He gave to me, With-
fall - ing, But He bids me go; through the voice of woe, His

Son of God dis-clos - es.
in my heart is ring - ing. And He walks with me, And He
voice to me is call - ing.

talks with me, And He tells me I am His own; And the

joy we share as we tar-ry there, None oth-er has ev-er known.

In the Garden

1912

...she turned around and saw Jesus standing there ... John 20:14

The art of meditating on Scripture involves using one's imagination. Instead of simply reading a passage, we must read it, close our eyes, and visualize the scene, perhaps even putting ourselves in the picture. That's what the author of this hymn did.

C. Austin Miles was a pharmacist who began writing gospel songs and eventually became an editor of hymnals and songbooks, as well as a popular music director at camp meetings, conventions, and churches. His hobby was photography, and he found his darkroom perfect for developing, not just his photographs, but his devotional life. In its privacy and strange blue glow, Miles could read his Bible in total privacy.

One day in March 1912, while waiting for some film to develop, he opened the Bible to his favorite chapter, John 20, the story of the first Easter. Miles later said, "As I read it that day, I seemed to be part of the scene . . . My hands were resting on the Bible while I stared at the light blue wall. As the light faded, I seemed to be standing at the entrance of a garden, looking down a gently winding path, shaded by olive branches. A woman in white, with head bowed, hand clasping her throat as if to choke back her sobs, walked slowly into the shadows. It was Mary. As she came to the tomb, upon which she placed her hand, she bent over to look in and hurried away. John, in flowing robe, appeared, looking at the tomb; then came Peter, who entered the tomb, followed slowly by John.

"As they departed, Mary reappeared, leaning her head upon her arm at the tomb. She wept. Turning herself, she saw Jesus standing; so did I. I knew it was He. She knelt before Him, with arms outstretched and looking into his face, cried, 'Rabboni!'

"I awakened in full light, gripping my Bible, with muscles tense and nerves vibrating. Under the inspiration of this vision I wrote as quickly as the words would be formed the poem exactly as it has since appeared. That same evening I wrote the music."

In addition to "In the Garden," Austin Miles is the author of several other gospel songs, including "A New Name in Glory," "Dwelling in Beulah Land," and "If Jesus Goes with Me I'll Go Anywhere."

The Old Rugged Cross

George Bennard

George Bennard

1. On a hill far a - way Stood an old rug-ged cross; The em-blem of
2. Oh, that old rug-ged cross, So de - spised by the world, Has a won-drous at -
3. To the old rug-ged cross I will ev - er be true, It's shame and re -

suf - fering and shame. And I love that old cross Where the dear-est and best,
trac - tion for me; For the dear Lamb of God, Left His glo - ry a-bove,
proach glad- ly bear; Then He'll call me some day To my home far a - way,

For a world of lost sin - ners was slain.
To bear it to dark Cal - va - ry. So I'll cher - ish the old rug - ged
Where His glo - ry for - ev - er I'll share.

cross, Till my tro - phies at last I lay down; I will cling to the

old rug - ged cross, And ex - change it some day for a crown.

The Old Rugged Cross
1913

For God so loved the world that He gave His only begotten Son, that whoever believes in Him should not perish but have everlasting life. John 3:16

George Beverly Shea recalls seeing George Bennard, author of this hymn, many times at Winona Lake Bible Conference in Indiana. "Though a preacher—a good one—he would sometimes sing," wrote Mr. Shea. "His voice was not trained or out of the ordinary, but he had great feeling and expression and could really put over any hymn. I remember how moved I was the first time I heard him sing his own 'The Old Rugged Cross' . . . What a distinguished looking man—slight of build, short, with glasses, the most memorable thing about him was his long, white hair."

George Bennard was born in Youngstown, Ohio, shortly after the end of the Civil War. His father, a coal miner, moved the family to Iowa, and there George came to Christ through the ministry of the Salvation Army. He felt impressed to train for the ministry, but his plans were disrupted when his father's death left him responsible for his mother and sisters. He was sixteen years old. Instead of theological school, he worked by day and devoted his spare time to books.

Eventually George's obligations lessened, and he was able to move to Chicago, marry, and begin in ministry with the Salvation Army. Later he was ordained by the Methodist Episcopal church and became a traveling evangelist.

On one occasion, after a difficult season of ministry, George realized he needed to better understand the power of the Cross of Christ. He later said, "I was praying for a full understanding of the Cross . . . I read and studied and prayed . . . The Christ of the Cross became more than a symbol . . . It was like seeing John 3:16 leave the printed page, take form, and act out the meaning of redemption. While watching this scene with my mind's eye, the theme of the song came to me."

It took several months for the words to formulate in his mind. As he preached through the Midwest, George would carry the words with him, working on them, polishing them, and sometimes singing them in his meetings. It always struck a chord with his audiences.

At last, his hymn finished, George went to the home of his friends, Rev. and Mrs. L. O. Boswick, and sang it for them. After the last note, he looked at them and asked, "Will it do?"

The Boswicks were so moved that they helped pay the fees to have it printed, and it soon began appearing in hymnbooks across America.

His Name Is Wonderful

Audrey Mieir   Audrey Mieir

His name is Won-der-ful, His name is Won-der-ful, His name is Won-der-ful,

Je - sus, my Lord; He is the Might-y King, Mas-ter of ev-'ry-thing;

His name is Won-der-ful, Je-sus, my Lord. He's the Great Shep-herd, The Rock of all

ag - es, Al-might-y God is He. Bow down be-fore Him, Love and a-

dore Him, His name is Won-der-ful, Je-sus my Lord.

His Name Is Wonderful
1959

Therefore God also has highly exalted Him and given Him the name which is above every name. Philippians 2:9

T his song was born in a small church. In an era when bigger is better and success is usually measured by statistics, it's important to remember that small churches can still do great things.

Audrey Mae Mieir was born on May 12, 1916, and attended L.I.F.E. Bible College. After marrying Charles B. Mieir in 1936, she was ordained to the Gospel ministry in the International Church of the Foursquare Gospel.

Audrey was a gifted pianist and an inspiring worship leader, song director, and choral clinician. In the 1950s, she was working in her brother-in-law's church, Bethel Union Church in Duarte, California, a suburb of Los Angeles. Christmas fell on Sunday that year, and the church was decorated with pine boughs. The choir loft was now a manger scene, and the young people had worked hard on the performance.

"As the morning service began," Audrey later said, "I was almost overwhelmed with the fragrance, the sounds, and most of all, with the gentle moving of the Spirit in that church. The pastor stood to his feet, opened the Bible, and said, 'His name shall be called Wonderful.' I tell you the truth, that's all it took. I wrote the words and music in the flyleaf of my Bible. In the Sunday evening service, I taught the chorus to a group of young people, and it was sung for the first time."

But Audrey had only written the first part of the song, and though it was well-received, it needed more. A friend told her, "Audrey, it's a good song but there just isn't enough of it. Maybe you could write a bridge for it." Audrey went to lunch that day with her friend's advice ringing in her ears. She ordered a hamburger, opened her Bible, and found a list of names given to Jesus in the Scripture. She jotted some of them down on her napkin. After returning to her office, Audrey went to the piano and began writing: "He's the great Shepherd, the Rock of all ages, Almighty God is He . . ."

Though it was inspired on Christmas day by a traditional Christmas text, "His Name Is Wonderful" has never been pegged as a Christmas hymn. It's been a favorite of Christians around the world throughout the year.

O Sacred Head, Now Wounded

Based on a Medieval Latin Poem
Ascribed to Bernard of Clairvaux

Hans Leo Hassler
Harmony by J. S. Bach

1. O sa - cred Head now wound - ed, With grief and shame weighed down,
2. What Thou, my Lord hast suf - fered Was all for sin - ners' gain:
3. What lan - guage shall I bor - row To thank thee, dear - est Friend,

Now scorn - ful - ly sur - round - ed With thorns, Thine on - ly crown;
Mine, mine was the trans - gres - sion, But Thine the dead - ly pain;
For this thy dy - ing sor - row, Thy pit - y with - out end?

How pale thou art with an - guish, with sore a - buse and scorn!
Lo, here I fall, my Sav - ior! 'Tis I de - serve Thy place;
O make me thine for - ev - er, And should I faint - ing be,

How does that vis - age lan - guish Which once was bright as morn!
Look on me with Thy fa - vor, Vouch - safe to me Thy grace.
Lord, let me nev - er, nev - er Out - live my love to thee.

O Sacred Head, Now Wounded

1153

Oh, give thanks to the LORD, for He is good! For His mercy endures forever.
Psalm 118:1

Bernard was born into a knight's family in a French castle in 1090. He was educated in the fashion of medieval aristocracy, but he later felt the Lord calling him to the monastic ministry. Being a born leader, he arrived at the monastery of Cîteaux with thirty other young men whom he had persuaded to join him.

Three years later, Bernard, twenty-five, founded his own monastery at Clairvaux, a town near the Swiss border. Here he would remain the rest of his life. He was a brilliant monk, and in time he advised kings and popes from his monastic cell. Historian Harold O. J. Brown wrote, "The ability of one man without political office or power to change history solely by his teaching and example is without parallel until the sixteenth century when Martin Luther would once again transform Europe from his pulpit and professor's chair in a small town in Saxony."

Bernard fought heresy and helped preserve the doctrine of the Trinity. Yet he also supported Christian military orders such as the Knights Templar—soldiers living under monastic discipline who fought to preserve European Christianity and fight Muslims in the Holy Land. He advocated a militant faith that depended on both sword and Spirit.

This man, then, is a paradox to us. We don't know whether to claim him or disdain him. Perhaps it's best to leave that judgment to God and to appreciate him for his songs, such as this pensive hymn on the sufferings of Christ, "O Sacred Head, Now Wounded."

Here are two lesser-known verses of this hymn. Transport yourself to Bernard's cloister, and hear these words echoing through the dimly lit corridors of the monastery. Consider what the Lord did for you during His six hours on Zion's cross.

Now from Thy cheeks has vanished their color once so fair;
From Thy red lips is banished the splendor that was there.
Grim death, with cruel rigor, hath robbed Thee of Thy life;
Thus Thou hast lost Thy vigor, Thy strength in this sad strife.

My burden in Thy Passion, Lord, Thou hast borne for me,
For it was my transgression which brought this woe on Thee.
I cast me down before Thee, wrath were my rightful lot;
Have mercy, I implore Thee; Redeemer, spurn me not!

When I Survey the Wondrous Cross

Gregorian Chant
Arranged by Lowell Mason

Isaac Watts

1. When I sur - vey the won - drous cross
2. For - bid it, Lord, that I should boast,
3. See, from His head, His hands, His feet,
4. Were the whole realm of na - ture mine,

On which the Prince of glo - ry died,
Save in the death of Christ, my God;
Sor - row and love flow min - gled down;
That were a pres - ent far too small;

My rich - est gain I count but loss,
All the vain things that charm me most,
Did e'er such love and sor - row meet,
Love so a - maz - ing, so di - vine,

And pour con - tempt on all my pride.
I sac - ri - fice them to His blood.
Or thorns com - pose so rich a crown?
De - mands my soul, my life, my all.

When I Survey the Wondrous Cross

1707

But God forbid that I should boast except in the cross of our Lord Jesus Christ, by whom the world has been crucified to me, and I to the world. Galatians 6:14

After Isaac Watts finished his college studies and returned home to Southampton, he wrote many of his now-immortalized hymns for Above Bar Congregational Church. In 1696, Isaac, twenty-two, left home for London to become a tutor.

All the while, he was feeling a clear tug toward ministry. On his twenty-fourth birthday, July 17, 1698, Isaac preached his first sermon. The following year, he became assistant pastor of London's Mark Lane Church.

In March of 1700, Isaac received a long letter from his brother, Enoch, urging him to publish the hymns he had written at Southampton. The letter said:

> Dear Brother, In your last [letter] you [mentioned] an inclination to oblige the world by showing it your hymns in print, and I heartily wish . . . that you were something more than inclinable thereunto . . . I am very confident whoever has the happiness of reading your hymns (unless he be either sot or atheist) will have a very favorable opinion of their author . . . There is . . . a great need of a pen, vigorous and lively as yours, to quicken and revive the dying devotion of the age . . . Yours now is the old truth, stripped of its ragged ornaments, and appears, if we may say so, younger by ages in a new and fashionable dress.

Isaac, however, hesitated. He had other obligations on his time. On March 8, 1702, he became Mark Lane's pastor. The next year, 1703, the church chose Samuel Price of Wales to assist Isaac, due to the latter's fragile health. Under the preaching of these two, the old, dying church revived. The building grew too small for the crowds, and a new house of worship was built down the street.

Finally in 1707, Watts published his hymns, selling the copyright to a Mr. Lawrence, the publisher, for ten pounds. This volume was an instant success. It was enlarged and republished in 1709.

"When I Survey the Wondrous Cross" appeared in his 1707 book of hymns. Inspired by Galatians 6:14, it was originally titled "Crucifixion to the World, by the Cross of Christ." Many consider it the finest hymn in English church history, and Charles Wesley reportedly said he would rather have written it than all his own.

Sweet Hour of Prayer

Attributed to William W. Walford   William B. Bradbury

1. Sweet hour of prayer, Sweet hour of prayer, That calls me from a world of care,
2. Sweet hour of prayer, Sweet hour of prayer, Thy wings shall my pe - ti - tion bear
3. Sweet hour of prayer, Sweet hour of prayer, May I Thy con - so - la - tion share,

And bids me at my Fa - ther's throne Make all my wants and wish - es known.
To Him whose truth and faith - ful - ness En - gage the wait - ing soul to bless;
'Til from Mount Pis - gah's loft - y height, I view my home and take my flight.

In sea - sons of dis - tress and grief My soul has of - ten found re - lief,
And since He bids me seek His face, Be - lieve His word, and trust His grace,
This robe of flesh I'll drop, and rise To seize the ev - er - last - ing prize;

And oft es - caped the temp - ter's snare, By Thy re - turn, sweet hour of prayer.
I'll cast on Him my ev - 'ry care, And wait for Thee, sweet hour of prayer.
And shout while pass - ing through the air, Fare - well, fare - well, sweet hour of prayer.

Sweet Hour of Prayer

1845

Hear my cry, O God; attend to my prayer. Psalm 61:1

weet Hour of Prayer" first appeared in the *New York Observer* on September 13, 1845, accompanied by this explanatory note by a Rev. Thomas Salmon, a British minister recently immigrated to America:

At Coleshill, Warwickshire, England, I became acquainted with W. W. Walford, the blind preacher, a man of obscure birth and connections and no education, but of strong mind and most retentive memory. In the pulpit he never failed to select a lesson well adapted to his subject, giving chapter and verse with unerring precision and scarcely ever misplacing a word in his repetition of the Psalms, every part of the New Testament, the prophecies, and some of the histories, so as to have the reputation of "knowing the whole Bible by heart." He actually sat in the chimney corner, employing his mind in composing a sermon or two for Sabbath delivery . . . On one occasion, paying him a visit, he repeated two or three pieces he had composed, and having no friend at home to commit them to paper, he had laid them up in the storehouse within. "How will this do?" asked he, as he repeated the following lines . . . I rapidly copied the lines with my pencil as he uttered them, and sent them for insertion in the *Observer.*

No one, however, has ever found a trace of a blind preacher named W. W. Walford in Coleshill, England. There was a Congregational minister named William Walford who wrote a book about prayer containing striking similarities to this poem, and some believe he was the author. But he was neither blind nor uneducated, and the authorship of this hymn remains a mystery.

There's yet another mystery—a deeper one—connected with this hymn. It's the question Jesus asked Simon Peter in Gethsemane: "What? Could you not watch with Me one hour?" If an hour spent with the Lord is so sweet, why do we race through our day prayerless, then squeeze all our requests into a two-minute segment at bedtime? If prayer is so powerful, why do we neglect it so consistently? An oft-omitted verse to this hymn says:

Sweet hour of prayer! Sweet hour of prayer! The joys I feel, the bliss I share,
Of those whose anxious spirits burn with strong desires for Thy return!
With such I hasten to the place where God my Savior shows His face,
And gladly take my station there, and wait for Thee, sweet hour of prayer!

I Love to Tell the Story

A. Katherine Hankey

William G. Fischer

1. I love to tell the sto - ry Of un - seen things a - bove,
2. I love to tell the sto - ry, More won - der - ful it seems
3. I love to tell the sto - ry, 'Tis pleas - ant to re - peat
4. I love to tell the sto - ry, For those who know it best

Of Je - sus and His glo - ry, Of Je - sus and His love.
Than all the gold - en fan - cies Of all our gold - en dreams.
What seems, each time I tell it, More won - der - ful - ly sweet.
Seem hun - ger - ing and thirst - ing To hear it like the rest.

I love to tell the sto - ry Be - cause I know 'tis true,
I love to tell the sto - ry, It did so much for me;
I love to tell the sto - ry, For some have nev - er heard
And when in scenes of glo - ry I sing the new, new song,

It sat - is - fies my long - ings As noth - ing else can do.
And that is just the rea - son I tell it now to thee.
The mes - sage of sal - va - tion From God's own ho - ly Word.
'Twill be the old, old sto - ry That I have loved so long.

92

I Love to Tell the Story

1866

Then they will see the Son of Man coming in the clouds with great power and glory.
Mark 13:26

W illiam Wilberforce, the Christian statesman and abolitionist, led a fierce campaign in nineteenth-century England to eradicate slavery from the British Empire. The geographical center of the campaign was a wealthy neighborhood in the south of London known as Clapham, where a group of Anglican evangelicals lived. The "Clapham Sect" also advocated prison reform, education for children, and the expansion of missionary efforts overseas. Though lampooned for their efforts, they changed the world.

Arabella Katherine Hankey was born into this environment in 1834. Her father was a banker in Clapham and a leader in the Clapham Group. Early in life, Kate became involved in religious work. As a young girl, she taught Sunday school, and when she was eighteen she organized a Bible study for factory girls in London. (This Bible study was never large, but the girls became close, and fifty years later, five of them met together at Kate's funeral.) When her brother fell ill in Africa, Kate traveled there to bring him home. That trip sparked a passion for foreign missions, and in later life Kate devoted all proceeds from her writing to missionary work.

During the winter of 1865–1866, Kate, thirty, became seriously ill. The doctors warned her to abandon her Christian activities and remain in bed for a full year. To occupy her time, Kate wrote a poem of one hundred stanzas entitled "The Old, Old Story." She began the first section, "The Story Wanted," on January 29, 1866. Later that year, she wrote a second section entitled "The Story Told."

The following year, at the international convention of the Young Men's Christian Association, Major General Russell ended his powerful sermon by quoting from Kate's poem. It left the audience breathless. Songwriter William Doane, in the crowd that day, put a portion of Kate's poem to music, giving birth to the hymn "Tell Me the Old, Old Story."

Another composer, William G. Fischer, set a second portion of Kate's poem to a musical score he named Hankey, and thus we have this hymn, "I Love to Tell the Story." It was first published in an American hymnbook in 1869, and was later popularized around the world in the great evangelistic campaigns of D. L. Moody and Ira Sankey.

Beneath the Cross of Jesus

Elizabeth C. Clephane

Frederick C. Maker

1. Be - neath the cross of Je - sus I fain would take my stand:
2. Up - on the cross of Je - sus Mine eyes at times can see
3. I take, O cross, thy shad - ow For my a - bid - ing place;

The shad-ow of a might - y Rock With - in a wea - ry land,
The ver - y dy - ing form of One Who suf - fered there for me;
I ask no oth - er sun-shine than The sun - shine of His face,

A home with - in the wil - der-ness, A rest up - on the way,
And from my strick-en heart with tears, Two won-ders I con - fess:
Con - tent to let the world go by, To know no gain nor loss,

From the burn-ing of the noon-tide heat And the bur-den of the day.
The won-ders of re - deem-ing love And my un - wor-thi - ness.
My sin - ful self, my on - ly shame, My glo-ry all the cross.

Beneath the Cross of Jesus

1868

For the message of the cross is . . . to us who are being saved . . . the power of God.
1 Corinthians 1:18

T he author of this hymn, Elizabeth Clephane, was born in Edinburgh, where her father was sheriff of Fife. One of her siblings later wrote, "My sister was a very quiet little child, shrinking from notice and was always absorbed in books. The loss of both her parents at an early age taught her sorrow. As she grew up she was recognized as the cleverest one of our family. She was first in her class and a favorite at school. Her love for poetry was a passion. Among the sick and suffering she won the name, 'My Sunbeam.'" (Elizabeth's own comment on her nickname is written into a line of this hymn: "I take, O Cross, thy shadow for my abiding place; / I ask no other sunshine than the sunshine of His face.")

At some point, Elizabeth's family moved to Melrose, southeast of Edinburgh, where she spent her remaining years. Though frail, she was a diligent Bible student, a sympathetic listener, and a worker among the poor. She and her sisters raised money for the unfortunate, on one occasion selling their horse and carriage for a needy family.

Elizabeth's poems were published in the Scottish magazine *The Family Treasury*. This one, appearing after her death, was discovered by Ira Sankey and introduced in the great Moody/Sankey meetings in Britain. In his autobiography, Sankey stated, "The author of this hymn, Elizabeth Celphane, also wrote the widely known hymn, 'The Ninety and Nine,' and these two were her only hymns. The first time this hymn was sung is still fresh in my memory. The morning after I had composed the music, Rev. W. H. Aitkin was to speak at our mission in London . . . Before the sermon, I sang 'Beneath the Cross of Jesus' as a solo; and as in the case of 'The Ninety and Nine,' much blessing came from its use for the first time. With eyes filled with tears and deeply moved, the preacher said to the audience: 'Dear friends, I had intended to speak to you this morning upon work for the Master, but this new hymn has made such an impression on my heart, and evidently upon your own, that I will defer my proposed address and speak to you on "The Cross of Jesus."'"

Sankey's tune has since been replaced in popular usage by St. Christopher, music composed for this hymn by Frederick C. Maker.

Near the Cross

Fanny J. Crosby

William H. Doane

1. Je - sus, keep me near the cross, There a pre - cious foun - tain,
2. Near the cross, a trem - bling soul, Love and mer - cy found me;
3. Near the cross! O Lamb of God, Bring its scenes be - fore me;
4. Near the cross I'll watch and wait, Hop - ing, trust - ing ev - er,

Free to all, a heal - ing stream, Flows from Cal - vary's moun - tain.
There the bright and Morn - ing Star Shed its beams a - round me.
Help me walk from day to day, With its shad - ows o'er me.
'Til I reach the gold - en strand Just be - yond the riv - er.

In the cross, in the cross, Be my glo - ry ev - er,

'Til my rap - tured soul shall find Rest be - yond the riv - er.

Near the Cross

1869

And He, bearing His cross, went out to a place called the Place of a Skull, which is called in Hebrew, Golgotha. John 19:17

Fanny Crosby was born in Putnam County, New York, in 1820, and was blinded in infancy through the malpractice of a doctor. In 1835, she enrolled in a school for the blind in New York City, staying there twelve years, first as a student, then as a teacher. Her remarkable poetry brought widespread acclaim to the school, and she frequently recited her work for visiting dignitaries.

In 1850, Fanny, then thirty years old, attended a revival meeting at New York's Thirtieth Street Methodist Church. During these services, she felt something was missing in her life. On two occasions during the meetings, she prayed with counselors, but without gaining assurance of a personal relationship with God. On November 20, 1850, as the altar call was given, Fanny went forward and found Christ as her Savior. The congregation was singing Isaac Watts's great hymn about the cross:

> *At the cross, at the cross where I first saw the light,*
> *And the burden of my heart rolled away,*
> *It was there by faith I received my sight,*
> *And now I am happy all the day.*

Shortly thereafter, Fanny turned her poetic skills to hymn writing, and many of her songs focused on the theme of the cross, such as "At the Cross, There's Room," "Blessed Cross," "Room at the Cross," "Save Me at the Cross," and this one, "Near the Cross." It was composed after Cincinnati businessman William Doane gave her a melody he had written. Fanny, listening to it, felt it said, "Jesus, keep me near the cross," and she promptly wrote the words.

Fanny Crosby wrote approximately eight thousand hymns. We aren't surprised, then, to discover that many of her later hymns were little more than rewritten versions of earlier ones. In 1893, she and Phoebe Knapp published a gospel song similar to "Near the Cross." The 1893 hymn, entitled "Nearer the Cross," said:

> *"Nearer the cross!" my heart can say I am coming nearer,*
> *Nearer the cross from day to day, I am coming nearer;*
> *Nearer the cross where Jesus died,*
> *Nearer the fountain's crimson tide,*
> *Nearer my Savior's wounded side,*
> *I am coming nearer, I am coming nearer.*

Christ Arose!

Robert Lowry

Christ Arose!

1874

He is not here, but is risen! Luke 24:6

What can exhausted pastors do to relax on Sunday nights after a hard day's work? Baptist preacher Robert Lowry went home to his wife and three sons—and wrote hymns. "Dr. Lowry will continue to preach the gospel in his hymns long after his sermons have been forgotten," Ira Sankey once wrote. "Many of his hymns were written after the Sunday evening service, when his body was weary but his mind refused to rest."

Robert Lowry was born in Pennsylvania in 1826. At his conversion at age seventeen, he joined a Baptist church. Shortly afterward, he enrolled at the University of Lewisburg (now Bucknell University in Lewisburg, Pennsylvania). After graduating, he pastored churches in New York, New Jersey, and Pennsylvania. He also taught at Bucknell and at one time served as its chancellor. Lowry gained a reputation for keen biblical scholarship and powerful, picturesque preaching.

When gospel song editor William Bradbury died in 1868, Lowry was chosen to replace him as a publisher of Sunday school music. He's best known, however, for his own gospel songs, including:

"Nothing but the Blood" (words and music)
"Shall We Gather at the River?" (words and music)
"Where Is My Wandering Boy Tonight?" (words and music)
"All the Way My Savior Leads Me" (music)
"I Need Thee Every Hour" (music)
"Marching to Zion" (music)

"Music, with me has been a side issue," he once said. "I would rather preach a gospel sermon to an appreciative audience than write a hymn. I have always looked upon myself as a preacher and felt a sort of depreciation when I began to be known more as a composer."

This hymn, "Christ Arose!," was written one evening during the Easter season of 1874 while Lowry was engaged in his devotions. He became deeply impressed with Luke 24:6–8, especially the words of the angel at the tomb of Christ: "Why do you seek the living among the dead? He is not here, but is risen!"

The words and music began forming together in his mind. Going to the little pump organ in his home, Lowry soon completed what was to become one of our greatest resurrection hymns.

Hallelujah, What a Savior!

Philip P. Bliss

Philip P. Bliss

1. "Man of sor - rows!" what a name
For the Son of God who came; Ru - ined sin - ners
to re - claim! Hal - le - lu - jah! What a Sav - ior!

2. Bear - ing shame and scoff - ing rude,
In my place con - demned He stood, Sealed my par - don
with His blood; Hal - le - lu - jah! What a Sav - ior!

3. Guilt - y, vile, and help - less we,
Spot - less Lamb of God was He; Full a - tone - ment!
Can it be? Hal - le - lu - jah! What a Sav - ior!

4. Lift - ed up was He to die,
"It is fin - ished!" was His cry; Now in heaven ex -
alt - ed high, Hal - le - lu - jah! What a Sav - ior!

5. When He comes, our glo - rious King,
All His ran - somed home to bring, Then a - new this
song we'll sing, Hal - le - lu - jah! What a Sav - ior!

Hallelujah, What a Savior!

1875

And my spirit has rejoiced in God my Savior. Luke 1:47

hilip Bliss and Lucy Young, deeply in love, were married on June 1, 1859. Philip was twenty years old at the time, with a strong physique and a remarkable talent for music. The young couple was devoted to Christ, and they often thrilled fellow church members with beautiful duets.

Believing God had given her husband a special talent, Lucy schemed for ways to afford him proper musical training. With her encouragement, he began traveling on an old horse from town to town, carrying a twenty-dollar melodeon and holding singing schools.

When Lucy's grandmother gave them thirty dollars, Philip attended a six-week course at the Normal Academy of Music in New York. Upon completion, he became a full-time music teacher and was soon recognized as a local music authority.

Philip and Lucy moved to Chicago so he could pursue a ministry of music there. Between 1865 and 1873, he held music conventions, singing schools, and church meetings. In 1869, he attracted the attention of evangelist D. L. Moody, who continually urged him to enter the full-time ministry of music.

Moody would later write, "In my estimate, he was the most highly honored of God of any man of his time as a writer and singer of gospel songs, and with all his gifts he was the most humble man I ever knew. I loved him as a brother."

With Lucy's encouragement, Philip joined Moody's associate, Major Daniel W. Whittle, as song leader in a series of evangelistic campaigns, and "Whittle and Bliss" became almost as famous as "Moody and Sankey." Successful crusades were held in Illinois, Wisconsin, Pennsylvania, Kentucky, Minnesota, Mississippi, Alabama, and Georgia.

Philip wrote such favorites as "Wonderful Words of Life," "Almost Persuaded," "Dare to Be a Daniel," "Hold the Fort," "Jesus Loves Even Me," "Let the Lower Lights Be Burning," "The Light of the World Is Jesus," "I Will Sing of My Redeemer," and the music to "It Is Well with My Soul." By 1876, Philip, only thirty-six, was known as one of the greatest hymnists of his generation.

Late that year, Philip conducted a service for inmates at the Michigan State Prison and sang one of his last hymns, "Hallelujah, What a Savior!" Many of the prisoners wept openly and confessed Christ as Savior.

No one dreamed that the young songwriter and his wife had but a month remaining to live.*

---

*See the story of "I Will Sing of My Redeemer."

Nothing but the Blood

Robert Lowry   Robert Lowry

1. What can wash a - way my sin? Noth-ing but the blood of Je - sus;
2. For my par-don, this I see, Noth-ing but the blood of Je - sus;
3. Noth-ing can for sin a - tone, Noth-ing but the blood of Je - sus;
4. This is all my hope and peace, Noth-ing but the blood of Je - sus;

What can make me whole a - gain? Noth-ing but the blood of Je - sus.
For my cleans-ing, this my plea, Noth-ing but the blood of Je - sus.
Naught of good that I have done, Noth-ing but the blood of Je - sus.
This is all my righ - teous-ness, Noth-ing but the blood of Je - sus.

O! pre-cious is the flow That makes me white as snow;

No oth - er fount I know; Noth-ing but the blood of Je - sus.

Nothing but the Blood

1876

Almost all things are purified with blood, and without shedding of blood there is no remission. Hebrews 9:22

s we thumb through our Bibles, we run across beloved and deeply underlined verses like these:

And when I see the blood, I will pass over you . . . It is the blood that makes atonement for the soul . . . For this is My blood of the new covenant, which is shed for many for the remission of sins . . . The church of God which He purchased with His own blood . . . Christ Jesus whom God set forth as propitiation by His blood . . . In Him we have redemption through His blood, the forgiveness of sins, according to the riches of His grace . . . With His own blood He entered the Most Holy Place once for all, having obtained eternal redemption . . . The precious blood of Christ, as of a lamb . . . The blood of Jesus Christ His Son cleanses us from all sin.*

We shouldn't be surprised, then, as we study the great hymnists of history, to find their souls thrilled and their songs filled with this theme.

In 1739, Count Zinzendorf wrote his great "Jesus, Thy Blood and Righteousness." That same year, Charles Wesley penned, "His blood can make the foulest clean, / His blood availed for me."

The melancholy William Cowper wrote, "There is a fountain filled with blood / drawn from Emmanuel's veins / And sinners plunged beneath that flood / Lose all their guilty stains."

Perhaps the most popular hymn about the blood is this one, written by two men who came to Christ as teenagers. Robert Lowry, author of the words, came to Christ at age seventeen. William Doane confessed Christ as his Savior while in high school. Together they wrote hymns and published gospel songbooks.

When "Nothing but the Blood" was published in 1876, the attached Scripture was from Hebrews 9:22: "Without shedding of blood there is no remission." Most of our hymnals omit Lowry's original final two stanzas:

Now by this I'll overcome—Nothing but the blood of Jesus,
Now by this I'll reach my home—Nothing but the blood of Jesus.

Glory! Glory! This I sing—Nothing but the blood of Jesus,
All my praise for this I bring—Nothing but the blood of Jesus.

---

*Exodus 12:13; Leviticus 17:11; Matthew 26:28; Acts 20:28; Romans 3:24–25; Ephesians 1:7; Hebrews 9:12; 1 Peter 1:18; 1 John 1:7

Are You Washed in the Blood?

Elisha A. Hoffman

Elisha A. Hoffman

1. Have you been to Je - sus for the cleans - ing power? Are you washed in the blood of the Lamb? Are you ful - ly trust - ing in His grace this hour? Are you washed in the blood of the Lamb?

2. Are you walk - ing dai - ly by the Sav - ior's side? Are you washed in the blood of the Lamb? Do you rest each mo - ment in the Cru - ci - fied? Are you washed in the blood of the Lamb?

3. Lay a - side the gar - ments that are stained with sin And be washed in the blood of the Lamb. There's a foun - tain flow - ing for the soul un - clean, O be washed in the blood of the Lamb!

Are you washed in the blood, in the soul-cleans-ing blood of the Lamb? Are your gar-ments spot-less? Are they white as snow? Are you washed in the blood of the Lamb?

Are You Washed in the Blood?

1878

To Him who loved us and washed us from our sins in His own blood . . . to Him be glory and dominion forever and ever. Amen. Revelation 1:5–6

A s a preacher, Elisha Hoffman was of average ability, but as a minister who cared for the poor and downtrodden, he excelled. He also stands among the giants of the gospel song era, the author of such favorites as "I Must Tell Jesus," "Down at the Cross," and "Leaning on the Everlasting Arms."

Elisha was born on May 7, 1839, in Orwigsburg, Pennsylvania, and died ninety years later, in 1929, in Chicago. His parents, Rev. Francis A. and Rebecca Ann Hoffman, were devoted to Christ and devoted to a denomination called the Evangelical Association. They gave their son the middle name of Albright in honor of Jacob Albright, the denomination's founder.

Elisha attended public school in Philadelphia, then enrolled in Union Bible Seminary at New Berlin, Pennsylvania, planning to follow his father's footsteps into the ministry. When the Civil War erupted, Elisha served with the Forty-seventh Pennsylvania Infantry Division. Near the war's end, he married Susan Orwig, the daughter of one of the bishops of the Evangelical Association. The couple moved to Cleveland, Ohio, where Elisha was hired as the publishing agent for the Board of Publications of the Evangelical Association. He later pastored churches in Ohio, Illinois, and Michigan.

In 1894, Elisha became the first music editor for the Hope Publishing Company of Chicago. He remained in that post until 1912. Through his years at Hope, he published fifty songbooks and hymnals and wrote the words or music to at least one thousand gospel and Sunday school songs. Some sources put the number at two thousand.

"Are You Washed in the Blood?" first appeared in *Spiritual Songs for Gospel Meetings and Sunday School,* published in 1878. Three years later, it was included in Ira Sankey's *Sacred Songs and Solos,* published in England.

Elisha Hoffman is credited for popularizing the element of "altar" into hymnology of his day. Consider this well-known hymn that came from his pen:

> You have longed for sweet peace, | And for faith to increase,
> And have earnestly, fervently prayed; | But you cannot have rest, or be perfectly blest,
> Until all on the altar is laid.

> Is your all on the altar of sacrifice laid? | Your heart does the Spirit control?
> You can only be blest, and have peace and sweet rest,
> As you yield Him your body and soul.

Because He Lives

Gloria Gaither and William J. Gaither

William J. Gaither

1. God sent His Son, they called Him Je-sus; He came to love, heal and for-give. He lived and died, to buy my par-don. An emp-ty grave is there to prove my Sav-ior lives!

2. How sweet to hold a new-born ba-by, And feel the pride, and joy he gives; But great-er still the calm as-sur-ance, This child can face un-cer-tain days be-cause He lives.

3. And then one day I'll cross that riv-er, I'll fight life's fi-nal war with pain; And then as death gives way to vic-tory, I'll see the lights of glo-ry and I'll know He reigns.

Be-cause He lives, I can face to-mor-row. Be-cause He lives, all fear is gone; Be-cause I know He holds the fu-ture, And life is worth the liv-ing, Just be-cause He lives!

Because He Lives

1971

There is hope in your future, says the LORD. Jeremiah 31:17

A s I prepared this volume of hymn stories, Gloria Gaither graciously shared with me the background for this beloved song:

"When Bill and I started our family in the sixties, racial tensions were tearing the country apart. Civil rights activists had suffered and some had been killed. The Vietnam conflict was claiming thousands of lives, and tensions boiled over on university campuses. Many young people were growing disillusioned and 'dropping out.'

"In this climate, Bill and I sought to write songs with lasting answers to the turmoil of the human spirit. But in the fall of 1969, several things happened to test the reality of our own convictions. We realized we were expecting another baby. Though we had always intended to have another child, we weren't planning on a baby so soon. My body hadn't quite recovered from the last pregnancy. Making matters worse, Bill contracted mononucleosis, which left him exhausted and depressed.

"This combination of national turmoil and personal trouble discouraged us, and we occasionally asked each other, 'If the world is like this now, what will it be in fifteen or sixteen years for our baby? What will this child face?'

"While pondering and praying about these things, we came to realize anew that our courage doesn't come from a stable world, for the world has never been stable. Jesus Himself was born in the cruelest of times. No, we have babies, raise families, and risk living because the Resurrection is true!

"Our baby arrived safe and sound, and we named him Benjamin, which means 'most beloved son.' A few weeks later 'Because He Lives' was born in our hearts and poured from our souls:

> *How sweet to hold our newborn baby*
> *And feel the pride and joy he gives;*
> *But greater still, the calm assurance—*
> *This child can face uncertain days because He lives.*

"Over the years this song has reassured us that our Lord's resurrection is the central truth of life. Because He lives, we can face tomorrow. Many times since, as our children grew, our business life changed, our fortunes shifted, or our direction clouded, our family has found assurance in this very personal song.

"It's 'our song,' but we're grateful others have loved it too."

Now Thank We All Our God

Martin Rinkart
Johann Crüger

1. Now thank we all our God, With heart and hands and voic-es,
2. O may this boun-teous God Through all our life be near us,
3. All praise and thanks to God The Fa-ther now be giv-en,

Who won-drous things hath done, In whom this world re - joic - es;
With ev - er joy - ful hearts And bless - ed peace to cheer us;
The Son, and Him who reigns With them in high-est heav - en,

Who, from our moth-ers' arms, Hath blessed us on our way
And keep us in His grace, And guide us when per - plexed,
The one e - ter - nal God, Whom earth and heav'n a - dore;

With count-less gifts of love, And still is ours to - day.
And free us from all ills In this world and the next.
For thus it was, is now, And shall be ev - er - more.

Now Thank We All Our God

1636

In everything give thanks; for this is the will of God in Christ Jesus for you.
1 Thessalonians 5:18

An old English preacher once said, "A grateful mind is a great mind," and the Bible agrees. There are 138 passages of Scripture on the subject of thanksgiving, and some of them are powerfully worded. Colossians 3:17 says, "And whatever you do in word or deed, do all in the name of the Lord Jesus, giving thanks to God the Father through Him." First Thessalonians 5:18 adds, "In everything give thanks; for this is the will of God in Christ Jesus for you."

Unfortunately, few hymns are devoted exclusively to thanking God. Among the small, rich handful we *do* have is "Now Thank We All Our God." The German Christians sing this hymn as American believers sing the "Doxology," yet it's loved on both sides of the Atlantic and around the world.

It was written by Martin Rinkart (1586–1649), a Lutheran pastor in the little village of Eilenberg, Saxony. He grew up as the son of a poor coppersmith, felt called to the ministry, and after his theological training began his pastoral work just as the Thirty Years' War was raging through Germany.

Floods of refugees streamed into the walled city of Eilenberg. It was the most desperate of times. The Swedish army encompassed the city gates, and inside the walls there was nothing but plague, famine, and fear. Eight hundred homes were destroyed, and people began dying in increasing numbers. There was a tremendous strain on the pastors, who expended all their strength in preaching the gospel, caring for the sick and dying, and burying the dead. One after another, the pastors themselves took ill and perished until at last only Martin Rinkart was left. Some days he conducted as many as fifty funerals.

Finally the Swedes demanded a huge ransom. It was Martin Rinkart who left the safety of the city walls to negotiate with the enemy, and he did it with such courage and faith that there was soon a conclusion of hostilities, and the period of suffering ended.

Rinkart, knowing there is no healing without thanksgiving, composed this hymn for the survivors of Eilenberg. It has been sung around the world ever since.

Now thank we all our God, with heart and hands and voices,
Who wondrous things has done, in Whom this world rejoices

Praise God, from Whom All Blessings Flow

Thomas Ken

Attributed to Louis Bourgeois

Praise God from whom all bless - ings flow.

Praise Him, all crea - tures here be - low.

Praise Him a - bove, ye heav'n - ly host.

Praise Fa - ther, Son and Ho - ly Ghost. A - men.

Praise God, from Whom All Blessings Flow

1674

Blessed be the God and Father of our Lord Jesus Christ, who has blessed us with every spiritual blessing in the heavenly places in Christ. Ephesians 1:3

Before Charles Wesley or Isaac Watts, there was Thomas Ken, who has been called "England's first hymnist." He was born in 1637 in Little Berkhampstead on the fringes of greater London. When his parents died, he was raised by his half sister and her husband, who enrolled him in Winchester College, an historic boys' school. Thomas was later ordained to the ministry and returned to Winchester as a chaplain.

To encourage the devotional habits of the boys, Thomas wrote three hymns in 1674. This was revolutionary because English hymns had not yet appeared. Only the Psalms were sung in public worship. Ken suggested the boys use the hymns privately in their rooms.

One hymn was to be sung upon waking, another at bedtime, and a third at midnight if sleep didn't come. His morning hymn had thirteen stanzas, beginning with:

> *Awake, my soul, and with the sun thy daily stage of duty run;*
> *Shake off dull sloth and joyful rise, to pay thy morning sacrifice.*

His evening hymn, equally meaningful, included this verse:

> *All praise to Thee, my God, this night, for all the blessings of the light!*
> *Keep me, O keep me, King of kings, beneath Thine own almighty wings.*

All three hymns ended with a common stanza, which has since become the most widely sung verse in the world.

> *Praise God, from Whom all blessings flow; / Praise Him, all creatures here below;*
> *Praise Him above, ye heavenly host; / Praise Father, Son, and Holy Ghost.*

In 1680, Thomas was appointed chaplain to England's King Charles II. It was a thankless job, as Charles kept a variety of mistresses. Once the king asked to lodge a mistress in the chaplain's residence. Thomas rebuked him, saying, "Not for the King's Kingdom!" Afterward the king referred to him as "that little man who refused lodging to poor Nellie."

During the reign of the next king, James II, Thomas, by now a bishop, was sent to the Tower of London for his Protestant convictions. After his release, Thomas retired to the home of a wealthy friend, where he died on March 11, 1711. He was buried at sunrise, and the "Doxology" was sung at his funeral.

Guide Me, O Thou Great Jehovah

William Williams

John Hughes

1. Guide me, O Thou great Je - ho - vah, Pil - grim through this bar - ren land; I am weak, but Thou art might - y, Hold me with Thy pow'r - ful hand. Bread of heav - en, Bread of heav - en, Feed me till I want no more; Feed me till I want no more.

2. O - pen now the crys - tal foun - tain, Whence the heal - ing stream doth flow; Let the fire and cloud - y pil - lar Lead me all my jour - ney through. Strong De - liv - 'rer, strong De - liv' - rer, Be Thou still my strength and shield; Be Thou still my strength and shield.

3. When I tread the verge of Jor - dan, Bid my an - xious fears sub - side; Death of death and Hell's de - struc - tion Land me safe on Ca - naan's side. Songs of prais - es, songs of prais - es, I will ev - er give to Thee; I will ev - er give to Thee.

Guide Me, O Thou Great Jehovah

1745

When you pass through the waters, I will be with you; and through the rivers, they shall not overflow you. When you walk through the fire, you shall not be burned, nor shall the flame scorch you. Isaiah 43:2

*T*he Great Awakening of the 1700s was a heaven-sent revival to many parts of the world. In America, the preaching of George Whitefield and Jonathan Edwards renewed Christian zeal and swept multitudes into the kingdom. In England, the open-air evangelism of Whitefield and the Wesley brothers did the same. In Wales, it was the electrifying preaching of Howell Harris and his convert, William Williams.

Williams, son of a wealthy farmer, graduated from the university as a physician, intending to become a medical doctor. But hearing a sermon that Harris preached while standing on a gravestone in Talgarth churchyard, he was converted. Soon thereafter, he changed professions to become a physician of the soul—a preacher.

During his forty-three years of itinerant ministry, Williams traveled over 95,000 miles, drawing crowds of 10,000 or more. Once he spoke to an estimated 80,000, noting in his journal, "God strengthened me to speak so loud that most could hear."

Williams is best remembered, however, for his hymns. He has been called the "Sweet Singer of Wales," and the "Watts of Wales." In all, he composed more than eight hundred hymns, his best known being this autobiographical prayer with its many Old Testament allusions, which first appeared in Williams's collection of Welsh hymns, *Alleluia* (1745), entitled "Strength to Pass Through the Wilderness."

Williams lived as a pilgrim, pressing through the snow of winter, the rains of springtime, and the heat of summer. He was both beaten by mobs (once nearly dying) and cheered by crowds, but in all his travels he sought only to do the will of God until his death at age seventy-four.

Many years later, when President James Garfield was dying of an assassin's bullet, he seemed to temporarily rally and was allowed to sit by the window. His wife began singing this hymn, and the president, listening intently, began to cry. To his doctor, Willard Bliss, he said, "Glorious, Bliss, isn't it?"

This hymn was also sung at the funeral of England's Princess Diana.

Several stanzas of this hymn are today seldom sung. One of the best reads:

Musing on my habitation, musing on my heav'nly home;
Fills my soul with holy longings: Come, my Jesus, quickly come.
Vanity is all I see; Lord, I long to be with Thee.

113

For the Beauty of the Earth

Folliott S. Pierpoint

Conrad Kocher

1. For the beau-ty of the earth, For the glo-ry of the skies, For the love which from our birth O - ver and a - round us lies;

2. For the won-der of each hour Of the day and of the night, Hill and vale and tree and flower, Sun and moon and stars of light:

3. For the joy of hu-man love, Broth-er, sist-er, par-ent, child; Friends on earth and friends a-bove, For all gen-tle thoughts and mild:

4. For Thy Church that ev-er-more Lift-eth ho-ly hands a-bove, Of-fering up on ev-ery shore Her pure sac-ri-fice of love:

5. For Thy-self, best gift di-vine, To our race so free-ly given; For that great, great love of Thine, Peace on earth and joy in heaven:

Lord of all, to Thee we raise This our hymn of grate-ful praise.

For the Beauty of the Earth

1864

Therefore You are great, O LORD GOD. For there is none like You, nor is there any God besides You, according to all that we have heard with our ears. 2 Samuel 7:22

olliot Sandford Pierpoint—that's the unlikely name of the author of this great hymn. Folliot was born October 7, 1835, in Bath, England. After graduating from Cambridge, he taught at Somersetshire College in his home area of Bath.

One day when he was twenty-nine, Folliot found himself walking in the countryside on a beautiful spring day. He saw the ocean of green, the blue dome of heaven, and the winding Avon River cutting through the flowery landscape. Overwhelmed with God's creative brilliance, he wrote this poem. He intended it primarily for communion services in the Anglican Church, but when it jumped the Atlantic, it quickly became associated with the American Thanksgiving holiday.

In Folliot's original version, each verse ended with, "Christ, Our God, to Thee we raise / This our sacrifice of praise." That line was eventually changed to, "Lord of all, to Thee we raise / This our hymn of grateful praise."

Little else is known about Folliot Sandford Pierpoint. He resigned from his position at Somersetshire and apparently moved from place to place, teaching some, writing hymns, and publishing his poetry. He died in 1917.

"For the Beauty of the Earth" is one of only a few songs devoted purely to giving thanks. One of the strange things about the "attitude of gratitude" is that we tend to exhibit it in reverse proportion to the number of blessings received. The more we have, the less thankful we are.

Among the lessons Viktor Frankl learned in the Nazi death camp Auschwitz was to take time to be thankful and to count your blessings. He wrote that prisoners in the camp dreamed at night about certain things more than others: bread, cakes, and nice warm baths—the very things we take for granted every day.

Ralph Waldo Emerson observed that if the constellations appeared only once in a thousand years, imagine what an exciting event it would be. But because they're there every night, we barely give them a look.

One of the evidences of the Holy Spirit's work in our lives is a gradual reversal of that twisted pattern. God wants to make us people who exhibit a thankfulness in proper proportion to the gifts and blessings we've received.

Why not take time to sing this hymn to the Lord right now?

This Is My Father's World

Maltbie D. Babcock

Traditional English Melody

1. This is my Fa-ther's world, And to my lis-t'ning ears;
2. This is my Fa-ther's world; The birds their car-ols raise.
3. This is my Fa-ther's world, O let me ne'er for - get

All na - ture sings and round me rings The mu - sic of the spheres.
The morn - ing light, the lil - y white, De - clare their Mak - er's praise;
That though the wrong seems oft so strong, God is the Rul - er yet.

This is my Fa - ther's world; I rest me in the thought
This is my Fa - ther's world; He shines in all that's fair;
This is my Fa - ther's world; The bat - tle is not done;

Of rocks and trees, of skies and seas; His hand the won - ders wrought.
In the rust - ling grass I hear Him pass, He speaks to me ev - ery - where.
Je - sus, who died, shall be sat - is - fied, And earth and heav'n be one.

116

This Is My Father's World

1901

For the world is Mine, and all its fullness. Psalm 50:12

Maltbie Babcock was arguably the most remarkable student Syracuse University had ever seen. Hailing from an aristocratic family, he was a brilliant scholar with a winning personality. Tall and steel-muscled, he was an outstanding athlete, expert swimmer, and captain of the baseball team. He also directed the university's orchestra, played several instruments, and composed original compositions. A proficient vocalist, he directed the university glee club. He entertained other students by drawing and doing impersonations. On the side, he was an avid fisherman.

He would have been successful in any profession, but God called him to the ministry; and after further training at Auburn Theological Seminary, he became pastor of the First Presbyterian Church in Lockport, New York. It was a beautiful area—midway between Lake Erie and Lake Ontario, not far from Niagara Falls—and Maltbie enjoyed hiking and running in the hills outside town. Telling his secretary, "I'm going out to see my Father's world," he would run or hike a couple of miles into the countryside, where he'd lose himself in nature.

It was during his pastorate at Lockport that he wrote a sixteen-stanza poem, each verse beginning with the words "This is my Father's world."

In 1886, Maltbie was called to the Brown Memorial Church in Baltimore. While there, he traveled widely and was in great demand on college campuses. He was a fresh, engaging speaker who never failed to stimulate students. In 1899, he moved to the Brick Presbyterian Church in New York City. Here he found it more difficult to take off on his hikes. The work load was enormous, but Maltbie faced it stoically, writing:

> *Be strong! We are not here to play, to dream, to drift,*
> *We have hard work to do and loads to lift;*
> *Shun not the struggle. Face it. 'Tis God's gift. Be strong!*

When he was forty-two, his church presented him with a special gift—a pilgrimage to the Holy Land. With great excitement, Maltbie departed by ship. While en route at Naples, Italy, he was seized with a deadly bacterial fever and died at the International Hospital on May 18, 1901.

After his death, his wife compiled his writings into a book entitled *Thoughts for Everyday Living*, published in 1901. Included was Maltbie's "This Is My Father's World."

Great Is Thy Faithfulness

Thomas O. Chisholm

William M. Runyan

1. Great is Thy faith - ful - ness, O God my Fa - ther,
2. Sum - mer and win - ter And spring - time and har - vest,
3. Par - don for sin And a peace that en - dur - eth,

There is no shad - ow Of turn - ing with Thee;
Sun, moon and stars In their cours - es a - bove;
Thine own dear pres - ence To cheer and to guide;

Thou chang - est not, Thy com - pas - sions they fail not;
Join with all na - ture In man - i - fold wit - ness
Strength for to - day And bright hope for to - mor - row,

As Thou hast been Thou for - ev - er wilt be.
To Thy great faith - ful - ness, Mer - cy and love.
Bless - ings all mine, With ten thou - sand be - side!

Great Is Thy Faithfulness

1923

Your mercy, O LORD, is in the heavens; Your faithfulness reaches to the clouds.
Psalm 36:5

*T*he author of this hymn, Thomas Obediah Chisholm, was born in a log cabin in Kentucky. At age sixteen, he began teaching school, despite the paucity of his own education. He came to Christ at age twenty-seven under the ministry of evangelist H. C. Morrison. But Chisholm's health was unstable, and he alternated between bouts of illness and gainful employment in which he did everything from journalism to insurance to evangelistic work. Through all the ups and downs, he discovered new blessings from God every morning. The third chapter of Lamentations 3 became precious to him: "His compassions fail not. They are new every morning; Great is Your faithfulness" (verses 22–23).

Thomas later admitted there was no dramatic story behind the writing of "Great Is Thy Faithfulness." While serving the Lord in Vineland, New Jersey, Thomas sent several poems to his friend, musician William Runyan, who was so moved by this one that he prayed earnestly for special guidance in composing the music. Runyan was in Baldwin, Kansas, at the time, and the hymn was published in 1923 in Runyan's private song pamphlets.

"It went rather slowly for several years," Thomas recalled. Then Dr. Will Houghton of the Moody Bible Institute of Chicago discovered it and would say in chapel, "Well, I think we shall have to sing 'Great Is Thy Faithfulness.'" It became an unofficial theme song for the Institute; and when Houghton died, it was sung at his funeral.

Still, it remained relatively unknown until popularized around the world by George Beverly Shea and the choirs at the Billy Graham Crusades.

Thomas spent his retirement years in a Methodist Home for the Aged in Ocean Park, New Jersey, where he was frequently seen walking by the ocean and along town streets. Tom Rich, a resident of Ocean Park, recalls his pleasant demeanor as he dropped by the diner, sat on park benches, and fellowshipped with friends at Ocean Park's summer Bible conferences.

Thomas died in Ocean Park in 1960. During his lifetime he wrote 1,200 poems and hymns. In addition to "Great Is Thy Faithfulness," he is the author of the well-known "O to Be Like Thee," and the hymn "Living for Jesus."

Living for Jesus, a life that is true,
Striving to please Him in all that I do;
Yielding allegiance, glad hearted and free,
This is the pathway of blessing for me.

We Gather Together

Anonymous Dutch Hymn

Dutch Folk Song

1. We gath-er to-geth-er to ask the Lord's bless-ing;
2. Be-side us to guide us, our God with us join-ing,
3. We all do ex-tol Thee, Thou Lead-er tri-um-phant,

He chas-tens and has-tens His will to make known;
Or-dain-ing, main-tain-ing His king-dom di-vine;
And pray that Thou still our De-fend-er wilt be.

The wick-ed op-press-ing now cease from dis-tress-ing,
So from the be-gin-ning the fight we were win-ning:
Let Thy con-gre-ga-tion es-cape tri-bu-la-tion:

Sing prais-es to His name: He for-gets not His own.
Thou, Lord, wast at our side, all glo-ry be Thine!
Thy Name be ev-er praised! O Lord, make us free!

We Gather Together

1597

So the nations shall fear the name of the LORD, and all the kings of the earth Your glory. Psalm 102:15

T hose who have visited the Netherlands, with its picturesque dikes and windmills, may be unaware of the terrific struggle for religious freedom that took place there in the sixteenth and seventeenth centuries. In 1555, the Low Country was given to King Philip II of Spain by his father, Emperor Charles V of Germany. Philip was an arch-Catholic, but the winds of Calvinistic Reformation had reached the Netherlands. Roman Catholic churches were plundered, and the authority of Spain was resisted.

In 1557, King Philip sent the dreaded Duke of Alba (Fernando Alvarez de Toledo) to bring the Netherlands back into the pope's fold. He established a reign of terror during which ten thousand people were executed and another forty thousand exiled. His ruling counsel was called the "Council of Troubles," but it's better known to history as the "Blood Council." The bodies of thousands of people were hung in the streets and on the doorposts of houses. Alva didn't hesitate to massacre whole cities. An attack on Leiden was stopped only by cutting the dikes and flooding the country-side.

On January 6, 1579, the Catholic southern regions of the Netherlands (modern Belgium) declared their allegiance to Philip, but three weeks later the northern part (modern Holland) refused to submit to the Catholic rule of Spain. In 1581, Holland declared its independence, led by the courageous William of Orange. Holland was devastated by warfare, and in the process William was cut down by an assassin's dagger. But the brave nation would not be denied, and eventually Spain lost its hold on the Dutch Republic.

This hymn, "We Gather Together," which Americans associate with their Thanksgiving holiday, was actually written sometime in 1597 to celebrate Holland's freedom from Spain. Its author, an unknown Dutchman, was full of thanksgiving that his people were finally free from Spanish tyranny and free to worship as they chose. Notice how he expressed this theme in these three beautiful verses:

The wicked oppressing now cease from distressing . . .

. . . so from the beginning the fight we were winning;
Thou, Lord, wast at our side, all glory be Thine!

We all do extol Thee, Thou Leader triumphant,
And pray that Thou still our Defender wilt be.
Let Thy congregation escape tribulation:
Thy Name be ever praised! O Lord, make us free!

121

Rejoice, the Lord Is King

Charles Wesley

John Darwall

1. Re - joice, the Lord is King! Your Lord and King a - dore!
2. Je - sus, the Sav - ior reigns, The God of truth and love;
3. His king-dom can - not fail, He rules o'er earth and heaven;
4. Re - joice in glo - rious hope! Je - sus, the judge shall come,

Mor - tals, give thanks, and sing, And tri-umph ev - er - more:
When He had purged our stains, He took His seat a - bove:
The keys of death and hell Are to our Je - sus given:
And take His ser - vants up To their e - ter - nal home:

Lift up your heart; Lift up your voice!
Lift up your heart; Lift up your voice!
Lift up your heart; Lift up your voice!
Lift up your heart; Lift up your voice!

Re - joice, a - gain I say, re - joice!
Re - joice, a - gain I say, re - joice!
Re - joice, a - gain I say, re - joice!
Re - joice, a - gain I say, re - joice!

Rejoice, the Lord Is King

1744

Rejoice greatly, O daughter of Zion! Shout, O daughter of Jerusalem! Behold, your King is coming to you . . . Zechariah 9:9

y the 1740s, Charles Wesley was regularly preaching to thousands in the open air, but opposition was developing. He first encountered physical danger when a doctor in Wales, angry over Charles's sermon, stormed up to him and demanded an apology for having been called a Pharisee.

Charles, who wasn't known for his tact, replied, "I still insist you are a Pharisee . . . My commission is to show you your sins, and I shall make no apology for so doing . . . You are a damned sinner."

The doctor struck Charles with his cane, causing a mêlée involving several men and women. This was the beginning of a period of dangerous ministry. Here's an entry in Charles's diary from July 22, 1743:

> I had just named my text at St. Ives . . . when an army of rebels broke in upon us . . . They began in a most outrageous manner, threatening to murder the people, if they did not go out that moment. They broke the sconces, dashed the windows in pieces, tore away the shutters . . . and all but the stone-walls. I stood silently looking on; but mine eyes were unto the Lord. They swore bitterly I should not preach there again; which I disproved, by immediately telling them Christ died for them all. Several times they lifted up their hands and clubs to strike me; but a stronger arm restrained them. They beat and dragged the women about, particularly one of a great age, and trampled on them without mercy. The longer they stayed, and the more they raged, the more power I found from above . . .

It was during these days of danger that Charles wrote his triumphant hymn "Rejoice, the Lord Is King," the third verse of which says:

> *His kingdom cannot fail, He rules o'er earth and heaven;*
> *The keys of death and hell are to our Jesus given:*
> *Lift up your heart; lift up your voice!*
> *Rejoice, again I say, rejoice!*

Interestingly, this entry appeared in Charles's journal a few years later, on Sunday, July 13, 1746: "At St. Ives no one offered to make the least disturbance. Indeed, the whole place is outwardly changed in this respect. I walk the streets with astonishment, scarce believing it St. Ives. It is the same throughout all the county. All opposition falls before us . . ."

All Things Bright and Beautiful

Cecil F. Alexander

17th-Century English Melody

Unison All things bright and beau - ti - ful, All crea - tures great and small,

All things wise and won - der - ful, The Lord God made them all.

1. Each lit - tle flow'r that o - pens, Each lit - tle bird that sings,
2. The pur - ple - head - ed moun - tains, The riv - er run - ning by,
3. The cold wind in the win - ter, The pleas - ant sum - mer sun,
4. He gave us eyes to see them, And lips that we might tell

He made their glow - ing col - ors, He made their ti - ny wings.
The sun - set and the morn - ing, That bright - ens up the sky.
The ripe fruits in the gar - den, He made them ev - 'ry one.
How great is God Al - might - y, Who has made all things well.

124

All Things Bright
and Beautiful
1848

Then God saw everything that He had made, and indeed it was very good.
Genesis 1:31

One day, Mrs. Cecil Frances Alexander was working with one of her pupils in Sunday school—a little boy who happened to be her godson. He was struggling to understand the Apostles' Creed and certain portions of the catechism. Mrs. Alexander began to mull the possibility of converting the Apostles' Creed into songs for children, using simple little hymns to explain the phrases and truths of the Christian faith to little ones.

The Apostles' Creed begins: "I believe in God, the Father Almighty, Maker of heaven and earth, and in Jesus Christ, His only Son, our Lord." For the phrase "Maker of heaven and earth . . ." she wrote this lovely little song, "All Things Bright and Beautiful." She based the hymn on Genesis 1:31: "Then God saw everything that He had made, and indeed it was very good."

The phrase, "suffered under Pontius Pilate, was crucified, died, and was buried," became the basis for Mrs. Alexander's hymn "There Is a Green Hill Far Away."

According to one account, the imagery Mrs. Alexander used for that hymn came about as she was driving into the city of Derry, Ireland, to do some shopping. Alongside the road near the old city walls was a little grass-covered hill. Somehow, this knoll helped her visualize Calvary, and from that came the inspiration for the hymn.

These hymns were published in 1848 in Mrs. Alexander's book *Hymns for Little Children.* She also published many other books and hymnals, including *Verses from the Holy Scriptures* (1846), *Narrative Hymns for Village Schools* (1853), *Poems on Subjects in the Old Testament* (1854), *Hymns Descriptive and Devotional* (1858), and *The Legend of the Golden Prayer* (1859). But nothing has stood the test of time like the powerful combination of the Apostles' Creed with her own gift for song.

The Star-Spangled Banner

Francis Scott Key

Attributed to John Stafford Smith

O say, can you see, by the dawn's ear - ly light,

What so proud - ly we hailed at the twi - light's last gleam-ing.

O say, does that star - span - gled ban - ner yet

wave O'er the land of the free and the home of the brave?

The Star-Spangled Banner

1814

For our citizenship is in heaven, from which we also eagerly wait for the Savior, the Lord Jesus Christ. Philippians 3:20

I t was a deadly September attack on America. Casualties on our own shores. The nation's capitol targeted. The White House in danger. Terror. Heroes.

One hero was Francis, a Georgetown attorney heavily involved in national politics. An evangelical Christian, Francis taught Bible classes and witnessed boldly, once telling a friend in Congress, "Christ alone can save you from the sentence of condemnation."

He also wrote hymns like this one:

Lord, with glowing heart I'd praise Thee, | For the bliss Thy love bestows,
For the pardoning grace that saves me, | And the peace that from it flows;
Help, O God, my weak endeavor; | This dull soul to rapture raise;
Thou must light the flame, or never
Can my love be warmed to praise.

But nothing prepared Francis for the hostage-recovery mission he undertook at the request of the president of the United States. He was seeking the release of a prominent physician, Dr. Beanes, who had been taken captive. During that assignment he was detained by enemy troops and forced to watch a brutal assault on the eastern seaboard.

Toward the morning of September 14, 1814, when it became clear that American forces had withstood the twenty-five–hour bombardment, Francis Scott Key penned another hymn, scribbling it on the back of an envelope. The first stanza we all know, but have you ever sung the last stanza of "The Star-Spangled Banner"?

Blest with victory and peace, may the heaven-rescued land
Praise the Power that hath made and preserved us a nation!
Then conquer we must when our cause it is just.
And this be our motto: "In God is our trust."
And the star-spangled banner in triumph shall wave
O'er the land of the free and the home of the brave.

After sunrise, the British released Francis, and back in Baltimore he wrote out this hymn in fuller form and showed it to his brother-in-law, who promptly gave it to a printer who ran off handbills for distribution on the streets. One copy landed in the hands of an unknown musician who adapted it to the tune "To Anacreon in Heaven." So was born the patriotic hymn that was to become our national anthem.

My Country, 'Tis of Thee

Samuel F. Smith

Thesaurus Musicus

1. My country, 'tis of Thee, Sweet land of
2. My native country, thee, Land of the
3. Let music swell the breeze, And ring from
4. Our fathers' God, to Thee, Author of

lib - er - ty, Of Thee I sing: Land where my
no - ble, free, Thy name I love: I love Thy
all the trees Sweet free - dom's song: Let mor - tal
lib - er - ty, To Thee we sing: Long may our

fa - thers died, Land of the pil - grims' pride,
rocks and rills, Thy woods and tem - pled hills;
tongues a - wake; Let all that breathe par - take;
land be bright With free - dom's ho - ly light;

From ev - ery moun - tain side Let free - dom ring!
My heart with rap - ture thrills Like that a - bove.
Let rocks their si - lence break, The sound pro - long.
Pro - tect us by Thy might, Great God, our King!

My Country, 'Tis of Thee

1831

Blessed is the nation whose God is the LORD ... Psalm 33:12

*T*his patriotic hymn was written by Samuel Francis Smith, a native Bostonian, born on October 21, 1808. After attending Boston Latin School, he enrolled in Harvard, then attended Andover Seminary. While there, Samuel became fascinated by the work of Adoniram Judson, America's first missionary, and he developed a lifelong passion for world evangelism.

It was also during Samuel's first year at Andover that hymn publisher Lowell Mason sought his help. Mason had a stack of German songs and materials needing translation. Learning that Samuel was proficient in German, he recruited the young student to translate them.

On a cold February afternoon, about a half hour before sunset, Samuel sat in his sparsely furnished room, pouring over the materials. He was struck by the words of *"Gott segne Sachsenland"* ("God Bless Our Saxon Land"), set to the tune we know as "America" (used in Great Britain for "God Save the Queen").

"I instantly felt the impulse to write a patriotic hymn of my own adapted to this tune," Samuel later said. "Picking up a scrap of paper which lay near me, I wrote at once, probably within half an hour, the hymn, 'America' as it is now known."

A friend, William Jenks, took a copy to the pastor of Boston's Park Street Congregational Church. There "America" was first sung by the Juvenile Choir at a Sunday School Rally, on July 4, 1831.

In the years that followed, Samuel Francis Smith grew into a powerful Baptist preacher, pastor, college professor, hymnist, linguist, writer, and missionary advocate. He traveled the world in support of evangelism, and he rejoiced when his son became a missionary to Rangoon. Samuel lived to ripe old age and remained active till the end. He died suddenly in his late eighties at the Boston train station en route to a preaching appointment.

But he has always been most revered for the patriotic hymn he wrote as a twenty-three-year-old student. As his friend and Harvard classmate Oliver Wendell Holmes put it at a class reunion:

> *And there's a nice youngster of excellent pith,—*
> *Fate tried to conceal him by naming him Smith;*
> *But he shouted a song for the brave and the free,—*
> *Just read on his medal, "My country, of thee!"*

Battle Hymn of the Republic

Julia Ward Howe

American Melody

1. Mine eyes have seen the glo - ry Of the com - ing of the Lord;
2. I have seen Him in the watch-fires Of a hun-dred cir - cling camps;
3. He has sound - ed forth the trum - pet That shall nev - er sound re - treat;
4. In the beau - ty of the lil - ies, Christ was born a - cross the sea,

He is tramp-ling out the vin - tage Where the grapes of wrath are stored;
They have build - ed Him an al - tar In the eve - ning dews and damps;
He is sift - ing out the hearts of men Be - fore His judg - ment seat;
With a glo - ry in His bos - om That trans - fig - ures you and me;

He hath loosed the fate - ful light - ning Of His ter - ri - ble swift sword;
I can read His righ - teous sen - tence By the dim and flar - ing lamps;
O be swift, my soul, to an - swer Him! Be ju - bi - lant, my feet!
As He died to make men ho - ly, Let us live to make men free,

His truth is march - ing on.
His day is march - ing on.
Our God is march - ing on.
While God is march - ing on.

130

Battle Hymn of the Republic

1861

Who is this King of glory? The LORD strong and mighty, the LORD mighty in battle.
Psalm 24:8

After the September 11, 2001, attacks on the Pentagon and the World Trade Center, a national service of prayer and remembrance was conducted at Washington's National Cathedral. America's most powerful leaders prayed together, listened to brief sermons by evangelist Billy Graham and others, then joined voices to sing the defiant anthem "Battle Hymn of the Republic." Its words seemed to perfectly signal America's intention to battle the forces of terror in the world.

"Battle Hymn of the Republic" was written by Julia Ward Howe, a leader in women's rights and an ardent foe of slavery. Julia, who came from a wealthy New York family, was married to prominent Boston philanthropist and humanitarian Dr. S. G. Howe. They were both crusaders for progressive political and moral issues of the day.

In 1861, during the darkest days of the Civil War, the Howes visited Washington, and Julia toured a nearby Union Army Camp on the Potomac in Virginia. There she heard soldiers singing a tribute to John Brown, who had been hanged in 1859 for attempting to lead an insurrection of slaves at Harper's Ferry: "John Brown's Body Lies a-mold'ring in the Grave." The music was rousing, but the words needed improvement. Julia's pastor, who accompanied her, asked her to consider writing new and better verses. That night, after the Howes retired to their room at the Willard Hotel, the words came.

> I went to bed and slept as usual, but awoke the next morning in the gray of the early dawn, and to my astonishment found that the wished-for lines were arranging themselves in my brain. I lay quite still until the last verse had completed itself in my thoughts, then hastily arose, saying to myself, I shall lose this if I don't write it down immediately. I searched for an old sheet of paper and an old stub of a pen which I had had the night before, and began to scrawl the lines almost without looking, as I learned to do by often scratching down verses in the darkened room when my little children were sleeping. Having completed this, I lay down again and fell asleep, but not before feeling that something of importance had happened to me.

Julia gave her song to a friend who worked at the *Atlantic Monthly*. The magazine published it in February 1862, sending her a check for five dollars.

131

America, the Beautiful

Katharine Lee Bates

Samuel A. Ward

1. O beau-ti-ful for spa-cious skies, For am-ber waves of grain,
2. O beau-ti-ful for pil-grim feet, Whose stern, im-pas-sioned stress
3. O beau-ti-ful for he-roes proved In lib-er-at-ing strife,
4. O beau-ti-ful for pa-triot dream That sees be-yond the years

For pur-ple moun-tains maj-es-ties A-bove the fruit-ed plain!
A thor-ough-fare for free-dom beat A-cross the wil-der-ness!
Who more than self their coun-try loved, And mer-cy more than life!
Thine al-a-bas-ter cit-ies gleam, Un-dimmed by hu-man tears!

A-mer-i-ca! A-mer-i-ca! God shed His grace on thee,
A-mer-i-ca! A-mer-i-ca! God mend thine ev-'ry flaw.
A-mer-i-ca! A-mer-i-ca! May God thy gold re-fine
A-mer-i-ca! A-mer-i-ca! God shed His grace on thee,

And crown thy good with broth-er-hood From sea to shin-ing sea!
Con-firm thy soul in self-con-trol, Thy lib-er-ty in law!
Till all suc-cess be no-ble-ness And ev-ery gain di-vine!
And crown thy good with broth-er-hood From sea to shin-ing sea.

America, the Beautiful

1893

The heavens are Yours, the earth also is Yours; the world and all its fullness, You have founded them. Psalm 89:11

I n 1892, the United States observed the 400th anniversary of the discovery of America by Christopher Columbus.

As part of the celebration, the city of Chicago sponsored a World's Fair, which carried over to the next year. It was in the early summer of 1893 that a group of professors from Wellesley College visited the Exposition on their way to teach summer school in Colorado. The women later compared the wonders of the man-made fair with the glory of God's handiwork in the Rockies.

At the close of school, the teachers decided to visit Pike's Peak, elevation 14,000 feet. One of them, Katharine Lee Bates, later wrote:

We hired a prairie wagon. Near the top we had to leave the wagon and go the rest of the way on mules. I was very tired. But when I saw the view, I felt great joy. All the wonder of America seemed displayed there, with the sea-like expanse . . .

It was then and there, as I was looking out over the sea-like expanse of fertile country spreading away so far under those ample skies, that the opening lines of the hymn floated into my mind. When we left Colorado Springs the four stanzas were penciled in my notebook . . . The Wellesley work soon absorbed time and attention again, the notebook was laid aside, and I do not remember paying heed to these verses until the second summer following, when I copied them out and sent them to *The Congregationalist*, where they first appeared in print July 4, 1895. The hymn attracted an unexpected amount of attention . . . In 1904, I rewrote it, trying to make the phraseology more simple and direct.

The new version first appeared in the *Boston Evening Transcript*, November 19, 1904.

There are two stories about the melody, MATERNA, which was written by Samuel A. Ward, originally for a hymn entitled "O Mother Dear, Jerusalem." Ward's son-in-law said that the tune was composed in memory of Ward's oldest daughter. One of the employees at Ward's music store in Newark insisted that he composed the tune in 1882 while crossing New York harbor after spending the day at Coney Island. The notes came to him so quickly he jotted them on the cuff of his shirt. Perhaps both stories are true.

God of Our Fathers

Daniel C. Roberts

George W. Warren

Trumpets before each stanza

1. God of our fa - thers, whose Al - might - y hand
2. Thy love di - vine hath led us in the past,
3. From war's a - larms, from dead - ly pes - ti - lence,
4. Re - fresh Thy peo - ple on their toil - some way,

Leads forth in beau - ty all the star - ry band
In this free land by Thee our lot is cast;
Be Thy strong arm our ev - er sure de - fense;
Lead us from night to nev - er end - ing day;

Of shin - ing worlds in splen - dor through the skies,
Be Thou our Rul - er, Guard - ian, Guide, and Stay,
Thy true re - li - gion in our hearts in - crease,
Fill all our lives with love and grace di - vine,

Our grate - ful songs be - fore Thy throne a - rise.
Thy word our law, Thy paths our cho - sen way.
Thy boun - teous good - ness nour - ish us in peace.
And glo - ry, laud, and praise be ev - er Thine!

God of Our Fathers

1876

The God of our fathers has chosen you that you should know His will, and see the Just One, and hear the voice of His mouth. Acts 22:14

This patriotic hymn represents a double celebration of America's one hundredth birthday. The words were written in 1876 by a New England pastor in honor of the one hundredth anniversary of the signing of the Declaration of Independence. The music was written twelve years later in celebration of the one hundredth anniversary of the adoption of the United States Constitution.

Daniel Crain Roberts, a thirty-four-year-old veteran of the Civil War, authored the words. Born on Long Island, New York, in 1841, Daniel attended college in Ohio and served as a private with the Eighty-fourth Ohio Volunteers during the War Between the States. As the war ended, he was ordained as a deacon in the Presbyterian Episcopalian church, and shortly afterward as a priest. He served for the next thirty years pastoring Episcopalian churches in New England, including a decades-long pastorate of St. Paul's Church in Concord, New Hampshire.*

It was while serving as rector of St. Thomas Episcopal Church in Brandon, Vermont, as the nation celebrated its one hundredth birthday, that Daniel wrote this hymn. He later submitted it anonymously to the committee for the Episcopal hymnal, and it was accepted. It is the only hymn for which he is remembered.

The majestic melody is not the one to which it was originally sung. When Daniel wrote "God of Our Fathers," he set the words to the tune of the Russian national anthem! It was twelve years later that George William Warren, a self-taught organist, composed the stately tune with its trumpet fanfares. It was called NATIONAL HYMN, written to commemorate the one hundredth anniversary of the U.S. Constitution.

George Warren, lacking formal training, had originally pursued a business career. But his natural talent soon shoved him into music, and he eventually became one of America's premier organists. During his career, he served various congregations in New York City, and he also composed anthems and edited *Warren's Hymns and Tunes as Sung at St. Thomas' Church* in 1888. He also wrote GUIDE ME for the words of the great Welsh hymn "Guide Me, O Thou Great Jehovah."

When George Warren died in 1902, there was a feeling that no organist could play as well as he could, so not a single note of music was played at his funeral, which was attended by thousands.

---

*Interestingly, this is the same church in which the controversial Rev. Gene Robinson was ordained in 2003 as the Episcopalians' first openly homosexual bishop.

The Lord Bless You and Keep You

Numbers 6:24–26

Peter C. Lutkin

The Lord Bless You and Keep You

FOURTEENTH CENTURY BC

The LORD bless you and keep you; the LORD make His face shine upon you, and be gracious to you; the LORD lift up His countenance upon you, and give you peace.
Numbers 6:24–26

T he Dead Sea Scrolls were, until recently, our oldest copies of biblical text. But in 1979, Villanova professor Judith Hadley was assisting archaeologist Gabriel Barkay in excavating a site in Jerusalem's Hinnom Valley. In a burial cave, she saw something resembling the metal cap of a pencil. It was a sensational find, a tiny silver scroll of great antiquity. Another was found nearby. These tiny amulets, dating to the Hebrew monarchy seven centuries before Christ, were so small and fragile they took several years to painstakingly clean and open.

When scientists finally unrolled them, they found the world's oldest extant copy of a biblical text, the words of Numbers 6:24–26: "The LORD bless you and keep you; The LORD make His face shine upon you, and be gracious to you; the LORD lift up His countenance upon you, and give you peace."

While the amulets date from the seventh century BC, the original words are far older, coming 1,400 years before Christ. As the Israelites wandered in the wilderness, the Lord commanded the priests to bless the people with this threefold blessing.

These ancient lyrics have been set to music many times, but never more beautifully than by Peter Christian Lutkin in his classic tune BENEDICTION. During the Fanny Crosby/Ira Sankey era of gospel music, when so much was written for easy congregational singing, Lutkin wrote more elaborate melodies with a classical flare.

Lutkin was born in Wisconsin in 1888, and devoted his life to church music, studying the masters in Europe, excelling on the organ, and founding the School of Music at Northwestern Illinois. He helped start the American Guild of Organists. He died in 1931 and was buried in Rosehill Cemetery in Chicago.

In his *Notes from My Bible,* D. L. Moody said about the priestly blessing of Numbers 6: "Here is a benediction that can give all the time without being impoverished. Every heart may utter it, every letter may conclude with it, every day may begin with it, every night may be sanctified by it. Here is blessing—keeping—shining—the uplifting upon our poor life of all heaven's glad morning. It is the Lord Himself who (gives us) this bar of music from heaven's infinite anthem."

The LORD bless you and keep you;
The LORD make His face shine upon you, and be gracious to you;
The LORD lift up His countenance upon you, and give you peace.

Be Thou My Vision

Irish Hymn, c. 8th Century

Irish Folk Melody

1. Be thou my Vi - sion, O Lord of my heart;
2. Be thou my Wis-dom, and thou my true Word;
3. Rich - es I heed not, nor man's emp - ty praise;
4. High King of heav - en, my vic - to - ry won,

Naught be all else to me, save that thou art;
I ev - er with thee and thou with me, Lord;
Thou mine in - her - i - tance, now and al - ways;
May I reach heav-en's joys, O bright heaven's Sun!

Thou my best thought, by day or by night,
Thou my great Fa - ther, and I thy true son,
Thou and thou on - ly, first in my heart,
Heart of my own heart, what - ev - er be - fall,

Wak - ing or sleep - ing, thy pres-ence my light.
Thou in my dwell - ing, and I with thee one.
High King of heav - en, my trea-sure thou art.
Still be my Vi - sion, O Rul - er of all.

Be Thou My Vision

EIGHTH CENTURY

Go therefore and make disciples of all the nations, baptizing them in the name of the Father and of the Son and of the Holy Spirit. Matthew 28:19

*O*nly one missionary is honored with a global holiday, and only one is known by his own distinct color of green—St. Patrick, of course, missionary to Ireland.

Patrick was born in AD 373, along the banks of the River Clyde in what is now called Scotland. His father was a deacon and his grandfather a priest. When Patrick was about sixteen, raiders descended on his little town and torched his home. When one of the pirates spotted him in the bushes, he was seized, hauled aboard ship, and taken to Ireland as a slave. There he gave his life to the Lord Jesus.

"The Lord opened my mind to an awareness of my unbelief," he later wrote, "in order that I might remember my transgressions and turn with all my heart to the Lord my God."

Patrick eventually escaped and returned home. His overjoyed family begged him to never leave again. But one night, in a dream reminiscent of Paul's vision of the Macedonian man in Acts 16, Patrick saw an Irishman pleading with him to come evangelize Ireland.

It wasn't an easy decision, but Patrick, about thirty, returned to his former captors with only one book, the Latin Bible, in his hand. As he evangelized the countryside, multitudes came to listen. The superstitious Druids opposed him and sought his death. But his preaching was powerful, and Patrick became one of the most fruitful evangelists of all time, planting about 200 churches and baptizing 100,000 converts.

His work endured, and several centuries later, the Irish church was still producing hymns, prayers, sermons, and songs of worship. In the eighth century, an unknown poet wrote a prayer asking God to be his Vision, his Wisdom, and his Best Thought by day or night.

In 1905, Mary Elizabeth Byrne, a scholar in Dublin, Ireland, translated this ancient Irish poem into English. Another scholar, Eleanor Hull of Manchester, England, took Byrne's translation and crafted it into verses with rhyme and meter. Shortly thereafter it was set to a traditional Irish folk song, "Slane," named for an area in Ireland where Patrick reportedly challenged local Druids with the gospel.

It is one of our oldest and most moving hymns:

Be Thou my vision, O Lord of my heart,
Naught be all else to me save that Thou art.
Thou my best thought by day or by night,
Waking or sleeping, Thy presence my light.

139

All Creatures of Our God and King

St. Francis of Assisi

Geistliche Kirchengesänge Cologne

1. All crea-tures of our God and King, Lift up your voice and with us
2. Let all things their Cre-a-tor bless, And wor-ship Him in humble-

sing, Al-le-lu-ia! Al-le-lu-ia! Thou burn-ing sun with
ness. O praise Him! Al-le-lu-ia! Praise, praise the Fa-ther,

gold-en beam, Thou sil-ver moon with soft-er gleam, O praise Him
praise the Son, And praise the spir-it, Three in One! O praise Him

O praise Him! Al-le-lu-ia! Al-le-lu-ia! Al-le-lu-ia!

All Creatures of Our God and King

1225

I tell you that if these should keep silent, the stones would immediately cry out.
Luke 19:40

S o many stories have arisen around St. Francis of Assisi that it's difficult to separate truth from fiction. We know he was born in 1182 in central Italy, son of a rich merchant. After a scanty education, Francis joined the army and was captured in war. He came to Christ shortly after his release, renounced his wealth, and began traveling about the countryside, preaching the gospel, living simply, seeking to make Christ real to everyone he met.

Francis loved nature, and many stories spotlight his interaction with animals. Once, as he hiked through Italy's Spoleto Valley, he came upon a flock of birds. When they didn't fly away, he decided to preach them a little sermon. "My brother and sister birds," he reportedly said, "you should praise your Creator and always love Him. He gave you feathers for clothes, wings to fly, and all other things you need. It is God who made your home in thin, pure air. Without sowing or reaping, you receive God's guidance and protection."

The flock, it is said, then flew off rejoicing.

That perspective is reflected in a hymn Francis composed just before his death in 1225, called *"Cantico di fratre sole"*—"Song of Brother Sun." It exhorts all creation to worship God. The sun and moon. All the birds. All the clouds. Wind and fire. All men of tender heart. All creatures of our God and King.

Though written in 1225, an English version didn't appear until 1919, when Rev. William H. Draper decided to use it for a children's worship festival in Leeds, England.

But is it sound theology to exhort birds and billowing clouds to lift their voices in praise? Yes! "All Creatures of Our God and King" simply restates an older hymn— Psalm 148—which says:

Praise Him, sun and moon; | Praise Him, all you stars of light . . .
You great sea creatures and all the depths; | Fire and hail, snow and clouds;
Stormy wind, fulfilling His word; | Mountains and all hills;
Fruitful trees and all cedars; | Beasts and all cattle;
Creeping things and flying fowl . . . | Let them praise the name of the LORD,
For His name alone is exalted . . . | Praise the LORD!

A Mighty Fortress Is Our God

Martin Luther   Martin Luther

1. A might-y for-tress is our God. A bul-wark nev-er fail - ing;
2. Did we in our own strength con-fide, Our striv-ing would be los - ing,
3. And though this world with dev-ils filled, Should threat-en to un-do us,
4. That word a-bove all earth-ly powers, No thanks to them, a-bid - eth;

Our help-er He a-mid the flood Of mor-tal ills pre-vail - ing.
Were not the right man on our side, The man of God's own choos - ing.
We will not fear, for God hath willed, His truth to tri-umph through us.
The Spir-it and the gifts are ours Through Him who with us sid - eth.

For still our an-cient foe Doth seek to work us woe- His craft and power are
Dost ask who that may be? Christ Je-sus, it is He- Lord Sab-a-oth His
The prince of dark-ness grim, We trem-ble not for him- His rage we can en-
Let goods and kin-dred go, This mor-tal life al-so- The bo-dy they may

great, And, armed with cru-el hate, On earth is not His e - qual.
name, From age to age the same, And He must win the bat - tle.
dure, For lo, his doom is sure: One lit-tle word shall fell him.
kill; God's truth a-bid-eth still: His king-dom is for-ev - er.

A Mighty Fortress
Is Our God

1529

God is our refuge and strength, a very present help in trouble. Psalm 46:1

We think of Martin Luther as a great reformer, Bible translator, political leader, fiery preacher, and theologian. But he was also a musician, having been born in an area of Germany known for its music. There in his little Thuringian village, young Martin grew up listening to his mother sing. He joined a boys' choir that sang at weddings and funerals. He became proficient with the flute (recorder), and his volcanic emotions often erupted in song.

When the Protestant Reformation began, Luther determined to restore worship to the German Church. He worked with skilled musicians to create new music for Christians, to be sung in the vernacular. He helped revive congregational singing and wrote a number of hymns.

Often he "borrowed" popular secular melodies for his hymns, though occasionally a tune brought criticism and he was "compelled to let the devil have it back again" because it was too closely associated with bars and taverns.

In the forward of a book, Luther once wrote, "Next to the Word of God, the noble art of music is the greatest treasure in the world. It controls our thoughts, minds, hearts, and spirits . . . A person who . . . does not regard music as a marvelous creation of God . . . does not deserve to be called a human being; he should be permitted to hear nothing but the braying of asses and the grunting of hogs."

Luther's most famous hymn is *"Ein' feste Burg ist unser Gott,"*—"A Mighty Fortress Is Our God." Based on Psalm 46, it reflects Luther's awareness of our intense struggle with Satan. In difficulty and danger, Luther would often resort to this song, saying to his associate, "Come, Philipp, let us sing the 46th Psalm."

This is a difficult hymn to translate because the original German is so vivid. At least eighty English versions are available. The most popular in America was done by Frederic Henry Hodge. But an older version appeared in the Pennsylvania Lutheran Church Book of 1868:

A mighty fortress is our God, | A trusty Shield and Weapon;
He helps us free from every need, | That hath us now o'ertaken.

The British version of "A Mighty Fortress" is Thomas Carlyle's translation:

A safe stronghold our God is still, | A trusty shield and weapon;
He'll help us clear from all the ill | That hath us now o'ertaken.

143

The Lord's My Shepherd

Scottish Psalter, 1650   Jessie S. Irvine

1. The Lord's my shepherd, I'll not want; He makes me down to lie In pastures green; He leadeth me The quiet waters by.
2. My soul He doth restore again, And me to walk doth make With in the paths of righteousness, E'en for His own name's sake.
3. Yea, though I walk in death's dark vale, Yet will I fear no ill, For Thou art with me, and Thy rod And staff me comfort still.
4. My table Thou hast furnished In presence of my foes; My head Thou dost with oil anoint, And my cup overflows.

The Lord's My Shepherd
1650

The LORD is my shepherd; I shall not want. Psalm 23:1

Our oldest hymnal is the book of Psalms, and Christians throughout history have wanted to obey the biblical injunction to praise the Lord using "*psalms,* hymns, and spiritual songs" (Ephesians 5:19; Colossians 3:16).

John Calvin, quoting Augustine, wrote, "We shall not find better songs nor more fitting for the purpose than the Psalms of David, which the Holy Spirit spoke . . . And moreover, when we sing them, we are certain that God puts in our mouths these, as if He Himself were singing in us to exalt His glory."

But the Psalms were originally written in Hebrew, and, when translated, they don't typically have the rhyme or rhythm for easy singing.

In the early 1640s, Francis Rouse, an English Puritan, rendered all 150 Psalms from the Hebrew into metrical English. The General Assembly of the Church of Scotland, meeting in Edinburgh, took Rouse's translation and submitted it to revision committees. These committees spent six years comparing the metered Psalms with the original Hebrew, seeking to develop a singable translation that was accurate to the original Hebrew. They worked as painstakingly as if creating a new translation of the Bible.

Finally, in 1650, the *Scottish Psalter* was released and approved for congregations of the Church of Scotland. Its full title was *The Psalms of David in Meeter: Newly translated, and diligently compared with the original Text, and former Translations: More plain, smooth, and agreeable to the Text, than any heretofore.*

Though the Scottish Psalter of 1650 is one of the great treasures of hymnody, the only portion widely sung beyond Scotland is its beautiful rendition of Psalm 23, set to the tune CRIMOND, which begins:

> *The Lord's my Shepherd, I'll not want.*
> *He makes me down to lie*
> *In pastures green; He leadeth me*
> *The quiet waters by.*

The melody, CRIMOND, was composed about 1870 by a woman named Jessie Seymour Irvine. She was the daughter of the parish minister in the little Scottish town of Crimond, which is also famous for its unusual clock in the church tower. The clockmaker accidentally put six marks into one of the five minute sections on the clock face. As a result, each hour in Crimond is sixty-one minutes, making a day there twenty-four minutes longer than anywhere else on earth.

Well, it just gives a little extra time for singing "The Lord's My Shepherd."

145

Fairest Lord Jesus

Anonymous German Hymn   *Schlesische Volkslieder* arr. by Richard S. Willis

1. Fair - est Lord Je - sus; Rul - er of all na - ture,
2. Fair are the mead - ows; Fair - er still the wood - lands,
3. Fair is the sun - shine; Fair - er still the moon - light
4. Beau - ti - ful Sav - ior! Lord of the na - tions!

O Thou of God and man the Son.
Robed in the bloom - ing garb of spring.
And all the twin - kling star - ry host.
Son of God and Son of man!

Thee will I cher - ish; Thee will I hon - or,
Je - sus is fair - er; Je - sus is pur - er,
Je - sus shines bright - er; Je - sus shines pur - er
Glo - ry and hon - or, Praise, ad - o - ra - tion,

Thou my soul's glo - ry, joy, and crown.
Who makes the woe - ful heart to sing.
Than all the an - gels heav'n can boast.
Now and for - ev - er - more be Thine!

Fairest Lord Jesus

1677

For unto us a Child is born, unto us a Son is given . . . and His name will be called Wonderful, Counselor, Mighty God, Everlasting Father, Prince of Peace. Isaiah 9:6

This hymn came from Roman Catholic Jesuits in Germany and originally had six verses. It first appeared in 1677 in a Jesuit hymnbook titled *Münster Gesangbuch*, but the text of the hymn was in existence at least fifteen years earlier, for it has been found in a manuscript dating back to 1662. Yet the origin of the words remains a mystery.

Who translated it into English? That, too, is largely a mystery. The first three stanzas are the work of an anonymous translator. The fourth stanza was by Joseph A. Seiss, and it first appeared in a Lutheran Sunday school book in 1873.

How appropriate that no human author draws attention from the great theme of this song. There's no source to distract from the subject, no story to detract from the Savior.

This hymn emphasizes the beauty and wonder of Christ, and it alludes to His dual nature, that He was both human and divine, God made flesh, the God-Man: "O Thou of God and man the Son . . . Son of God and Son of Man . . ."

It brings to mind one of the greatest observations ever made about Christ, uttered by the "Golden-mouthed" preacher of Antioch, John Chrysostom, in a fourth-century sermon: "I do not think of Christ as God alone, or man alone, but both together. For I know He was hungry, and I know that with five loaves He fed five thousand. I know He was thirsty, and I know that He turned the water into wine. I know He was carried in a ship, and I know that He walked on the sea. I know that He died, and I know that He raised the dead. I know that He was set before Pilate, and I know that He sits with the Father on His throne. I know that He was worshiped by angels, and I know that He was stoned by the Jews. And truly some of these I ascribe to the human, and others to the divine nature. For by reason of this He is said to have been both God and man."

Beautiful Savior! Lord of all the nations!
Son of God and Son of Man!
Glory and honor, praise, adoration,
Now and forever more be Thine.

Praise Ye the Lord, the Almighty

Joachim Neander

Straslund Gesangbuch

1. Praise to the Lord, the Al-might-y, The King of cre-a-tion!
2. Praise to the Lord, Who o'er all things So won-drous-ly reign-eth,
3. Praise to the Lord! O let all that is in me a-dore Him!
4. Praise to the Lord, Who doth pros-per Thy work and de-fend thee;

O my soul, praise Him, For He is thy health and sal-va-tion!
Shel-ters thee un-der His wings, Yes, so gent-ly sus-tain-eth!
All that hath life and breath, Come now with prais-es be-fore Him.
Sure-ly His good-ness and mer-cy Here dail-y at-tend thee.

All ye who hear, Now to His tem-ple draw near;
Hast Thou not seen How all thy long-ings have been
Let the a-men sound from His peo-ple a-gain:
Pon-der a-new what the Al-might-y can do,

Join me in glad ad-o-ra-tion!
Grant-ed in what He or-dain-eth?
Glad-ly for aye we a-dore Him.
If with His love He be-friend thee.

148

Praise Ye the Lord, the Almighty

1680

Where were you when I laid the foundations of the earth? Tell Me, if you have understanding. Job 38:4

This hymn was written by Joachim Neander, born in 1650, whose father, grandfather, great-grandfather, and great-great-grandfather—all Joachim Neanders—had been preachers of the gospel. But as a student, Joachim was wild and rebellious. At twenty, he joined a group of students who descended on St. Martin's Church in Bremen to ridicule and scoff the worshippers. But the sermon that day by Rev. Theodore Under-Eyck arrested him and led to his conversion. A few years later, he was the assistant preacher at that very church.

Joachim often took long walks near his home in Hochdal, Germany. They were worship walks, and he frequently composed hymns as he strolled, singing them to the Lord. He was the first hymnwriter from the Calvinist branch of Protestantism. When he was thirty—the year he died—he wrote this while battling tuberculosis:

> *Praise ye the Lord, the Almighty, the King of Creation.*
> *O my soul praise Him, for He is Thy health and Salvation.*

One of Joachim's favorite walking spots was a beautiful gorge a few miles from Dusseldorf. The Dussel River flowed through the valley, and Joachim Neander so loved this spot that it eventually was named for him—Neander Valley. The Old German word for "valley" was *tal* or *thal* with a silent *h.*

Two hundred years later, Herr von Beckersdorf owned the valley, which was a source for limestone used to manufacture cement. In 1856, miners discovered caves that contained human bones. Beckersdorf took the bones to a local science teacher, who speculated they belonged to one who died in the Flood.

But when William King, an Irish professor of anatomy, saw the bones, he claimed they were proof of evolution's famous "missing link." Other Neanderthal fossils were found, and for many years they were used to "prove" Darwin's theory of evolution. Today we know the Neanderthal was fully human, an extinct people group of great strength.

But as one expert put it, "when Joachim Neander walked in his beautiful valley so many years ago, he could not know that hundreds of years later his name would become world famous, not for his hymns celebrating creation but for a concept that he would have totally rejected: human evolution."*

---

*Marvin L. Lubenow, *Bones of Contention* (Grand Rapids: Baker Book House, 1992), 77. I am indebted to Lubenow for much of the information in this story, gleaned from chapter 6 of this excellent book, subtitled "A Creation's Assessment of Human Fossils."

I Sing the Mighty Power of God

Isaac Watts

from *Gesangbuch der Herzogl*, Württemberg

1. I sing the might-y power of God, That made the mountains rise;
2. I sing the good-ness of the Lord, That filled the earth with food;
3. There's not a plant or flow'r be-low But makes Thy glo-ries known,

That spread the flow-ing seas a-broad, And built the loft-y skies.
He formed the crea-tures with His word, And then pro-nounced them good.
and clouds a-rise and tem-pests blow, By or-der from Thy throne.

I sing the wis-dom that or-dained The sun to rule the day;
Lord, how Thy won-ders are dis-played, Wher-e'er I turn my eye;
While all that bor-rows life from Thee Is ev-er in Thy care;

The moon shines full at His com-mand, And all the stars o-bey.
If I sur-vey the ground I tread, Or gaze up-on the sky.
And ev-ery-where that man can be, Thou, God, art pres-ent there.

I Sing the Mighty Power of God

1715

He has made the earth by His power; He has established the world by His wisdom, and stretched out the heaven by His understanding. Jeremiah 51:15

A s Isaac Watts quietly pastored Mark Lane Chapel in London, the growing popularity of his hymns was causing a tempest. "Christian congregations have shut out divinely inspired Psalms," one man complained, "and taken in Watts' flights of fancy." The issue of singing hymns versus Psalms split churches, including the one in Bedford, England, once pastored by John Bunyan.

The controversy jumped the Atlantic. In May 1789, Rev. Adam Rankin told the General Assembly of the Presbyterian Church, meeting in Philadelphia: "I have ridden horseback all the way from my home in Kentucky to ask this body to refuse the great and pernicious error of adopting the use of Isaac Watts' hymns in public worship in preference to the Psalms of David."

We don't know Isaac's reactions. Dr. Samuel Johnson later reported that "by his natural temper he was quick of resentment; but, by his established and habitual practice, he was gentle, modest, and inoffensive." But in 1712, Isaac suffered a breakdown from which he never fully recovered. He asked his church to discontinue his salary, but they raised it and hired a co-pastor who assumed the bulk of the pastoral duties. Watts remained as pastor the rest of his life, preaching whenever he could.

A wealthy couple in the church, Sir Thomas and Lady Abney, invited him to spend a week on their estate. Isaac accepted—and lived with them until his death thirty-six years later. He enjoyed the children in the home, and in 1715, he published *Divine and Moral Songs for Children.* It sold 80,000 copies in a year and has been selling ever since. In his preface, he said, "Children of high and low degree, of the Church of England or Dissenters, baptized in infancy or not, may all join together in these songs. And as I have endeavored to sink the language to the level of a child's understanding . . . to profit all, if possible, and offend none."

One hymn in this volume, intended for children, became popular with adults. Entitled "Praise for Creation and Providence," it said:

> *I sing the mighty power of God, that made the mountains rise,*
> *That spread the flowing seas abroad, and built the lofty skies.*
> *I sing the wisdom that ordained the sun to rule the day;*
> *The moon shines full at God's command, and all the stars obey.*

And Can It Be That I Should Gain?

Charles Wesley

Thomas Campbell

1. And can it be that I should gain An in-t'rest in the Sa-vior's blood? Died He for me, who caused His pain? For me, who Him to death pur-sued? A-maz-ing love! How can it be That Thou, my God, shouldst die for me?

2. He left His Fa-ther's throne a-bove, So free, so in-fi-nite His grace; Emp-tied Him-self of all but love, And bled for A-dam's help-less race. 'Tis mer-cy all, im-mense and free! For, O my God it found out me!

3. No con-dem-na-tion now I dread; Je-sus, and all in Him, is mine! A-live in Him my liv-ing Head, And clothed in righ-teous-ness di-vine, Bold I ap-proach th'e-ter-nal throne, And claim the crown, through Christ my own.

4. Long my im-pris-oned spir-it lay Fast bound in sin and na-ture's night; Thine eye dif-fused a quick-'ning ray, I woke, the dun-geon flamed with light; My chains fell off, my heart was free; I rose, went forth and fol-lowed Thee.

And Can It Be That I Should Gain?

1738

But He was wounded for our transgressions, He was bruised for our iniquities;
The chastisement for our peace was upon Him, and by His stripes we are healed.
Isaiah 53:5

 harles Wesley was born just before Christmas in 1707. He was premature and neither cried nor opened his eyes. His mother, Susanna, kept him tightly wrapped in wool until his actual due date, whereupon he opened his eyes and cried.

At age eight, he was taken to London to attend Westminster School. At thirteen, he became a King's Scholar at Westminster, and upon graduating, Charles enrolled at Oxford. He was nineteen and full of life. He later said, "My first year at college I lost in diversions."

During his second year at Oxford, he grew serious about spiritual things. Neither he nor his brother, John, had yet received Christ as Savior, but they began seeking to live the Christian life so methodically they were dubbed "Methodists" by fellow students.

Their studies completed, the brothers volunteered to go to Georgia, a new colony in America for those in Britain's debtors' prisons, founded by Colonel James Oglethorpe. But as a missionary, Charles was an utter failure. He was demanding and autocratic, and he insisted on baptizing infants, not by sprinkling, but by immersing them three times in succession. One angry woman fired a gun at him.

Charles left America ill and depressed. Some time later, John also returned in low spirits. Finding themselves in spiritual crisis, the brothers began attending meetings led by the Moravian Christian, Peter Boehler. Finally, on Sunday, May 21, 1738, Charles, thirty-one, wrote, "I now found myself at peace with God, and rejoiced in hope of loving Christ. I saw that by faith I stood."

John came to Christ about the same time, saying, "I felt my heart strangely warmed."

On Tuesday, May 23, Charles wrote in his journal, "I began a hymn upon my conversion." We aren't certain which hymn he meant, but many historians think it was "And Can It Be," because of the vivid testimony of verse 4:

> *Long my imprisoned spirit lay,*
> *Fast bound in sin and nature's night;*
> *Thine eye diffused a quickening ray—*
> *I woke, the dungeon flamed with light;*
> *My chains fell off, my heart was free,*
> *I rose, went forth, and followed Thee.*

153

O for a Thousand Tongues to Sing

Charles Wesley

Carl G. Gläser; arranged by Lowell Mason

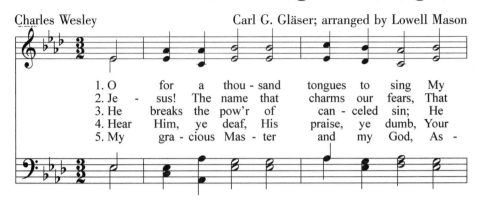

1. O for a thou - sand tongues to sing My
2. Je - sus! The name that charms our fears, That
3. He breaks the pow'r of can - celed sin; He
4. Hear Him, ye deaf, His praise, ye dumb, Your
5. My gra - cious Mas - ter and my God, As -

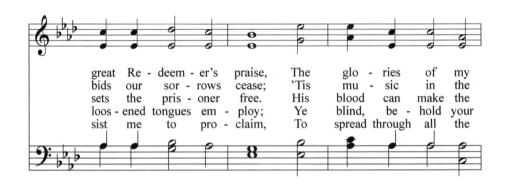

great Re - deem - er's praise, The glo - ries of my
bids our sor - rows cease; 'Tis mu - sic in the
sets the pris - oner free. His blood can make the
loos - ened tongues em - ploy; Ye blind, be - hold your
sist me to pro - claim, To spread through all the

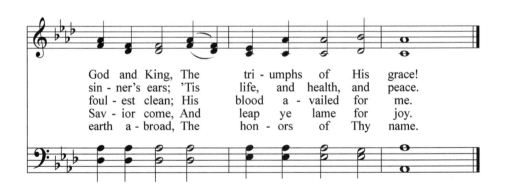

God and King, The tri - umphs of His grace!
sin - ner's ears; 'Tis life, and health, and peace.
foul - est clean; His blood a - vailed for me.
Sav - ior come, And leap ye lame for joy.
earth a - broad, The hon - ors of Thy name.

O for a Thousand Tongues to Sing

1739

The whole multitude . . . began to rejoice and praise God with a loud voice for all the mighty works they had seen. Luke 19:37

T he Wesley brothers sent word of their conversion to their sainted mother, Susanna, who didn't know what to make of it. "I think you have fallen into an odd way of thinking," she replied. "You say that till within a few months you had no spiritual life and no justifying faith . . . I heartily rejoice that you have attained to a strong and lively hope in God's mercy through Christ. Not that I can think that you were totally without saving faith before, but it is one thing to have faith, and another thing to be sensible we have it."

Well, Charles was now very sensible of having it. His life changed, and he gained victory over both his temper and his unfortunate drinking habit. "I was amazed to find my old enemy, intemperance, so suddenly subdued, that I almost forgot I was ever in bondage to him."

He also began to spread the news of what had happened to him. "In the coach to London," he wrote, "I preached faith in Christ. A lady was extremely offended . . . (and) threatened to beat me. I declared I deserved nothing but hell; so did she; and must confess it, before she could have a title to heaven. This was most intolerable to her."

New vitality came into Charles's public preaching. He discontinued the practice of reading his sermons and began preaching extemporaneously.

He found a fruitful arena for ministry at the infamous Newgate Prison and allowed himself to be locked up with condemned men on nights before their executions, that he might comfort and witness to them during their final hours.

As the first anniversary of his conversion approached, Charles wrote an eighteen-stanza hymn describing his praise to the Lord. It was titled "For the Anniversary Day of One's Conversion," and the first stanza began, "Glory to God, and praise, and love . . ." Verse 7 began, "O for a thousand tongues to sing," inspired by a statement Charles had once heard: "Had I a thousand tongues, I would praise Him with them all."

Beginning with a 1767 hymnbook, the seventh stanza was made the first, and when John Wesley compiled his *Collection of Hymns* in 1780, he chose this for the first hymn in the book. Congregations today usually sing verses 7, 8, 9, and 10 of Wesley's original, which we know today as "O for a Thousand Tongues to Sing."

Come, Thou Fount of Every Blessing

Robert Robinson   Traditional American Melody

1. Come, Thou fount of ev-ery bless-ing, Tune my heart to sing Thy grace.
2. Here I raise my Eb-e - ne - zer; Hith-er by Thy help I come.
3. Oh, to grace how great a debt - or Dai-ly I'm con-strained to be!

Streams of mer-cy, nev-er ceas-ing, Call for songs of loud-est praise.
And I hope, by Thy good plea-sure, Safe-ly to ar-rive at home.
Let thy grace, Lord, like a fet-ter, Bind my wan-d'ring heart to Thee:

Teach me some me-lo-dious son-net, Sung by flam-ing tongues a-bove.
Je - sus sought me when a stran-ger Wand'ring from the fold of God;
Prone to wan-der, Lord, I feel it, Prone to leave the God I love.

Praise the mount! I'm fixed up-on it, Mount of God's un-chang-ing love.
He, to res-cue me from dan-ger, In-ter-posed His pre-cious blood.
Here's my heart, Lord, take and seal it, Seal it for Thy courts a-bove.

Come, Thou Fount of Every Blessing

1758

The Lord is not slack concerning His promise, as some count slackness, but is longsuffering toward us, not willing that any should perish but that all should come to repentance. 2 Peter 3:9

R obert Robinson had a rough beginning. His father died when he was young, and his mother, unable to control him, sent him to London to learn barbering. What he learned instead was drinking and gang life. When he was seventeen, he and his friends reportedly visited a fortune-teller. Relaxed by alcohol, they laughed as she tried to tell their futures. But something about the encounter bothered Robert, and that evening he suggested to his buddies they attend the evangelistic meeting being held by George Whitefield.

Whitefield was one of history's greatest preachers, with a voice that was part foghorn and part violin. That night he preached from Matthew 3:7: "But when he saw many of the Pharisees and Sadducees coming to his baptism, he said to them, 'Brood of vipers! Who warned you to flee from the wrath to come?'" Bursting into tears, Whitefield exclaimed, "Oh, my hearers! The wrath to come! The wrath to come!"

Robert immediately sobered up and sensed Whitefield was preaching directly to him. The preacher's words haunted him for nearly three years, until December 10, 1755, when he gave his heart to Christ.

Robert soon entered the ministry, and three years later at age twenty-three, while serving Calvinist Methodist Chapel in Norfolk, England, he wrote a hymn for his sermon on Pentecost Sunday. It was a prayer that the Holy Spirit flood into our hearts with His streams of mercy, enabling us to sing God's praises and remain faithful to Him. "Come, Thou Fount of Every Blessing" has been a favorite of the church since that day.

Robinson continued working for the Lord until 1790, when he was invited to Birmingham, England, to preach for Dr. Joseph Priestly, a noted Unitarian. There, on the morning of June 8, he was found dead at age fifty-four, having passed away quietly during the night.

Take a few moments to offer this hymn as a personal prayer, especially remembering those last insightful lines:

> *Let thy goodness, like a fetter, bind my wandering heart to thee.*
> *Prone to wander, Lord, I feel it, prone to leave the God I love;*
> *Here's my heart, O take and seal it, seal it for Thy courts above.*

Rock of Ages

Augustus M. Toplady

Thomas Hastings

1. Rock of A - ges, cleft for me, Let me hide my - self in Thee. Let the wa - ter and the blood, From Thy wound - ed side which flowed, Be of sin the dou - ble cure, Save from wrath and make me pure.

2. Could my tears for - ev - er flow? Could my zeal no lan - guor know? These for sin could not a - tone; Thou must save, and Thou a - lone. In my hand no price I bring; Sim - ply to thy cross I cling.

3. While I draw this fleet - ing breath, When my eyes shall close in death, When I rise to worlds un - known, And be - hold Thee on Thy throne, Rock of A - ges cleft for me, Let me hide my - self in Thee.

Rock of Ages

<u>1776</u>

My Father, who has given them to Me, is greater than all; and no one is able to snatch them out of My Father's hand. John 10:29

n November 4, 1740, a baby in Farnham, England, was given the formidable name of Augustus Montague Toplady. His father died in a war, his mother spoiled him, his friends thought him "sick and neurotic," and his relatives disliked him.

But Augustus was interested in the Lord. "I am now arrived at the age of eleven years," he wrote on his birthday. "I praise God I can remember no dreadful crime; to the Lord be the glory." By age twelve he was preaching sermons to whoever would listen. At fourteen he began writing hymns. At sixteen he was soundly converted to Christ while attending a service in a barn. And at twenty-two he was ordained an Anglican priest.

As a staunch Calvinist, he despised John Wesley's Arminian theology and bitterly attacked the great Methodist leader. "I believe him to be the most rancorous hater of the gospel-system that ever appeared on this island," Augustus wrote.

"Wesley is guilty of satanic shamelessness," he said on another occasion, "of acting the ignoble part of a lurking, shy assassin."

In 1776, Augustus wrote an article about God's forgiveness, intending it as a slap at Wesley. He ended his article with an original poem:

> *Rock of Ages, cleft for me,*
> *Let me hide myself in Thee;*
> *Let the water and the blood,*
> *From Thy wounded side which flowed,*
> *Be of sin the double cure,*
> *Save from wrath and make me pure.*

Augustus Toplady died at age thirty-eight, but his poem outlived him and has been called "the best known, best loved, and most widely useful" hymn in the English language. Oddly, it is remarkably similar to something Wesley had written thirty years before in the preface of a book of hymns for the Lord's Supper: "O Rock of Salvation, Rock struck and cleft for me, let those two Streams of Blood and Water which gushed from thy side, bring down Pardon and Holiness into my soul."

Perhaps the two men were not as incompatible as they thought.*

---

*Robert J. Morgan, "Rock of Ages," November 4, *On This Day* (Nashville: Thomas Nelson Publishers, 1997).

All Hail the Power of Jesus' Name

Edward Perronet

Oliver Holden

1. All hail the power of Je - sus' name! Let an - gels pros - trate
2. Ye cho - sen seed of Is - rael's race, Ye ran - somed from the
3. Let ev - ery kin - dred, ev - ery tribe, On this ter - res - trial
4. O that with yon - der sa - cred throng, We at His feet may

fall; Bring forth the roy - al di - a - dem, And
fall, Hail Him who saves you by His grace, And
ball, To Him all maj - es - ty as - cribe, And
fall! We'll join the ev - er - last - ing song, And

crown Him Lord of all; Bring forth the roy - al
crown Him Lord of all; Hail Him who saves you
crown Him Lord of all; To Him all maj - es -
crown Him Lord of all; We'll join the ev - er -

di - a - dem, And crown Him Lord of all.
by His grace, And crown Him Lord of all.
ty as - cribe, And crown Him Lord of all.
last - ing song, And crown Him Lord of all.

All Hail the Power of Jesus' Name

<u>1779</u>

Who has gone into heaven and is at the right hand of God, angels and authorities and powers having been made subject to Him. 1 Peter 3:22

 n the November 1799 issue of the *Gospel Magazine*, edited by Augustus Toplady, there appeared an anonymous hymn entitled "On the Resurrection, the Lord Is King":

> *All hail the power of Jesus' Name! Let angels prostrate fall;*
> *Bring forth the royal diadem, and crown Him Lord of all.*

The author, it was later revealed, was Rev. Edward Perronet.

Edward's Protestant grandparents had fled Catholic France, going first to Switzerland, then to England. Edward's father had become a vicar in the Anglican Church, and Edward followed in his footsteps.

For several years, he became closely allied with the Wesleys, traveling with them and sometimes caught up in their adventures. In John Wesley's journal, we find this entry: "Edward Perronet was thrown down and rolled in mud and mire. Stones were hurled and windows broken."

In time, however, Edward broke with the Wesleys over various Methodist policies, and John Wesley excluded his hymns from Methodist hymnals. Edward went off to pastor a small independent church in Canterbury, where he died on January 22, 1792. His last words were: "Glory to God in the height of His divinity! Glory to God in the depth of His humanity! Glory to God in His all-sufficiency! Into His hands I commend my spirit."

Edward Perronet's hymn, "All Hail the Power," has earned him an indelible place in the history of church music. It also has a place in missionary history, being greatly used in evangelistic endeavors. Rev. E. P. Scott, for example, missionary to India, wrote of trying to reach a savage tribe in the Indian subcontinent. Ignoring the pleadings of his friends, he set off into the dangerous territory. Several days later, he met a large party of warriors who surrounded him, their spears pointed at his heart.

Expecting to die at any moment, Scott took out his violin, breathed a prayer, closed his eyes, and began singing "All Hail the Power of Jesus' Name!" When he reached the words, "Let every kindred, every tribe," he opened his eyes. There stood the warriors, some in tears, every spear lowered. Scott spent the next two years evangelizing the tribe.

161

Amazing Grace

John Newton

Traditional American Melody

1. A - maz - ing grace! How sweet the sound! That saved a wretch like me! I once was lost, but now am found; Was blind, but now I see.

2. 'Twas grace that taught my heart to fear, And grace my fears re - lieved. How pre - cious did that grace ap - pear, The hour I first be - lieved.

3. Thro' man - y dan - gers, toils and snares I have al - read - y come. 'Tis grace that brought me safe thus far, And grace will lead me home.

4. When we've been there ten thou - sand years, Bright shin - ing as the sun, We've no less days to sing God's praise, Than when we first be - gun.

162

Amazing Grace
1779

In Him we have redemption through His blood, the forgiveness of sins, according to the riches of His grace. Ephesians 1:7

I t's hard to shake off a mother's influence. John Newton's earliest memories were of his godly mother, who, despite fragile health, devoted herself to nurturing his soul. At her knee he memorized Bible passages and hymns. Though she died when he was about seven, he later recalled her tearful prayers for him.

After her death, John alternated between boarding school and the high seas, wanting to live a good life but nonetheless falling deeper and deeper into sin. Pressed into service with the British Navy, he deserted, was captured, and after two days of suspense, was flogged. His subsequent thoughts vacillated between murder and suicide. "I was capable of anything," he recalled.

More voyages, dangers, toils, and snares followed. It was a life unrivaled in fiction. Then, on the night of March 9, 1748, John, twenty-three, was jolted awake by a brutal storm that descended too suddenly for the crew to foresee. The next day, in great peril, he cried to the Lord. He later wrote, "That tenth of March is a day much remembered by me; and I have never suffered it to pass unnoticed since the year 1748—the Lord came from on high and delivered me out of deep waters."

The next several years saw slow, halting spiritual growth in John, but in the end he became one of the most powerful evangelical preachers in British history, a powerful foe of slavery, and the author of hundreds of hymns.

Here are some things you may not know about Newton's most famous hymn. His title for it wasn't originally "Amazing Grace" but "Faith's Review and Expectation." It is based in Newton's study of 1 Chronicles 17:16–17: "King David . . . said: 'Who am I, O LORD God? And what is my house, that You have brought me this far? And yet . . . You have also spoken of Your servant's house for a great while to come, and have regarded me according to the rank of a man of high degree . . .'"

And here's a nearly forgotten verse that Newton added near the end of "Amazing Grace." Try singing it for yourself:

The earth shall soon dissolve like snow, the sun forbear to shine;
But God, Who called me here below, shall be forever mine.

How Firm a Foundation

Rippon's *Selection of Hymns*

Early American Melody

1. How firm a foun - da - tion, ye saints of the Lord,
2. Fear not; I am with thee. O be not dis - mayed,
3. When through fi - ery tri - als Thy path - way shall lie,
4. The soul that on Je - sus Hath leaned for re - pose,

Is laid for your faith In His ex - cel - lent Word!
For I am thy God, I will still give thee aid.
My grace, all suf - fi - cient, Shall be thy sup - ply.
I will not, I will not De - sert to its foes;

What more can He say Than to you He hath said,
I'll strength - en thee, help thee, And cause thee to stand,
The flames shall not hurt thee; I on - ly de - sign
That soul, though all hell Should en - deav - or to shake,

To you who for ref - uge To Je - sus have fled?
Up - held by My righ - teous, Om - nip - o - tent hand.
Thy dross to con - sume and thy gold to re - fine.
I'll nev - er, no nev - er, No nev - er for - sake.

How Firm a Foundation

1787

Fear not, for I am with you; be not dismayed, for I am your God. I will strengthen you, yes, I will help you, I will uphold you with My righteous right hand. Isaiah 41:10

T alk about long pastorates! John Rippon pastored Carter's Lane Baptist Church in London for sixty-three years, beginning in 1775. He had been born in 1751, so he was in his mid-twenties when he first mounted the Carter's Lane pulpit following his education at the Baptist College in Bristol, England.

During the years of Carter's Lane, John developed a vision for a church hymnal, which he edited, assisted by his minister of music, Robert Keene. The resulting volume, *A Selection of Hymns from the Best Authors, Intended to Be an Appendix to Dr. Watts' Psalms and Hymns,* was published in 1787. It was a runaway hit, especially among the Baptists, going through eleven British editions during Rippon's lifetime. An American edition appeared in 1820.

"How Firm a Foundation" first appeared here. No one knows its author, for the line reserved for the author's name simply bore the letter *K.* Many scholars attribute the composition to Keene.

The unique power of this hymn is due to the fact that each of the seven original stanzas was based on various biblical promises. The first verse established the hymnist's theme—God's Word is a sufficient foundation for our faith. The author then selected precious promises from the Bible, and converted these into hymn stanzas, among them:

- Isaiah 41:10—"Fear not, for I am with you; be not dismayed, for I am your God. I will strengthen you, yes, I will help you, I will uphold you with My righteous right hand."
- Isaiah 43:2—"When you pass through the waters, I will be with you; and through the rivers, they shall not overflow you. When you walk through the fire, you shall not be burned, nor shall the flame scorch you."
- 2 Corinthians 12:9—"My grace is sufficient for you, for My strength is made perfect in weakness. Therefore most gladly I will rather boast in my infirmities, that the power of Christ may rest upon me."
- Hebrews 13:5—"For He Himself has said, 'I will never leave you nor forsake you.'"

No wonder this hymn was first published under the title "Exceedingly Great and Precious Promises."

There Is a Balm in Gilead

Traditional Spiritual

Traditional Spiritual

There is a balm in Gil-e-ad to make the wound-ed whole;

There is a balm in Gil-e-ad to heal the sin-sick soul.

1. Some - times I feel dis - cour - aged, And think my work's in vain,
2. If you can't preach like Pet - er, If you can't pray like Paul,

But then the Ho - ly Spir - it Re - vives my soul a - gain.
Just tell the love of Je - sus, And say He died for all.

There Is a Balm in Gilead

About 1800

Who Himself bore our sins in His own body on the tree, that we, having died to sins, might live for righteousness—by whose stripes you were healed. 1 Peter 2:24

T he first Africans on American shores arrived in chains. Their hellish voyage aboard slave ships was only the beginning of their sorrows. The breakup of their families, the oppression of bondage, the whips and shackles, their loss of dignity . . . it all combined to kill both body and spirit.

But the souls of the slaves found release through singing, and a unique form of music evolved called the "Negro spiritual." Spirituals differed greatly from the hymns we've thus far studied. The classics of English hymnody were largely written by pastors like Isaac Watts and John Newton out of their studies of Scripture. African-American slaves, on the other hand, composed their songs in the fields and barns, the words dealing with daily pain and future hope.

Often the slaves were allowed to sing while working. If, for example, they were hauling a fallen tree, they would combine muscles and voices, using the musical rhythms for a "heave-ho" effect. Other times, risking the lash or branding iron, they'd slip into torch-lit groves to worship the Lord. With swaying bodies, they would stand, eyes half-closed, singing "Go Down, Moses," "Roll, Jordan, Roll, "He's Got the Whole World in His Hands," and the classic "There Is a Balm in Gilead" based on Jeremiah 8:22.

"Hymns more genuine than these have never been sung since the psalmists of Israel relieved their burdened hearts," wrote Edith A. Talbot.

Fisk University, in Nashville, Tennessee, was established after the Civil War, and the famous Fisk Jubilee Singers popularized these Negro spirituals around the world. Composers began arranging spirituals in a way that appealed to the larger population, and this gave rise to another type of Christian music, tagged by composer Thomas A. Dorsey as "gospel songs."

Few Negro spirituals can be precisely dated, nor are many specific authors known, but they have mightily influenced American Christian music. The roots of the children's Sunday school chorus "Do Lord," for example, is in this old spiritual:

O do, Lord, remember me!
For Death is a simple thing,
And he go from door to door
And he knock down some, and he cripple up some,
And he leave some here to pray.
O do Lord, remember me!

Holy, Holy, Holy! Lord God Almighty

Reginald Heber   John B. Dykes

1. Ho-ly, ho-ly, ho - ly, Lord God Al - might - y!
2. Ho-ly, ho-ly, ho - ly! All the saints a - dore Thee,
3. Ho-ly, ho-ly, ho - ly! Though the dark-ness hide Thee,
4. Ho-ly, ho-ly, ho - ly! Lord God Al - might - y!

Ear - ly in the morn - ing our song shall rise to Thee.
Cast - ing down their gold-en crowns A - round the glass-y sea;
Though the eye of sin - ful man Thy glo - ry may not see.
All Thy works shall praise Thy name In earth, and sky, and sea.

Ho - ly, ho-ly, ho - ly! Mer - ci - ful and might - y!
Cher - u - bim and ser - a - phim Fall - ing down be - fore Thee,
On - ly Thou art ho - ly; There is none be - side, Thee
Ho - ly, ho-ly, ho - ly! Mer - ci - ful and might - y!

God in three Per - sons, Bless - ed Trin - i - ty!
Which wert, and art, And ev - er - more shall be.
Per - fect in power, In love, and pur - i - ty.
God in three Per - sons, Bless - ed Trin - i - ty.

Holy, Holy, Holy! Lord God Almighty

1826

And they do not rest day or night, saying: "Holy, holy, holy, Lord God Almighty, Who was and is and is to come!" Revelation 4:8

R eginald Heber was born April 21, 1783, to a minister and his wife in an English village. After a happy childhood and a good education in the village school, he enrolled at Oxford, where he excelled in poetry and became fast friends with Sir Walter Scott. Following graduation, he succeeded his father as vicar in his family's parish, and for sixteen years he faithfully served his flock.

His bent toward poetry naturally gave him a keen and growing interest in hymnody. He sought to lift the literary quality of hymns, and he also dreamed of publishing a collection of high-caliber hymns corresponding to the church year for use by liturgical churches. But the bishop of London wouldn't go along with it, and Heber's plans were disappointed.

He continued writing hymns for his own church, however, and it was during the sixteen years in the obscure parish of Hodnet that Heber wrote all fifty-seven of his hymns, including the great missionary hymn "From Greenland's Icy Mountains," which exhorted missionaries to take the gospel to faraway places like "Greenland's icy mountains," and "India's coral strand."

> *From Greenland's icy mountains, | From India's coral strand,*
> *Where Afric's sunny fountains | Roll down their golden sand;*
> *From many an ancient river, | From many a palmy plain,*
> *They call us to deliver | Their land from error's chain.*

This hymn represented an earnest desire for Reginald, for he felt God was calling him as a missionary to "India's coral strand." His desire was fulfilled in 1822, when, at age forty, he was appointed to oversee the Church of England's ministries in India.

Arriving in Calcutta, he set out on a sixteen-month tour of his diocese, visiting mission stations across India. In February of 1826, he left for another tour. While in the village of Trichinopoly on April 3, 1826, he preached to a large crowd in the hot sun, and afterward plunged into a pool of cool water. He suffered a stroke and drowned.

It was after his death that his widow, finding his fifty-seven hymns in a trunk, succeeded in publishing his *Hymns Written and Adapted to the Weekly Service of the Church Year.* In this volume was the great Trinitarian hymn based on Revelation 4:8–11, "Holy, Holy, Holy! Lord God Almighty."

169

O Worship the King

Robert Grant

Johann Michael Haydn

1. O wor-ship the King, All glo-rious a-bove, And
2. O tell of His might, And sing of His grace, Whose
3. Thy boun-ti-ful care, What tongue can re-cite? It
4. Frail child-ren of dust, And fee-ble as frail, In

grate-ful-ly sing His power and His love: Our
robe is the light, Whose can-o-py space. His
breathes in the air; It shines in the light. It
Thee do we trust, Nor find Thee to fail. Thy

Shield and De-fend-er, The An-cient of Days, Pa-
char-iots of wrath, The deep thun-der-clouds form, And
streams from the hills; It de-scends to the plain, And
mer-cies how ten-der! How firm to the end! Our

vil-ioned in splen-dor, And gird-ed with praise.
dark is His path On the wings of the storm.
sweet-ly dis-tills In the dew and the rain.
Mak-er, De-fend-er, Re-deem-er, and Friend!

O Worship the King

1833

I will sing to the LORD as long as I live; I will sing praise to my God while I have my being. Psalm 104:33

harles Grant, director of the East India Company, was respected throughout India as one of Britain's finest statesmen. He was also a deeply committed Christian, an evangelical in the Anglican Church, who used his position in India to encourage missionary expansion there.

In 1778, just as England was reeling from the American Revolution, Charles returned to the British Isles to become a member of Parliament from Inverness, Scotland.

His son, Robert, six years old at the time, grew up in a world of power, politics, and privilege. But he also grew up as a devout and dedicated follower of Christ. As a young man, Robert attended Magdalene College, Cambridge, then entered the legal profession. His intelligence and integrity were obvious. He became King's Sargent in the Court of the Duchy of Lancaster, and in 1818, he entered Parliament. Among his legislative initiatives was a bill to remove civil restrictions against the Jews.

One day in the early 1830s, as Robert studied Psalm 104, he compared the greatness of the King of kings with the majesty of British royalty. Psalm 104:1 says of God: "O LORD my God, You are very great: You are clothed with honor and majesty." Verses 2–3 add that God covers Himself "with light as with a garment" and "makes the clouds His chariot." Verse 5 reminds us that God "laid the foundations of the earth." All of creation reflects God's greatness, verse 24 proclaiming, "O LORD, how manifold are Your works!" Verse 31 says, "May the glory of the LORD endure forever."

Robert filled his heart with these verses, and from his pen came one of the most magnificent hymns in Christendom:

> *O worship the King, all glorious above,*
> *And gratefully sing His power and His love;*
> *Our Shield and Defender, the Ancient of Days,*
> *Pavilioned in splendor and girded with praise.*

In 1832, Robert was appointed judge advocate general, this hymn was published in 1833, and he was knighted in 1834. Soon thereafter, at age fifty, Sir Robert returned to India, land of his early childhood, to be governor of Bombay. He died there on July 9, 1838. A nearby medical college was built in his honor and named for him. But his most lasting memorial is this majestic hymn of praise, calling us to worship the King of kings.

The Solid Rock

Edward Mote

William B. Bradbury

1. My hope is built on noth-ing less Than Je-sus' blood and
2. When dark-ness seems to hide His face, I rest on His un-
3. His oath, His cov - e - nant, His blood, Sup - port me in the
4. When He shall come with trum-pet sound, O may I then in

righ - teous-ness. I dare not trust the sweet-est frame, But whol-ly
chang - ing grace. In ev - ery high and storm - y gale, My an - chor
whelm-ing flood. When all a - round my soul gives way, He then is
Him be found! Dressed in His righ-teous - ness a - lone, Fault - less to

lean on Je - sus' name.
holds with - in the veil.   On   Christ the sol - id   Rock I stand, All
all my Hope and Stay.
stand be - fore the throne!

oth-er ground is sink-ing sand. All oth-er ground is sink-ing sand.

The Solid Rock

1834

For no other foundation can anyone lay than that which is laid, which is Jesus Christ. 1 Corinthians 3:11

dward Mote was born into poverty on January 21, 1797, in London. His parents, innkeepers, wouldn't allow a Bible in their house, but somehow Edward heard the gospel as a teenager and came to Christ. He eventually became a skilled carpenter and the owner of his own cabinet shop.

"One morning," he recalled, "it came into my mind as I went to labor to write a hymn on the 'Gracious Experience of a Christian.' As I went up to Holborn, I had the chorus: 'On Christ the solid Rock I stand / All other ground is sinking sand.' In the day I had four verses complete, and [I] wrote them off.

"On the Sabbath following, I met brother King . . . who informed me that his wife was very ill, and [he] asked me to call and see her. I had an early tea and called afterwards. He said that it was his usual custom to sing a hymn, read a portion, and engage in prayer before he went to meeting. He looked for his hymnbook but could find it nowhere. I said, 'I have some verses in my pocket;' if he liked, we would sing them. We did, and his wife enjoyed them so much that after service he asked me, as a favor, to leave a copy of them for his wife.

"I went home and by the fireside composed the last two verses, wrote the whole off, and took them to sister King . . . As these verses so met the dying woman's case, my attention to them was the more arrested, and I had a thousand printed for distribution."

In 1852, Edward, then fifty-five, gave up his carpentry to pastor the Baptist Church in Horsham, Sussex, where he ministered twenty-one years. He resigned in 1873, in failing health, saying, "I think I am going to heaven; yes, I am nearing port. The truths I have been preaching, I am now living upon, and they'll do very well to die upon. Ah! The precious blood." He passed away at age seventy-seven.

Here's an interesting verse from Mote's original that is omitted from most hymnals today:

I trust His righteous character,
His council, promise, and His power;
His honor and His Name's at stake
To save me from the burning lake;
On Christ, the solid Rock, I stand,
All other ground is sinking sand.

Just as I Am

Charlotte Elliott

William B. Bradbury

1. Just as I am, with-out one plea, But
2. Just as I am, and wait - ing not To
3. Just as I am, though tossed a - bout With
4. Just as I am, poor, wretch - ed, blind; Sight,
5. Just as I am, Thou wilt re - ceive, Wilt

that Thy blood was shed for me, And that Thou bidst me
rid my soul of one dark blot; To Thee whose blood can
many a con-flict, many a doubt, Fight - ings and fears with-
rich - es, heal-ing of the mind. Yea, all I need, in
wel - come, par-don, cleanse, re - lieve. Be - cause Thy prom - ise

come to Thee, O Lamb of God, I come, I come!
cleanse each spot, O Lamb of God, I come, I come!
in, with - out, O Lamb of God, I come, I come!
Thee to find, O Lamb of God, I come, I come!
I be - lieve, O Lamb of God, I come, I come!

Just as I Am

1836

All that the Father gives Me will come to Me, and the one who comes to Me I will by no means cast out. John 6:37

She was an embittered woman, Charlotte Elliott of Brighton, England. Her health was broken, and her disability had hardened her. "If God loved me," she muttered, "He would not have treated me this way."

Hoping to help her, a Swiss minister, Dr. Cesar Malan, visited the Elliotts on May 9, 1822. Over dinner, Charlotte lost her temper and railed against God and family in a violent outburst. Her embarrassed family left the room, and Dr. Malan was left alone with her.

"You are tired of yourself, aren't you?" he asked. "You are holding to your hate and anger because you have nothing else in the world to cling to. Consequently, you have become sour, bitter, and resentful."

"What is your cure?" asked Charlotte.

"The faith you are trying to despise."

As they talked, Charlotte softened. "If I wanted to become a Christian and to share the peace and joy you possess," she finally asked, "what would I do?"

"You would give yourself to God just as you are now, with your fightings and fears, hates and loves, pride and shame."

"I would come to God just as I am? Is that right?"

Charlotte did come just as she was, and her heart was changed that day. As time passed she found and claimed John 6:37 as a special verse for her: "The one who comes to Me I will by no means cast out."

Years later, her brother, Rev. Henry Elliott, was raising funds for a school for the children of poor clergymen. Charlotte wrote a poem, and it was printed and sold across England. The leaflet said, *Sold for the Benefit of St. Margaret's Hall, Brighton: Him That Cometh to Me I Will in No Wise Cast Out.* Underneath was Charlotte's poem—which has since become the most famous invitational hymn in history.

Charlotte lived to be eighty-two and wrote about 150 hymns, though she never enjoyed good health. As her loved ones sifted through her papers after her death, they found over a thousand letters she had kept in which people expressed their gratitude for the way this hymn had touched their lives.

Nearer, My God, to Thee

Sarah F. Adams　　　　　　　　　　　　　　　　　　　　Lowell Mason

1. Near - er, my God, to Thee, Near - er to Thee,
2. Though like the wan - der - er, The sun gone down,
3. There let the way ap - pear, Steps un - to heav'n;
4. Then, with my wak - ing tho'ts Bright with Thy praise,
5. Or if, on joy - ful wing Cleav - ing the sky,

E'en though it be a cross That rais - eth me!
Dark - ness be o - ver me, My rest a stone;
All that Thou send - est me, In mer - cy giv'n;
Out of my ston - y griefs Beth - el I'll raise,
Sun, moon, and stars for - got, Up - ward I fly,

Still all my song shall be, Near - er, my God, to Thee;
Yet in my dreams I'd be, Near - er, my God, to Thee;
An - gels to beck - on me, Near - er, my God, to Thee;
So by my woes to be, Near - er, my God, to Thee;
Still all my song shall be, Near - er, my God, to Thee;

Near - er, my God, to Thee, Near - er to Thee!
Near - er, my God, to Thee, Near - er to Thee!
Near - er, my God, to Thee, Near - er to Thee!
Near - er, my God, to Thee, Near - er to Thee!
Near - er, my God, to Thee, Near - er to Thee!

176

Nearer, My God, to Thee

1840

Then he dreamed, and behold, a ladder was set up on the earth, and its top reached to heaven. Genesis 28:12

I t was reported that the band aboard the *Titanic* gallantly played "Nearer, My God, to Thee" as the great liner sank to its watery grave on April 14, 1912. A Canadian survivor told of being comforted by its strains. Historians, however, have never been able to nail down the validity of the story.

Never mind. It's a great hymn anyway, written by a woman named Sarah Flower Adams. She was born in Harlow, England, in the winter of 1805. Her father was a newspaper editor and a man of prominence.

Sarah herself grew up enjoying the spotlight. She showed great interest in the stage and dreamed of being an actress. In 1834, she married William Bridges Adams, a civil engineer. The couple lived in London where Sarah could be near the great theaters. In 1837, she played "Lady MacBeth" in the Richmond Theater in London to rave reviews.

Her frail health hampered her career, however, and she found herself focusing more on her literary gifts. It's said that she wrote quickly, as if under compulsion, and seldom did editors find anything to change in her work. Among her compositions were hymns of praise to the Lord. Sarah's sister, Eliza, a gifted musician, often wrote the music for her hymns. The two were very close.

One day in 1841, their pastor, Rev. William Johnson Fox of London's South Place Unitarian Church, paid a visit. He was compiling a church hymnbook and he wanted to include some of their hymns. He further mentioned that he was frustrated at his inability to find a hymn to go along with the upcoming Sunday's message, which was from the story of Jacob at Bethel in Genesis 28:20–22.

Sarah offered to write a hymn based on those verses. For the rest of the week she pored over the passage, visualizing Jacob's sleeping with a stone for his pillow as he dreamed of a ladder reaching to heaven. The following Sunday, South Place Unitarian Church sang Sarah's "Nearer, My God, to Thee."

Eliza, who was suffering from tuberculosis, died in 1846. Sarah had faithfully cared for her sister during the illness, but by the time Eliza died, Sarah, too, was showing signs of consumption.

She passed away on August 14, 1848, at age forty-three.

Abide with Me

Henry F. Lyte

W. H. Monk

1. A - bide with me! Fast falls the e - ven - tide.
2. Swift to its close ebbs out life's lit - tle day.
3. I need Thy pres - ence Ev - ery pass-ing hour.
4. I fear no foe, With Thee at hand to bless;

The dark - ness deep - ens; Lord, with me a - bide!
Earth's joys grow dim; Its glo - ries pass a - way.
What but Thy grace Can foil the temp-ter's power?
Ills have no weight, And tears no bit - ter - ness.

When oth - er help - ers fail And com-forts flee,
Change and de - cay In all a - round I see;
Who, like Thy - self, My guide and stay can be?
Where is death's sting? Where, grave, thy vic - to - ry?

Help of the help - less, O a - bide with me!
O Thou, who chang - est not, a - bide with me!
Through cloud and sun - shine, Lord, a - bide with me.
I tri - umph still, If Thou a - bide with me.

Abide with Me

<u>1847</u>

If you abide in Me, and My words abide in you, you will ask what you desire, and it shall be done for you. John 15:7

Henry Francis Lyte, vicar in the fishing village of Lower Brixham, Devonshire, England, ministered faithfully for twenty-three years to his seafaring people.

Though a humble couple, he and his wife, Anne, lived in an elegant estate, Berry Head. It had reportedly been provided by King William IV, who had been impressed with Henry's ministry. At water's edge, its coastal views were among the most beautiful on the British Isles. Henry laid out walking trails through the estate's forty-one acres and enjoyed the tranquillity of the house and grounds. There he wrote most of his sermons, poems, and hymns.

But Henry's lung condition hung over the home like a blackening cloud. Lower Brixham suffered damp winters, and while in his early fifties, Henry realized his lung disorder had deteriorated into tuberculosis. On September 4, 1847, age fifty-four, he entered his pulpit with difficulty and preached what was to be his last sermon. He had planned a therapeutic holiday in Italy. "I must put everything in order before I leave," he said, "because I have no idea how long I will be away."

That afternoon he walked along the coast in pensive prayer, then retired to his room, emerging an hour later with a written copy of "Abide with Me." Some accounts indicate he wrote the poem during that hour; others say that he discovered it in the bottom of his desk as he packed for his trip to Italy, and that it had been written a quarter century earlier. Probably both stories are true. It is likely that, finding sketches of a poem he had previously started, he prayerfully revised and completed it that evening.

Shortly afterward, Henry embraced his family a final time and departed for Italy. Stopping in Avignon, France, he again revised "Abide with Me"—it was evidently much on his mind—and posted it to his wife. Arriving on the French Riviera, he checked into the Hotel de Angleterre in Nice, and there, on November 20, 1847, his phthisic lungs finally gave out. Another English clergyman, a Rev. Manning of Chichester, who happened to be staying in the same hotel, attended him during his final hours. Henry's last words were, "Peace! Joy!"

When news of his death reached Brixham, the fishermen of the village asked Henry's son-in-law, also a minister, to hold a memorial service. It was on this occasion that "Abide with Me" was first sung.

What a Friend We Have in Jesus

Joseph M. Scriven

Charles C. Converse

1. What a Friend we have in Je-sus, All our sins and griefs to bear!
2. Have we tri-als and temp-ta-tions? Is there trou-ble an-y-where?
3. Are we weak and heav-y-lad-en, Cum-bered with a load of care?

What a priv-i-lege to car-ry, Ev-ery-thing to God in prayer!
We should nev-er be dis-cour-aged; Take it to the Lord in prayer.
Pre-cious Sav-ior, still our ref-uge! Take it to the Lord in prayer.

Oh, what peace we of-ten for-feit, Oh, what need-less pain we bear.
Can we find a friend so faith-ful, Who will all our sor-rows share?
Do Thy friends de-spise, for-sake Thee? Take it to the Lord in prayer.

All be-cause we do not car-ry Ev-ery-thing to God in prayer!
Je-sus knows our ev-ery weak-ness; Take it to the Lord in prayer.
In His arms He'll take and shield Thee; Thou wilt find a so-lace there.

What a Friend We Have in Jesus

1855

The peace of God, which surpasses all understanding, will guard your hearts and minds through Christ Jesus. Philippians 4:6–7

Joseph Scriven watched in shock as the body of his fiancée was pulled from the lake. Their wedding had been planned for the next day. Reeling from the tragedy, he made up his mind to immigrate to America. Packing up his belongings in Dublin, Ireland, he sailed for Canada, leaving his mother behind. He was about twenty-five years old.

Ten years later, in 1855, he received word that his mother was facing a crisis. Joseph wrote this poem and sent it to her. Mrs. Scriven evidently gave a copy to a friend who had it published anonymously, and it quickly became a popular hymn, though no one knew who had written it.

Meanwhile, Joseph fell in love again. But tragedy struck a second time when his bride, Eliza Catherine Roche, contracted tuberculosis and died in 1860 before their wedding could take place.

To escape his sorrow, Joseph poured himself into ministry, doing charity work for the Plymouth Brethren and preaching among the Baptists. He lived a simple, obscure life in Port Hope, Canada, cutting firewood for widows, giving away his clothes and money to those in need. He was described as "a man of short stature, with iron-gray hair, close-cropped beard, and light blue eyes that sparkled when he talked." Ira Sankey later wrote:

> Until a short time before his death it was not known that he had a poetic gift. A neighbor, sitting up with him in his illness, happened upon a manuscript copy of "What a Friend We Have in Jesus." Reading it with great delight and questioning Mr. Scriven about it, he said that he had composed it for his mother, to comfort her in a time of special sorrow, not intending that anyone else should see it. Some time later, when another Port Hope neighbor asked him if it was true he composed the hymn, his reply was, "The Lord and I did it between us."

On October 10, 1896, Joseph became critically ill. In his delirium, he rose from his bed and staggered outdoors, where he fell into a small creek and drowned at age sixty-six. His grave was arranged so that his feet were opposite those of his lost love, Eliza Catherine Roche, that at the resurrection they might arise facing one another.

Stand Up, Stand Up for Jesus

George Duffield Jr.

George J. Webb

1. Stand up, stand up for Je - sus, Ye sol - diers of the cross;
2. Stand up, stand up for Je - sus, The trum - pet call o - bey;
3. Stand up, stand up for Je - sus, Stand in His strength a - lone;
4. Stand up, stand up for Je - sus, The strife will not be long,

Lift high His roy - al ban - ner, It must not suf - fer loss;
Forth to the might - y con - flict In this His glo - rious day.
The arm of flesh will fail you, Ye dare not trust your own.
This day, the noise of bat - tle, The next, the vic - tor's song.

From vic - t'ry un - to vic - t'ry His ar - my shall He lead,
Ye that are men, now serve Him A - gainst un - num - bered foes;
Put on the Gos - pel a - rmor, Each piece put on with prayer;
To Him that o - ver - com - eth, A crown of life shall be;

Till ev - 'ry foe is van - quished And Christ is Lord in - deed.
Let cou - rage rise with dan - ger, And strength to strength op - pose.
Where du - ty calls, or dan - ger, Be nev - er want - ing there.
He with the King of Glo - ry Shall reign e - ter - nal - ly.

Stand Up, Stand Up for Jesus

1858

Stand therefore, having girded your waist with truth, having put on the breastplate of righteousness. Ephesians 6:14

Dudley Tyng served as his father's assistant at Philadelphia's Church of the Epiphany and was elected its pastor when his father retired in 1854. He was only twenty-nine when he succeeded his father at this large Episcopal church, and at first it seemed a great fit. But the honeymoon ended when Dudley began vigorously preaching against slavery. Loud complaints rose from the more conservative members, resulting in Dudley's resignation in 1856.

He and his followers organized the Church of the Covenant elsewhere in the city, and his reputation grew. He began noontime Bible studies at the YMCA, and his ministry reached far beyond his own church walls. Dudley had a burden for leading husbands and fathers to Christ, and he helped organize a great rally to reach men.

On Tuesday, March 30, 1858, five thousand men gathered. As Dudley looked over the sea of faces he felt overwhelmed. "I would rather this right arm were amputated at the trunk than that I should come short of my duty to you in delivering God's message," he told the crowd.

Over a thousand men were converted that day.

Two weeks later Dudley was visiting in the countryside, watching a corn-thrasher in the barn. His hand moved too close to the machine and his sleeve was snared. His arm was ripped from its socket, the main artery severed. Four days later his right arm was amputated close to the shoulder. When it appeared he was dying, Dudley told his aged father, "Stand up for Jesus, Father, and tell my brethren of the ministry to stand up for Jesus."

Rev. George Duffield of Philadelphia's Temple Presbyterian Church was deeply stirred by Dudley's funeral, and the following Sunday he preached from Ephesians 6:14 about standing firm for Christ. He read a poem he had written, inspired by Dudley's words:

> *Stand up, stand up for Jesus, / Ye soldiers of the cross;*
> *Lift high His royal banner, / It must not suffer loss.*

The editor of a hymnal heard the poem, found appropriate music, and published it. "Stand Up, Stand Up for Jesus" soon became one of America's favorite hymns, extending Dudley's dying words to millions.

Jesus Loves Me

Anna B. Warner

William B. Bradbury

1. Je-sus loves me! this I know, For the Bi-ble tells me so;
2. Je-sus loves me! He who died, Heav-en's gate to o-pen wide;
3. Je-sus take this heart of mine, Make it pure and whol-ly Thine;
4. Je-sus loves me! He will stay, Close be-side me all the way;

Lit - tle ones to Him be-long, They are weak, but He is strong.
He will wash a - way my sin, Let His lit - tle child come in.
Thou has bled and died for me, I will hence-forth live for Thee.
He's pre-pared a home for me, And some-day His face I'll see.

Yes, Je - sus loves me, Yes, Je - sus loves me,

Yes, Je - sus loves me, The Bi - ble tells me so.

Jesus Loves Me

<u>1860</u>

That Christ may dwell in your hearts through faith; that you, being rooted and grounded in love, may be able to comprehend with all the saints what is the width and length and depth and height—to know the love of Christ which passes knowledge; that you may be filled with all the fullness of God. Ephesians 3:17–19

Anna and Susan Warner lived in a lovely townhouse in New York City, where their father, Henry Whiting Warner, was a successful lawyer. But the Panic of 1837 wrecked the family's finances, forcing them to move into a ramshackle Revolutionary War–era home on Constitution Island on the Hudson, right across from the Military Academy at West Point.

Needing to contribute to the family income, Anna and Susan began writing poems and stories for publication. Anna wrote "Robinson Crusoe's Farmyard," and Susan wrote "The Wide, Wide World." The girls thus launched parallel literary careers that resulted in 106 publications, 18 of them coauthored.

One of their most successful joint projects was a novel titled *Say and Seal* in which a little boy named Johnny Fox is dying. His Sunday school teacher, John Linden, comforts him by taking him in his arms, rocking him, and making up a little song: "Jesus loves me, this I know, for the Bible tells me so . . ."

The novel became a bestseller, second only to *Uncle Tom's Cabin*; when hymnwriter William Bradbury read the words of John Linden's little song (written by Anna), he composed a childlike musical score to go along with them. "Jesus Loves Me" soon became the best-known children's hymn on earth.

Despite their success, the Warner sisters never seemed able to recover from the staggering financial reverses of 1836. Years later a friend wrote, "One day when sitting with Miss Anna in the old living room, she took from one of the cases a shell so delicate that it looked like lace work, and holding it in her hand, with eyes dimmed with tears, she said, 'There was a time when I was very perplexed, bills were unpaid, necessities must be had, and someone sent me this exquisite thing. As I held it, I realized that if God could make this beautiful home for a little creature, He would take care of me.'"

For forty years, Susan and Anna conducted Bible classes for cadets at West Point, and both were buried with full military honors. They are the only civilians buried in the military cemetery at West Point. To this day, their home on Constitution Island is maintained by West Point as a museum to their memory.

He Leadeth Me

Joseph H. Gilmore

William B. Bradbury

1. He lead-eth me, O bless-ed thought! O words with heaven-ly com-fort fraught!
2. Some-times 'mid scenes of deep-est gloom, Some-times where E - den's bow-ers bloom,
3. Lord, I would clasp Thy hand in mine, Nor ev - er mur - mur nor re - pine;
4. And when my task on earth is done, When by Thy grace the vic-t'ry's won,

What -e'er I do, where-e'er I be, Still 'tis God's hand that lead-eth me.
By wa - ters still, o'er trou-bled sea, Still 'tis His hand that lead-eth me!
Con -tent what - ev - er lot I see, Since 'tis my God that lead-eth me.
E'en death's cold wave I will not flee, Since God through Jor - dan lead-eth me.

He lead-eth me, He lead-eth me, By His own hand He lead-eth me;

His faith-ful fol-lower I would be, For by His hand He lead-eth me.

He Leadeth Me

1862

He leads me in the paths of righteousness for His name's sake. Psalm 23:3

On autumn nights as we sleep peacefully in our beds, millions of songbirds travel under cover of darkness, heading south. Somehow, they know their way. God has given them a state-of-the-art internal guidance system.

We're more valuable than many sparrows. If God guides His creation, will He not also guide His children? The psalmist thought so, saying, "He leadeth me . . . He leadeth me . . ." (Psalm 23:2–3).

Dr. Joseph H. Gilmore, son of a Governor of New Hampshire, gave this account of writing his famous hymn on this theme:

As a young man recently graduated . . . I was supplying for a couple of Sundays the pulpit of the First Baptist Church in Philadelphia. At the mid-week service, on the 26th of March, 1862, I set out to give the people an exposition of the Twenty-third Psalm, which I had given before on three or four occasions, but this time I did not get further than the words "He Leadeth Me." Those words took hold of me as they had never done before, and I saw in them a significance . . . of which I had never dreamed.

It was the darkest hour of the Civil War. I did not refer to that fact—that is, I don't think I did—but it may subconsciously have led me to realize that God's leadership is the one significant fact in human experience, that it makes no difference how we are led, or whither we are led, so long as we are sure God is leading us.

At the close of the meeting a few of us in the parlor of my host, Deacon Watson, kept on talking about the thought I had emphasized; and then and there, on a blank page of the brief from which I had intended to speak, I penciled the hymn, talking and writing at the same time, then handed it to my wife and thought no more about it. She sent it to *The Watchman and Reflector*, a paper published in Boston, where it was first printed. I did not know until 1865 that my hymn had been set to music by William B. Bradbury. I went to Rochester to preach as a candidate before the Second Baptist Church. Going into their chapel . . . I picked up a hymnal to see what they were singing, and opened it at my own hymn, "He Leadeth Me."

Shall We Gather at the River?

Robert Lowry   Robert Lowry

1. Shall we gath-er at the riv-er, Where bright an-gel feet have trod;
2. On the mar-gin of the riv-er, Wash-ing up its sil-ver spray,
3. Ere we reach the shin-ing riv-er, Lay we ev-ery bur-den down;
4. Soon we'll reach the shin-ing riv-er, Soon our pil-grim-age will cease,

With its crys-tal tide for - ev - er Flow-ing by the throne of God?
We will walk and wor-ship ev - er, All the hap-py gold-en day.
Grace our spir-its will de - liv - er, And pro-vide a robe and crown.
Soon our hap-py hearts will quiv-er With the mel-o - dy of peace.

Yes, we'll gath-er at the riv-er, The beau-ti-ful, the beau-ti-ful riv - er;

Gath-er with the saints at the riv-er That flows by the throne of God.

Shall We Gather at the River?

1864

And he showed me a pure river of water of life, clear as crystal, proceeding from the throne of God and of the Lamb. Revelation 22:1

O ften called the "Good Doctor," Robert Lowry was a cheerful man with a big beard and a quick mind. He pastored Baptist churches in the Eastern United States during the mid-1800s. One friend said, "Very few men had greater ability in painting pictures from imagination. He could thrill an audience with his vivid descriptions, inspiring them with the same thoughts that inspired him."

But he is best remembered for his hymns. Even in childhood he had composed tunes, and as he became acquainted with leaders in America hymnology—many of them based in New York—he realized he could reach more people through his songs than through his sermons.

He set many of Fanny Crosby's hymns to music, including the classic "All the Way My Savior Leads Me." And he wrote both words and music to the popular gospel song, "What can wash away my sins? / Nothing but the blood of Jesus."

The doctor's best-known hymn is "Shall We Gather at the River?" Though often used at baptisms, it's actually a song about heaven. It came to Lowry on a midsummer's day in New York, when, in the sweltering heat, he began musing about the cool, crystal river that flows through the city of God as described in Revelation 22:

One afternoon in July, 1864, when I was pastor at Hanson Place Baptist Church, Brooklyn, the weather was oppressively hot, and I was lying on a lounge in a state of physical exhaustion. I felt almost incapable of bodily exertion, and my imagination began to take itself wings. Visions of the future passed before me with startling vividness. The imagery of the apocalypse took the form of a tableau. Brightest of all were the throne, the heavenly river, and the gathering of the saints. My soul seemed to take new life from that celestial outlook. I began to wonder why the hymn writers had said so much about the "river of death" and so little about the "pure water of life, clear as crystal, proceeding out of the throne of God and the Lamb." As I mused, the words began to construct themselves. They came first as a question of Christian inquiry, "Shall we gather?" Then they broke out in a chorus, "Yes, we'll gather." On this question and answer the hymn developed itself. The music came with the hymn.

Day by Day

Karolina Sandell-Berg

Oskar Ahnfelt

1. Day by day and with each pass-ing mo-ment, Strength I find to meet my tri-als here;
2. Ev - 'ry day the Lord Him-self is near me With a spe-cial mer-cy for each hour;
3. Help me then in ev - 'ry trib - u - la - tion, So to trust Your prom-is-es, O Lord;

Trust-ing in my Fa-ther's wise be - stow-ment, I've no cause for wor-ry or for fear.
All my cares He fain would bear and cheer me, He whose name is Coun - se - lor and Pow'r.
That I lose not faith's sweet con - so - la - tion, Of - fered me with - in Your ho-ly Word.

He whose heart is kind be-yond all mea-sure, Give un - to each day what He deems best;
The pro - tec - tion of His child and trea-sure, Is a charge that on Him-self He laid;
Help me, Lord, when toil and trou-ble meet-ing, E'er to take, as from a Fa-ther's hand,

Lov-ing -ly, its part of pain and plea-sure, Min-gling toil with peace and rest.
"As your days, your strength shall be in mea-sure," This the pledge to me He made.
One by one, the days, the mo-ments fleet-ing, Till I reach the prom - ised land.

Day by Day

<u>1865</u>

The LORD is my light and my salvation; whom shall I fear? The LORD is the strength of my life; of whom shall I be afraid? Psalm 27:1

This is a Scandinavian hymn, written by the "Fanny Crosby of Sweden," Karolina W. Sandell-Berg.

Lina was born in Frvderyd on October 3, 1832, the daughter of Jonas Sandell, pastor of the village's Lutheran church. Though frail in body, she had a strong spirit, feasting on the artistic, literary, and religious influences of her home life.

But tragedy struck when she was twenty-six. Lina and her father were enjoying a boat trip on the east coast of Sweden near Gothenburg when the ship suddenly lurched. Before her eyes, Rev. Sandell pitched overboard and drowned. Returning home alone, Lina began processing her grief through the Scriptures and expressing her faith in poetry. Fourteen poems were published that year, 1858, one of which is sung to this day:

> *Children of the heavenly Father | Safely in His bosom gather;*
> *Nestling bird nor star in heaven | Such a refuge e'er was given.*

Seven years later, her best-known hymn, "Day by Day," was published. In it, Lina spoke from personal experience about the daily strength the Lord provides for His struggling children.

> *Day by day, and with each passing moment, | Strength I find, to meet my trials here;*
> *Trusting in my Father's wise bestowment, | I've no cause for worry or for fear.*

If you need strength for a particular trial, take this grand old hymn into the day with you, and claim some of the wonderful promises God has given:

- "The LORD is my strength and song, and He has become my salvation."—Exodus 15:2
- "As your days, so shall your strength be."—Deuteronomy 33:25
- "Do not sorrow, for the joy of the LORD is your strength."—Nehemiah 8:10
- "God is our refuge and strength, a very present help in trouble."—Psalm 46:1
- "Those who wait on the LORD shall renew their strength."—Isaiah 40:31
- "My grace is sufficient for you, for My strength is made perfect in weakness."—2 Corinthians 12:9
- "I can do all things through Christ who strengthens me."—Philippians 4:13

Onward Christian Soldiers

Sabine Baring-Gould

Arthur S. Sullivan

1. On-ward, Chris-tian sol - diers, March-ing as to war, With the cross of
2. At the sign of tri - umph, Sa-tan's host doth flee; On, then, Chris-tian

Je - sus Go - ing on be - fore! Christ, the roy - al Mas - ter, Leads a-
sol - diers, On to vic - to - ry! Hell's foun - da - tions quiv - er At the

gainst the foe; For - ward in - to bat - tle, See His ban-ners go!
shouts of praise; Broth - ers, lift your voi - ces, Loud your an-thems raise!

On - ward, Chris - tian sol - diers, March - ing as to war,

With the cross of Je - sus Go - ing on be - fore!

Onward Christian Soldiers

1865

You will not need to fight in this battle. Position yourselves, stand still and see the salvation of the LORD, Who is with you . . . 2 Chronicles 20:17

Rev. Sabine Baring-Gould was born in Exeter in 1834. His father, an officer with the East India Company, had a disabling carriage accident and decided that if he couldn't work, he could at least travel. As a result, little Sabine was dragged from one end of Europe to the other, year after year. It gave him an unsettled childhood, spotty schooling, and a wanderlust he never outgrew. He later managed to scrape through Cambridge, but for the most part he is remembered as a brilliant, self-taught scholar. That helps explain why he developed certain eccentric habits. When he taught school, for example, he kept a pet bat on his shoulder.

From Sabine's original mind flowed an endless number of books, articles, poems, hymns, and tracts. This particular hymn, "Onward Christian Soldiers," was written on a Whitsunday's evening in the mid-1860s.

Whitsunday is better known as Pentecost Sunday. It got its nickname because it became a popular day for new Christians to be baptized. The baptismal candidates marched to the rivers or fonts wearing robes of white. Thus it came to be called "White Sunday" or Whitsunday.

It was on this day in 1865, in the little town of Horbury, England, that Sabine stayed up late searching through hymnbooks for a martial-type hymn for children. The next day, Monday, all the village children were marching to the neighboring town for a Sunday school rally. Sabine wanted to give them a "marching song" for the trip. Searching his hymnals and finding nothing, he began scribbling on a piece of paper, playing with words, dashing off lines until he had written a hymn of his own just for the occasion:

> *Onward, Christian soldiers, / Marching as to war,*
> *With the cross of Jesus / Going on before.*

"It was written in great haste," he later said, "and I am afraid some of the rhymes are faulty. Certainly, nothing has surprised me more than its popularity."

Perhaps you've noticed that several of our greatest "adult" hymns were originally written or translated for children. See, for example, the stories behind "All Creatures of Our God and King," "I Sing the Mighty Power of God," "I Heard the Voice of Jesus Say," and "O Little Town of Bethlehem." Add "Onward, Christian Soldiers" to that list, and visualize this eccentric preacher, singing in step, marching alongside the children—perhaps with a pet bat on his shoulder.

193

Safe in the Arms of Jesus

Fanny J. Crosby

William H. Doane

1. Safe in the arms of Je - sus, safe on His gen-tle breast,
2. Safe in the arms of Je - sus, safe from cor-rod-ing care,
3. Je - sus, my heart's dear Ref - uge, Je - sus has died for me;

There by His love o'er - shad - ed, sweet - ly my soul shall rest.
Safe from the world's temp - ta - tions, sin can-not harm me there.
Firm on the Rock of A - ges, ev - er my trust shall be.

Hark! 'tis the voice of an - gels, borne in a song to me.
Free from the blight of sor - row, free from my doubts and fears;
Here let me wait with pa - tience, wait till the night is o'er;

O - ver the fields of glo - ry, o - ver the jas - per sea.
On - ly a few more tri - als, on - ly a few more tears!
Wait till I see the morn - ing break on the gold - en shore.

Safe in the Arms of Jesus

1868

And He took them up in His arms, laid His hands on them, and blessed them.
Mark 10:16

On March 5, 1858, Fanny Crosby, the blind hymnist and America's "Queen of Gospel Songs," quietly married Alexander Van Alsteine. A year later, the couple suffered a tragedy that shook the deepest regions of Fanny's heart.

She gave birth to a child—no one knows if it was a boy or a girl. In later years, she never spoke about it except to say in her oral biography, "God gave us a tender babe," and "soon the angels came down and took our infant up to God and His throne."

One of Fanny's relatives, Florence Paine, lived with the poet for six years and could never get her to talk about this. The child's death seemed to have devastated her, and she privately bore the sadness all her life.

Years later, on April 30, 1868, musician Howard Doane knocked on the door of Fanny's apartment in Manhattan. "I have exactly forty minutes," he said, "before I must meet a train for Cincinnati. I have a tune for you. See if it says anything to you. Perhaps you can commit it to memory and then compose a poem to match it." He then hummed the tune.

Fanny clapped her hands and said, "Why, that says, 'Safe in the arms of Jesus!'" She retreated to the other room of her tiny apartment, knelt on the floor, and asked God to give her the words quickly. Within half an hour, she had composed the poem in her mind and dictated it to Doane, who dashed off to catch his train.

During her lifetime, "Safe in the Arms of Jesus" was among the most widely sung of Fanny's hymns, and she considered it in a class by itself. She claimed it was written for the bereaved, especially for mothers who had lost children. Often when comforting a grief-stricken mother, she would say, "Remember, my dear, your darling cherub is safe in the arms of Jesus." Rev. John Hall of New York's Fifth Avenue Presbyterian Church told Fanny that her hymn had given more "peace and satisfaction to mothers who have lost their children than any other hymn I have ever known."

It isn't hard to understand why.

Safe in the arms of Jesus, safe on His gentle breast;
There by His love o'ershaded, sweetly my soul shall rest.

Sweet By and By

Sanford F. Bennett

Joseph P. Webster

1. There's a land that is fair-er than day, And by faith we can see it a - far; For the Fa-ther waits o - ver the way, To pre-pare us a dwell-ing place there.

2. We shall sing on that beau-ti-ful shore The me - lo - di - ous songs of the blest, And our spir-its shall sor-row no more, Not a sigh for the bless-ing of rest.

3. To our boun-ti-ful Fa - ther a - bove We will of - fer our trib - ute of praise, For the glo - ri - ous gift of His love And the bless - ings that hal - low our days.

In the sweet by and by We shall meet on that beau - ti - ful shore. In the sweet by and by, We shall meet on that beau-ti-ful shore.

Sweet By and By

1868

In My Father's house are many mansions; if it were not so, I would have told you. I go to prepare a place for you. John 14:2

I n 1868, a pharmacist named Sanford Fillmore Bennett, thirty-one, was filling prescriptions and handling sales at his apothecary in Elkhorn, Wisconsin. His friend Joseph Webster entered the store. Joseph was a local musician, vocalist, violinist, and amateur composer who suffered from periods of depression. The two men had occasionally collaborated on hymns and songs, Sanford writing the words and Joseph the music.

On this particular day, Joseph was unusually blue and his face was long. Looking up, Sanford asked, "What is the matter now?"

"It's no matter," Joseph replied, "it will be all right by and by."

An idea for a hymn hit Sanford like a flash of sunlight. Sitting at his desk, he began writing as fast as he could. The words came almost instantly. Two customers entered the drugstore, but no attempt was made to assist them—Sanford was too absorbed in his poem—so they sallied over to the stove and visited with Joseph. Finally, Sanford rose and joined them, handing a sheet of paper to his friend.

"Here is your prescription, Joe," he said. "I hope it works." Webster read the words aloud:

> *There's a land that is fairer than day,*
> *And by faith we can see it afar;*
> *For the Father waits over the way,*
> *To prepare us a dwelling place there.*
> *In the sweet by and by,*
> *We shall meet on that beautiful shore.*
> *In the sweet by and by,*
> *We shall meet on that beautiful shore.*

Instantly a tune suggested itself, and Joseph jotted down some notes. Picking up his fiddle, he played his melody over a time or two, then said to the others, "We four make a good male quartet. Let's try the new song and see how it sounds."

As "Sweet By and By" was being sung for the first time, another customer, R. R. Crosby, entered the store. "Gentlemen," he said, "I never heard that song before but it is immortal."

He was right. For more than a hundred years, we've been singing an immortal hymn that was written in a drugstore in less than half an hour.

I Need Thee Every Hour

Annie S. Hawks; Robert Lowry, Refrain

Robert Lowry

1. I need Thee ev-'ry hour, Most gra - cious Lord;
2. I need Thee ev-'ry hour, Stay Thou near by;
3. I need Thee ev-'ry hour In joy or pain;
4. I need Thee ev-'ry hour, Most Ho - ly One.

No ten - der voice like Thine Can peace af - ford.
Temp - ta - tions lose their power When Thou art nigh.
Come quick - ly and a - bide Or life is vain.
Oh, make me Thine in - deed, Thou bless - ed Son!

I need Thee, O I need Thee; Ev - 'ry hour I need Thee;

O bless me now, my Sav - ior, I come to Thee!

I Need Thee Every Hour

1872

Not that we are sufficient of ourselves to think of anything as being from ourselves, but our sufficiency is from God. 2 Corinthians 3:5

In his book *The Practice of the Presence of God*, Brother Lawrence claimed to be as close to God while working in the kitchen as when praying in the chapel. The Lord, after all, is *always* near us; thus, wherever we are is holy ground. That was the experience of Annie Hawks, a housewife and mother of three in Brooklyn, New York.

As a child, Annie Sherwood had dabbled in poetry, her first verse being published when she was fourteen. In 1857, she married Charles Hawks, and they established their home in Brooklyn, joining Dr. Robert Lowry's Hanson Place Baptist Church.* With the good doctor's encouragement, she began writing Sunday school songs for children, and he set many of them to music.

"I Need Thee Every Hour" was written on a bright June morning in 1872. Annie later wrote, "One day as a young wife and mother of 37 years of age, I was busy with my regular household tasks. Suddenly, I became so filled with the sense of nearness to the Master that, wondering how one could live without Him, either in joy or pain, these words, 'I Need Thee Every Hour,' were ushered into my mind, the thought at once taking full possession of me."

The next Sunday, Annie handed these words to Dr. Lowry, who wrote the tune and chorus while seated at the little organ in the living room of his Brooklyn parsonage. Later that year, it was sung for the first time at the National Baptist Sunday School Association meeting in Cincinnati, Ohio, and published in a hymnbook the following year.

When Annie's husband died sixteen years later, she found that her own hymn was among her greatest comforts. "I did not understand at first why this hymn had touched the great throbbing heart of humanity," Annie wrote. "It was not until long after, when the shadow fell over my way, the shadow of a great loss, that I understood something of the comforting power in the words which I had been permitted to give out to others in my hour of sweet serenity and peace."

Some time after Charles's death, Annie moved to Bennington, Vermont, to live with her daughter and son-in-law. All in all, she wrote more than four hundred hymns during her eighty-three years, though only this one is still widely sung.

---

*See the story of "Shall We Gather at the River?"

Blessed Assurance

Fanny J. Crosby

Phoebe P. Knapp

1. Bless-ed as-sur-ance, Je-sus is mine! Oh, what a fore-taste of
2. Per - fect sub - mis-sion, per-fect de - light! Vi - sions of rap-ture now
3. Per - fect sub - mis-sion, all is at rest. I in my Sav - ior am

glo - ry di - vine! Heir of sal - va - tion, pur - chase of God,
burst at my sight! An - gels de - scend - ing bring from a - bove
hap - py and blest; Watch-ing and wait - ing, look - ing a - bove,

Born of His Spir - it, washed in His blood!
Ech - oes of mer - cy, whis - pers of love. This is my sto - ry,
Filled with His good-ness, lost in His love.

this is my song, Prais-ing my Sav - ior all the day long. This is my

sto - ry, this is my song, Prais-ing my Sav - ior all the day long.

Blessed Assurance

1873

Nevertheless I am not ashamed, for I know whom I have believed and am persuaded that He is able to keep what I have committed to Him until that Day.
2 Timothy 1:12

rances Ridley Havergal and Frances (Fanny) Crosby never met, but they became dear pen pals—the two most famous women hymnists of their age, the former in England and the latter in America. Havergal once wrote a poem about her American counterpart:

Sweet, blind singer over the sea, / Tuneful and jubilant! How can it be,
That the songs of gladness, which float so far, / As if they fell from the evening star
Are the notes of one who may never see / 'Visible music' of flower and tree . . .
Oh, her heart can see, her heart can see! / And its sight is strong and swift and free . . .

Another of Fanny's dearest friends was Phoebe Knapp. While Fanny lived in the Manhattan slums and worked in rescue missions, Phoebe lived in the Knapp Mansion, a palatial residence in Brooklyn, where she entertained lavishly. She was an extravagant dresser with a wardrobe full of elaborate gowns and diamond tiaras. Her music room contained one of the finest collections of instruments in the country, and Fanny was a frequent houseguest.

One day in 1873, while Fanny was staying at the Knapp Mansion, Phoebe said she had a tune she wanted to play. Going to the music room, she sat at the piano and played a new composition of her own while the blind hymnist listened. Fanny immediately clapped her hands and exclaimed, "Why, that says, 'Blessed Assurance!' " She quickly composed the words, and a great hymn was born.

Many years later D. L. Moody was preaching in New York at the 23rd Street Dutch Reformed Church. The Moody/Sankey meetings had popularized Fanny Crosby's hymns around the world and had made the blind poetess a household name. But whenever she attended a Moody/Sankey meeting, she refused to be recognized, disavowing acclaim.

This day the church was so crowded she could find nowhere to sit. Moody's son, Will, seeing her, offered to find her a seat. To her bewilderment, he led her onto the platform just as the crowd was singing "Blessed Assurance." Moody Sr. jumped to his feet, raised his hand, and interrupted the singing. "Praise the Lord!" he shouted. "Here comes the authoress!"

Fanny took her seat amid thunderous ovation, humbly thanking God for making her a blessing to so many.

It Is Well with My Soul

Horatio G. Spafford

Philip P. Bliss

1. When peace like a riv-er, At-tend-eth my way, When sor-rows, Like
2. My sin, O the bliss Of this glo-ri-ous tho't, My sin not in
3. O, Lord haste the day When my faith shall be sight, The clouds be rolled

sea bil-lows roll; What-ev-er my lot, Thou hast taught me to say,
part But the whole Is nailed to the cross And I bear it no more.
back As a scroll; The trump shall re-sound And the Lord shall de-scend,

"It is well, It is well, with my soul." It is well,
Praise the Lord, Praise the Lord, O my soul!
"E-ven so" it is well With my soul. It is well

with my soul, It is well, It is well, with my soul.
with my soul,

It Is Well with My Soul

1873

Many are the afflictions of the righteous, but the LORD delivers him out of them all. Psalm 34:19

W hen the great Chicago fire consumed the Windy City in 1871, Horatio G. Spafford, an attorney heavily invested in real estate, lost a fortune. About that time, his only son, age four, succumbed to scarlet fever. Horatio drowned his grief in work, pouring himself into rebuilding the city and assisting the 100,000 who had been left homeless.

In November of 1873, he decided to take his wife and daughters to Europe. Horatio was close to D. L. Moody and Ira Sankey, and he wanted to visit their evangelistic meetings in England, then enjoy a vacation.

When an urgent matter detained Horatio in New York, he decided to send his wife, Anna, and their four daughters, Maggie, Tanetta, Annie, and Bessie, on ahead. As he saw them settled into a cabin aboard the luxurious French liner *Ville du Havre*, an unease filled his mind, and he moved them to a room closer to the bow of the ship. Then he said good-bye, promising to join them soon.

During the small hours of November 22, 1873, as the *Ville du Havre* glided over smooth seas, the passengers were jolted from their bunks. The ship had collided with an iron sailing vessel, and water poured in like Niagara. The *Ville du Havre* tilted dangerously. Screams, prayers, and oaths merged into a nightmare of unmeasured terror. Passengers clung to posts, tumbled through darkness, and were swept away by powerful currents of icy ocean. Loved ones fell from each other's grasp and disappeared into foaming blackness. Within two hours, the mighty ship vanished beneath the waters. The 226 fatalities included Maggie, Tanetta, Annie, and Bessie. Mrs. Spafford was found nearly unconscious, clinging to a piece of the wreckage. When the forty-seven survivors landed in Cardiff, Wales, she cabled her husband: "Saved Alone."

Horatio immediately booked passage to join his wife. En route, on a cold December night, the captain called him aside and said, "I believe we are now passing over the place where the *Ville du Havre* went down." Spafford went to his cabin but found it hard to sleep. He said to himself, "It is well; the will of God be done."

He later wrote his famous hymn based on those words.

⌒

The melody for "It Is Well," titled VILLE DU HAVRE, was written by Philip Bliss, who was himself soon to perish, along with his wife, in a terrible train wreck in Ohio.*

---

*See the story of "I Will Sing of My Redeemer."

Bringing in the Sheaves

Knowles Shaw

George A. Minor

1. Sow - ing in the morn - ing, sow - ing seeds of kind - ness,
2. Sow - ing in the sun - shine, sow - ing in the shad - ows,
3. Go - ing forth with weep - ing, sow - ing for the Mas - ter,

Sow - ing in the noon - tide and the dew - y eve, Wait - ing for the har - vest
Fear - ing nei - ther clouds nor win - ter's chill - ing breeze; By and by the har - vest
Though the loss sus - tained our spir - it oft - en grieves; When our weep - ing's o - ver

and the time of reap - ing- We shall come re - joic - ing, bring - ing in the sheaves.
and the la - bor end - ed- We shall come re - joic - ing, bring - ing in the sheaves.
He will bid us wel - come- We shall come re - joic - ing, bring - ing in the sheaves.

Bring - ing in the sheaves, bring - ing in the sheaves, We shall come re - joic - ing,

1.

bring - ing in the sheaves. We shall come re - joic - ing, bring - ing in the sheaves.

2.

Bringing in the Sheaves

1874

The harvest truly is plentiful, but the laborers are few. Matthew 9:37

Knowles Shaw, the "Singing Evangelist," wrote this gospel song in 1874. Four years later, on June 7, 1878, he and Elder Kirk Baxter boarded a train in Dallas, en route to McKinney, Texas, where Shaw was beginning an evangelistic campaign. As the train chugged across Texas, the two men fell into conversation with a Methodist minister named Malloy. Baxter later wrote:

Malloy asked him to tell the secret of his success in protracted meetings, which Brother Shaw proceeded to do in an earnest manner, saying he depended much on the power of song; preached Christ; always kept Jesus before the people; made them feel that they were sinners and needed just such a Savior as he preached; that he never became discouraged; had confidence in the gospel truth as the power of God; that he loved his work, and became wholly absorbed in it; and added: "Oh, it is a grand thing to rally people to the Cross of Christ."

At that moment, I felt the car was off the track, bouncing over the ties. I saw Brother Shaw rise from his seat and realized at once the car was going over. All became dark as night. When I came to myself, the coach was at the bottom of the embankment. I looked round, but all were gone. When I got out, I saw the passengers on the railroad track above me, and made my way up to them. The first one I met was Mr. Malloy. I said, "Have you seen Brother Shaw?" "No," said he, "I fear he is under the wreck; but he saved my life by pushing me from the position in which he himself fell."

I waited to hear no more, but ran down to the wreck, looked in, and saw a man's hand pointing upward out of the water. It was Brother Shaw's. I called for help, and in about fifteen minutes he was taken lifeless from the water.

I sent a telegram to Dallas, telling the sad news. In a short time, a deep gloom pervaded the whole city, as from house to house passed the sad words, "Brother Shaw is dead."

But his life proved his song. According to records found in his diary, Shaw recorded more than 11,400 conversions to Christ under his nineteen years of preaching. He entered heaven rejoicing, bringing in the sheaves.

Take My Life and Let It Be

Frances R. Havergal

Henri A. Cesar Malan

1. Take my life and let it be Con - se - crat - ed,
2. Take my feet, and let them be Swift and beau - ti -
3. Take my lips, and let them be Filled with mes - sa -
4. Take my love, my God, I pour At Thy feet its

Lord to Thee. Take my hands and let them move,
ful for Thee. Take my voice, and let me sing
ges for Thee. Take my sil - ver and my gold;
trea - sure store. Take my - self and I will be

At the im - pulse of Thy love,
Al - ways, on - ly, for my King.
Not a mite would I with - hold,
Ev - er, on - ly, all for Thee,

At the im - pulse of Thy love.
Al - ways, on - ly, for my King.
Not a mite would I with - hold.
Ev - er, on - ly, all for Thee.

Take My Life and Let It Be

1874

Yet indeed I also count all things loss for the excellence of the knowledge of Christ Jesus my Lord, for whom I have suffered the loss of all things, and count them as rubbish, that I may gain Christ. Philippians 3:8

Although hymnist Frances Havergal, thirty-six, had served the Lord for years, she felt something was missing in her Christian experience. Then one day in 1873, she received a little book called *All for Jesus*, which stressed the importance of making Christ the King of every corner and cubicle of one's life. Soon thereafter she made a fresh and complete consecration of herself to Christ.

Years later when asked about it, she replied, "Yes, it was on Advent Sunday, December 2, 1873, I first saw clearly the blessedness of true consecration. I saw it as a flash of electric light, and what you see you can never un-see. There must be full surrender before there can be full blessedness."

Not long afterward, she found herself spending several days with ten people in a house, some of them unconverted. Others were Christians, but not fully surrendered to Christ. "Lord, give me all in this house," she prayed. She went to work witnessing, and before she left, all ten were yielded Christians. On the last night of her visit, Frances—too excited to sleep—wrote this great consecration hymn, "Take My Life . . ."

In the years that followed, Frances frequently used this hymn in her own devotions, especially every December 2, on the anniversary of her consecration.

On one occasion, as she pondered the words, "Take my voice and let me sing / Always only for my King," she felt she should give up her secular concerts. Her beautiful voice was in demand, and she frequently sang with the Philharmonic. But from that moment, her lips were exclusively devoted to the songs of the Lord.

On another occasion she was praying over the stanza that says, "Take my silver and my gold / Not a mite would I withhold." She had accumulated a great deal of jewelry, but she now felt she should donate it to the Church Missionary Society. Writing to a friend, she said, "I retain only a brooch for daily wear, which is a memorial to my dear parents; also a locket with the holy portrait I have of my niece in heaven. Evelyn, I had no idea I had such a jeweler's shop; nearly fifty articles are being packed off. I don't think I need to tell you I never packed a box with such pleasure."

Have you given your whole life—everything—over to Jesus? Why not make this the date of your own complete consecration?

O the Deep, Deep Love of Jesus

Samuel Trevor Francis

Thomas J. Williams

1. O the deep, deep love of Je-sus, Vast, un - mea - sured, bound - less, free!
2. O the deep, deep love of Je-sus, Spread His praise from shore to shore!
3. O the deep, deep love of Je-sus, Love of ev - 'ry love the best!

Roll-ing as a might-y o - cean In its full - ness o - ver me!
How He lov-eth, ev - er lov - eth, Chang-eth nev - er, nev - er-more!
'Tis an o-cean full of bless - ing, 'Tis a ha - ven giv - ing rest!

Un - der - neath me, all a - round me, Is the cur - rent of Thy love,
How He watch - es o'er His loved ones, Died to call them all His own;
O the deep, deep love of Je - sus, 'Tis a heav'n of heav'ns to me;

Lead-ing on-ward, lead-ing home - ward, To my glo - rious rest a - bove!
How for them He in - ter - ced - eth, Watch-eth o'er them from the throne!
And it lifts me up to glo - ry, For it lifts me up to Thee!

O the Deep, Deep Love of Jesus

1875

For I am persuaded that neither death nor life, nor angels nor principalities nor powers, nor things present nor things to come, nor height nor depth, nor any other created thing, shall be able to separate us from the love of God which is in Christ Jesus our Lord. Romans 8:38–39

Few hymns paint such a vivid picture of God's love as this one by Samuel Trevor Francis: ". . . vast, unmeasured, boundless free; / Rolling as a mighty ocean in its fullness over me. / Underneath me, all around me, is the current of Thy love . . ." It helps us visualize the immensity of Christ's liquid-love, overwhelming and submerging us in the depths of His tender, triumphant heart.

Samuel was born on November 19, 1834, in a village north of London, but his parents soon moved to the city of Hull midway up the English coast. His father was an artist. As a child, Samuel enjoyed poetry and even compiled a little handwritten volume of his own poetry. He also developed a passion for music, joining the church choir at age nine. But as a teenager, he struggled spiritually, and when he moved to London to work, he knew things weren't right in his heart.

One day, as he later wrote, "I was on my way home from work and had to cross Hungerford Bridge to the south of the Thames. During the winter's night of wind and rain and in the loneliness of that walk, I cried to God to have mercy on me. I stayed for a moment to look at the dark waters flowing under the bridge, and the temptation was whispered to me: 'Make an end of all this misery.' I drew back from the evil thought, and suddenly a message was borne into my very soul: 'You do believe in the Lord Jesus Christ?' I at once answered, 'I do believe,' and I put my whole trust in Him as my Savior."

Francis went on to become a London merchant, but his real passion was kingdom work—especially hymn writing and open-air preaching—which occupied his remaining seventy-three years. He traveled widely and preached around the world for the Plymouth Brethren. He died on December 28, 1925, at age ninety-two.

⌒⌒

EBENEZER, the ponderous, rolling melody for this hymn, is traditionally called "*Ton-Y-Botel*" ("Tune in a Bottle") because of a legend that it was found in a bottle along the Welsh Coast. It was actually composed by Thomas J. Williams and first appeared as a hymn tune in 1890 in a Welsh hymnal entitled *Llawlyfn Moliant*.

'Tis So Sweet to Trust in Jesus

Louisa M. R. Stead

William J. Kirkpatrick

1. 'Tis so sweet to trust in Je - sus, Just to take Him at His word;
2. O how sweet to trust in Je - sus, Just to trust His cleans-ing blood;
3. Yes, 'tis sweet to trust in Je - sus, Just from sin and self to cease;
4. I'm so glad I learned to trust Thee, Pre-cious Je - sus, Sav - ior friend;

Just to rest up - on His prom - ise; Just to know "Thus saith the Lord."
Just in sim - ple faith to plunge me, Neath the heal - ing, cleans-ing flood!
Just from Je - sus sim - ply tak - ing Life and rest and joy and peace.
And I know that Thou art with me, Wilt be with me to the end.

Je - sus, Je - sus how I trust Him! How I've proved Him o'er and o'er!

Je - sus, Je - sus, pre - cious Je - sus! O for grace to trust Him more!

'Tis So Sweet to Trust in Jesus

1882

In God I have put my trust; I will not be afraid. Psalm 56:11

How fitting that a missionary should write this hymn about faith and trust. Louisa M. R. Stead was born about 1850 in Dover, England, and became a Christian at age nine. She felt a burden to become a missionary in her teenage years. When she was twenty-one or so, she immigrated to the United States and attended a revival meeting in Urbana, Ohio. There the Lord deeply impressed her with a ringing missionary call.

She made plans to go to China, but her hopes were dashed when her health proved too frail for the climate there. Shortly afterward, she married a man named Stead. But sometime around 1879 or 1880, Mr. Stead drowned off the coast of Long Island. Some accounts say that he saved a boy who was drowning, and other accounts say both Mr. Stead and the boy perished. Other records suggest it was his own four-year-old daughter, Lily, that he saved. In any event, the family's beachside picnic ended in tragedy for Louisa.

Shortly afterward, taking little Lily, Louisa went to South Africa as a missionary, and it was there during those days she wrote "'Tis So Sweet to Trust in Jesus."

Louisa served in South Africa for fifteen years, and while there she married Robert Wodehouse. When her health forced a return to America, Robert pastored a local Methodist Church. In 1900, her health restored, Robert and Louisa attended a large missionary conference in New York, and were so enthused by the experience they again offered themselves as missionary candidates.

They arrived as Methodist missionaries in Rhodesia on April 4, 1901. "In connection with this whole mission there are glorious possibilities," she wrote. "One cannot in the face of the peculiar difficulties help saying, 'Who is sufficient for these things?' but with simple confidence and trust we may and do say, 'Our sufficiency is of God.'"

Louisa retired in 1911, and passed away in 1917; but her daughter, Lily, married missionary D. A. Carson and continued the work for many years at the Methodist mission station in southern Rhodesia (Zimbabwe).

How Great Thou Art

Carl Boberg

Swedish Folk Melody

1. O Lord, my God, When I in awe-some won-der, Con-sid-er
2. When thru the woods and for-est glades I wan-der, And hear the
3. And when I think that God, His Son not spar-ing, Sent Him to
4. When Christ shall come With shout of ac-cla-ma-tion And take me

all the worlds Thy hands have made; I see the stars, I hear the roll-ing
birds sing sweet-ly in the trees; When I look down from loft-y moun-tain
die, I scarce can take it in; That on the cross my bur-den glad-ly
home, What joy shall fill my heart! Then I shall bow In hum-ble ad-o-

thun-der, Thy pow'r through-out The u-ni-verse dis-played.
gran-deur And hear the brook and feel the gent-le breeze.
bear-ing, He bled and died To take a-way my sin.
ra-tion, And there pro-claim, "My God, how great Thou art!"

Then sings my soul, My Sav-ior God, to Thee, How great Thou art! How great Thou art!

Then sings my soul, My Sav-ior God, to Thee, How great Thou art! How great Thou art!

How Great Thou Art

1885

For thus says the LORD, Who created the heavens, Who is God, Who formed the earth and made it, Who has established it, Who did not create it in vain, Who formed it to be inhabited: "I am the LORD, and there is no other." Isaiah 45:18

arl Boberg, a twenty-six-year-old Swedish minister, wrote a poem in 1885 that he called *"O Store Gud"*—"O Mighty God." The words, literally translated to English, said:

When I the world consider | Which Thou has made by Thine almighty Word
And how the webb of life Thou wisdom guideth | And all creaion feedeth at Thy board.
Then doth my soul burst forth in song of praise | Oh, great God, Oh, great God!

His poem was published and "forgotten"—or so he thought. Several years later Carl was surprised to hear it being sung to the tune of an old Swedish melody, but the poem and hymn did not achieve widespread fame.

Hearing this hymn in Russia, English missionary Stuart Hine was so moved he modified and expanded the words and made his own arrangement of the Swedish melody. He later said his first three verses were inspired, line upon line, by Russia's rugged Carpathian Mountains. The first verse was composed when he was caught in a thunderstorm in a Carpathian village, the second as he heard the birds sing near the Romanian border, and the third as he witnessed many of the Carpathian mountain-dwellers coming to Christ. The final verse was written after Dr. Hine returned to Great Britain.

Some time later, Dr. J. Edwin Orr heard "How Great Thou Art" being sung by Naga tribespeople in Assam, in India, and decided to bring it back to America for use in his own meetings. When he introduced it at a conference in California, it came to the attention of music publisher Tim Spencer, who contacted Mr. Hine and had the song copyrighted. It was published and recorded.

During the 1954 Billy Graham Crusade in Harringay Arena, George Beverly Shea was given a leaflet containing this hymn. He sang it to himself and shared it with other members of the Graham team. Though not used in London, it was introduced the following year to audiences in Toronto.

In the New York Crusade of 1957, it was sung by Bev Shea ninety-nine times, with the choir joining the majestic refrain:

Then sings my soul, my Savior God to Thee,
How great Thou art! How great Thou art!

Leaning on the Everlasting Arms

Elisha A. Hoffman

Anthony J. Showalter

1. What a fel-low-ship, what a joy di - vine, Lean-ing on the ev-er - last-ing arms!
2. Oh how sweet to walk in this pilgrim way, Lean-ing on the ev-er - last-ing arms!
3. What have I to dread, what have I to fear, Lean-ing on the ev-er - last-ing arms?

What a bless - ed-ness, what a peace is mine, Lean-ing on the ev-er - last-ing arms!
Oh how bright the path Grows from day to day, Lean-ing on the ev-er - last-ing arms.
I have bless - ed peace with my Lord so near, Lean-ing on the ev-er - last-ing arms.

Lean - ing, lean - ing, Safe and se-cure from all a - larms;
Lean-ing on Je - sus, lean-ing on Je-sus,

Lean - ing, lean - ing, Lean-ing on the ev-er - last-ing arms.
Lean-ing on Je-sus, lean-ing on Je-sus,

Leaning on the Everlasting Arms

1887

The eternal God is your refuge, and underneath are the everlasting arms . . .
Deuteronomy 33:27

T he idea for this song came from Anthony Showalter, principal of the Southern Normal Musical Institute in Dalton, Georgia. Showalter, a Presbyterian elder, was a well-known advocate of gospel music. He published more than 130 music books with combined sales of two million copies, and he became known through the South for his singing schools in local churches.

Showalter took a personal interest in his students and enjoyed keeping up with them as the years passed. One evening in 1887, he was leading a singing school in a local church in Hartselle, Alabama. After dismissing the class for the evening, he gathered his materials and returned to his boardinghouse.

Two letters had arrived, both from former pupils. Each of the young men was heartbroken, having just lost his wife. Professor Showalter went to the Bible, looking for a verse to comfort them. He selected Deuteronomy 33:27: "The eternal God is your refuge, and underneath are the everlasting arms . . ." As he pondered that verse, these words came to mind:

Leaning, leaning, safe and secure from all alarms; | Leaning, leaning, leaning on the everlasting arms.

He scribbled replies to his bereaved friends, then, reaching for another piece of paper, he wrote to his friend, hymnist Elisha Hoffman. "Here is the chorus for a good hymn from Deuteronomy 33:27," his letter said, "but I can't come up with any verses." Hoffman wrote three stanzas and sent them back. Showalter set it all to music, and ever since, these words have cheered us in adversity:

What have I to dread, what have I to fear, | Leaning on the everlasting arms.
I have blessed peace with my Lord so near, | Leaning on the everlasting arms.

⌒

"God, the eternal God, is our support at all times, especially when we are sinking into deep trouble. There are seasons when we sink quite low . . . Dear child of God, even when you are at your lowest, underneath are the everlasting arms."—Charles Spurgeon

⌒

"However low the people of God are at any time brought, everlasting arms are underneath them to keep the spirit from fainting and the faith from failing, even when they are pressed above measure . . . everlasting arms with which believers have been wonderfully sustained and kept cheerful in the worst of times. Divine grace is sufficient."—Matthew Henry

My Faith Has Found a Resting Place

Lidie H. Edmunds

Norwegian Folk Melody arr. by William J. Kirkpatrick

1. My faith has found a rest-ing place, Not in de-vice or creed;
2. E - nough for me that Je - sus saves, This ends my fear and doubt;
3. My heart is lean - ing on the Word, The writ-ten Word of God,
4. My great Phy - si - cian heals the sick, The lost He came to save;

I trust the Ev - er - liv - ing One, His wounds for me shall plead.
A sin - ful soul, I come to Him, He'll nev - er cast me out.
Sal - va - tion by my Sav-ior's name, Sal - va - tion through His blood.
For me His pre-cious blood He shed, For me His life He gave.

I need no oth - er ar - gu-ment, I need no oth - er plea,

It is e - nough that Je - sus died, And that He died for me.

My Faith Has Found a Resting Place

1891

Who through Him believe in God, who raised Him from the dead and gave Him glory, so that your faith and hope are in God. 1 Peter 1:21

*T*his hymn was written by the mysterious Lidie H. Edmunds. For years no one seemed to know who she was. As it turns out, this was a pseudonym for a popular hymnwriter named Eliza Edmunds Hewitt.

In those days, hymnists often used pen names because publishers were nervous about having too many hymns from one author in their books. Fanny Crosby, for example, published under the names Carrie Hawthorne, Maud Marion, Louise W. Tilden, Lillian G. Frances, Mrs. Edna Forest, Eleanor Craddock—and 198 others!

The music for "My Faith Has Found a Resting Place" was written by the prolific William J. Kirkpatrick, who was born in Pennsylvania in 1838. His father was his earliest music teacher, and William edited his first hymnbook, *Devotional Melodies*, at age twenty-one. He went on to write the melodies of some of our favorite hymns, including:

- COMING HOME—"I've Wandered Far Away from God" (music and words)
- DUNCANNON—"King of My Life, I Crown Thee Now"
- JESUS SAVES—"We Have Heard the Joyful Sound"
- KIRKPATRICK—"A Wonderful Savior Is Jesus My Lord"
- TRUST IN JESUS—"'Tis So Sweet to Trust in Jesus"
- REDEEMED—"Redeemed, How I Love to Proclaim It"
- And this one, LÅNDES, a traditional Norwegian melody—"My Faith Has Found a Resting Place"

On the evening of September 21, 1921, Professor Kirkpatrick huddled away in his study in Germantown, Pennsylvania, working on a poem he was planning to put to music. His wife, sleeping in a nearby bedroom, awoke and noticed his study light was on. "Professor," she called, "it's very late; don't you think you'd better come to bed?"

"I'm all right, dear," he replied. "I have a little work I want to finish. Go back to sleep; everything is all right."

Mrs. Kirkpatrick went back to sleep, but awakened again later. The study light was still on, and again she called. This time there was no response. She found the professor slumped over, his last hymn on the desk before him. It said:

Just as Thou wilt, Lord, this is my cry / Just as Thou wilt, to live or die.
I am Thy servant, Thou knowest best, / Just as Thou wilt, Lord, labor or rest.

217

When the Roll Is Called Up Yonder

James M. Black

James M. Black

1. When the trum - pet of the Lord shall sound, and
2. On that bright and cloud - less morn - ing when the
3. Let us la - bor for the Mas - ter from the

time shall be no more, And the morn-ing breaks e - ter - nal bright and fair.
dead in Christ shall rise, And the glo - ry of His res - ur - rec - tion share;
dawn 'til set - ting sun, Let us talk of all His won-drous love and care;

When the saints on earth shall gath - er o - ver on the oth - er shore,
When the cho - sen ones shall gath - er to their home be - yond the skies,
And when all of life is o - ver and our work on earth is done,

And the roll is called up yon - der I'll be there.
And the roll is called up yon - der I'll be there.
And the roll is called up yon - der I'll be there.

When the Roll Is Called Up Yonder

1893

I am the resurrection and the life. He who believes in Me, though he may die, he shall live. John 11:25

This old favorite was inspired by disappointment. James Black was calling roll one day for a youth meeting at his Methodist church in Williamsport, Pennsylvania. One name didn't answer—young Bessie, the daughter of an alcoholic. Crestfallen at her absence, James commented, "O God, when my own name is called up yonder, may I be there to respond!" Returning home, a thought struck him while opening the gate. Entering the house, he went to the piano and wrote the words and music effortlessly.

⌒⁀⊃

Years later, this song comforted a group of traumatized children in a Japanese concentration camp. In his book *A Boy's War*, David Mitchell tells of being in boarding school in Chefoo, China, during the Japanese invasion. On November 5, 1942, the students and faculty were marched from their campus and eventually ended up in Weihsien Concentration Camp.

Among the students was Brian Thompson, a lanky teenager. One evening about a year before the war ended, Brian was restless, waiting for the evening roll call that was long overdue. A bare wire from the searchlight tower was sagging low, and some of the older boys were jumping up and touching it with their fingers. "Whew, I got a shock off that," said one.

Brian decided to try. Being taller than the others, his hand was drawn into the wire, and it came down with him. When his bare feet hit the damp ground, the electricity shot through him like bolts of lightning. His mother, who had been interred with the students, tried to reach him, but the others held her back or she, too, would have been electrocuted. Finally someone found an old wooden stool and managed to detach the electrical wire, but it was too late.

At roll call that night, when the name *Brian Thompson* was called, there was no answer. David Mitchell later wrote, "Our principal and Mr. Houghton led a very solemn yet triumphant funeral service the next day. The shortness of life and the reality of eternity were brought home to us with force as Paul Bruce related that Brian had missed the roll call in camp but had answered one in Heaven. How important it was for us to sing and know, 'When the Roll is called up yonder, I'll be there.'"

Jesus Loves the Little Children

C. H. Woolston and Joseph Barlowe

George F. Root

1. Je-sus calls the chil-dren dear, "Come to me and nev-er fear, For I
2. Je-sus is the Shep-herd true, And He'll al-ways stand by you, For He
3. I am com-ing, Lord, to Thee, And Your sol-dier I will be, For You

love the lit-tle chil-dren of the world; I will take you by the hand, Lead you
loves the lit-tle chil-dren of the world; He's a Sav-ior great and strong, And He'll
love the lit-tle chil-dren of the world; And Your cross I'll al-ways bear, And for

to the bet-ter land, For I love the lit-tle chil-dren of the world."
shield you from the wrong, For He loves the lit-tle chil-dren of the world.
You I'll do and dare, For You love the lit-tle chil-dren of the world.

Je-sus loves the lit-tle chil-dren, All the chil-dren of the world. Red and yel-low, black and

white, They are pre-cious in His sight, Je-sus loves the lit-tle chil-dren of the world.

Jesus Loves the Little Children

Before 1895

Let the little children come to Me, and do not forbid them; for of such is the kingdom of God. Luke 18:16

A lmost everyone knows "Jesus Loves the Little Children," but few of us have sung the three verses that go along with that chorus. Nor do many people realize this was originally a Civil War ballad.

George Frederick Root was born into a large family in Sheffield, Massachusetts, in 1820, and showed signs of musical genius. By age thirteen, he boasted that he could play thirteen different instruments. As a young adult, he taught music in Boston and New York, and he also composed music and served as church organist.

In 1855, he offered a song called "Rosalie, the Prairie Flower" to his publisher for the hefty sum of one hundred dollars. Root's publisher, not thinking it worth that much, offered Root a royalty plan instead. In time, Root grossed *thousands* of dollars from "Rosalie," which helped establish him financially.

The outbreak of the Civil War deeply affected Root, and he immediately began using his gifts to advance the Union war effort, writing a host of patriotic songs to rally the moral of the North. As a serious, classical composer, he was embarrassed at the simple martial music coming from his pen, so he signed them with the name *Wurzel*, the German word for "root." Among his most popular pieces was a ballad entitled "Tramp! Tramp! Tramp!"

In the prison cell I sit,
Thinking, mother, dear of you,
And our bright and happy home so far away,
And the tears, they fill my eyes,
'Spite of all that I can do,
Tho' I try to cheer my comrades and be gay.

CHORUS:
Tramp! Tramp! Tramp! The boys are marching,
Cheer up, comrades, they will come,
And beneath the starry flag
We shall breathe the air again
Of the free land in our own beloved home.

After the Civil War, the melody remained popular, but the words were dated. A minister named Clare Herbert Woolston, a lyricist whom Root occasionally used, wrote new verses and a chorus. And that's how a Civil War ballad about a soldier in prison became one of the most popular children's choruses in history.

221

I Surrender All

Judson W. Van De Venter

Winfield S. Weeden

1. All to Je-sus I sur-ren-der, All to Him I free-ly give;
2. All to Je-sus I sur-ren-der, Hum-bly at His feet I bow,
3. All to Je-sus I sur-ren-der, Make me Sav-ior whol-ly Thine;
4. All to Je-sus I sur-ren-der, Lord, I give my-self to Thee.

I will ev-er love and trust Him, In His pres-ence dai-ly live.
World-ly pleas-ures all for-sak-en, Take me, Je-sus, take me now.
Let me feel the Ho-ly Spir-it, Tru-ly know that Thou art mine.
Fill me with Thy love and pow-er; Let Thy bless-ings fall on me.

I sur-ren-der all, I sur-ren-der all.
I sur-ren-der all, I sur-ren-der all.

All to Thee my bless-ed Sav-ior, I sur-ren-der all.

I Surrender All

1896

But now, O LORD, You are our Father; we are the clay, and You our potter; and all we are the work of Your hand. Isaiah 64:8

Someone once said, "Only in the Christian life does surrender bring victory." Judson Wheeler Van De Venter learned that for himself.

Born on a farm in Monroe Country, Michigan, in 1855, Judson grew up interested in art and music. He was converted to Christ at age seventeen. After graduating from college in Hillsdale, Michigan, Judson became an art teacher and then supervisor of art for the high school in Sharon, Pennsylvania. In 1885, he toured Europe, visiting art galleries and museums and studying painting. He was also a musician, having studied in numerous singing schools.

All the while, Judson was heavily involved in his local Methodist Episcopal church where he sang in the choir. He found himself especially fulfilled when participating in evangelistic rallies and revivals in which people received Christ as their personal Savior. Friends encouraged him to resign from the school system to enter full-time music evangelism, but for five years he struggled with the decision.

Finally falling to his knees, he said, "Lord, if you want me to give my full time to Thy work, I'll do it, I surrender all to Thee." For the next several years he traveled extensively through the United States, England, and Scotland, assisting in evangelistic work, leading the singing for Wilber Chapman and other evangelists, and winning men and women to Christ.

While engaged in meetings in East Palestine, Ohio, Judson stayed in the home of George Sebring (whose family founded Sebring, Ohio, and who himself later founded Sebring, Florida). It was there that he wrote the hymn "I Surrender All," while recalling his own personal submitting to full-time ministry.

Moving to Tampa in 1923, he began teaching hymnology at Florida Bible Institute. He retired after several years, but still occasionally showed up on campus to lecture or to speak in chapel. In the 1930s, a student at Florida Bible Institute sat wide-eyed, listening to Judson Van De Venter. That student, Billy Graham, later wrote, "One of the evangelists who influenced my early preaching was also a hymnist who wrote 'I Surrender All,' the Rev. J. W. Van De Venter. He was a regular visitor at the Florida Bible Institute [now Trinity Bible College] in the late 1930s. We students loved this kind, deeply spiritual gentleman and often gathered in his winter home at Tampa, Florida, for an evening of fellowship and singing."

When We All Get to Heaven

Eliza E. Hewitt

Emily D. Wilson

1. Sing the won-drous love of Je - sus, Sing His mer - cy and His grace;
2. While we walk the pil - grim path - way, Clouds will o - ver - spread the sky;
3. Let us then be true and faith - ful, Trust - ing, serv - ing ev - ery day;
4. On - ward to the prize be - fore us! Soon His beau - ty we'll be - hold;

In the man - sions bright and bless - ed, He'll pre - pare for us a place.
But when trav - 'ling days are o - ver, Not a shad - ow, not a sigh.
Just one glimpse of Him in glo - ry Will the toils of life re - pay.
Soon the pearl - y gates will o - pen, We shall tread the streets of gold.

When we all get to heav - en, What a day of re-
When we all What a

joic - ing that will be! When we all see
day of re - joic - ing that will be! When we all

Je - sus, We'll sing and shout the vic - tor - y.
shout, and shout the vic - to - ry.

When We All Get to Heaven

1898

And I will give you the keys of the kingdom of heaven, and whatever you bind on earth will be bound in heaven, and whatever you loose on earth will be loosed in heaven. Matthew 16:19

E liza Edmunds Hewitt was one of the premier women hymnwriters of the late 1800s and the early 1900s. She wrote the popular hymn "Singing I Go Along Life's Road," which was to have such a profound influence on soloist George Beverly Shea.* She is also the author of "Will There Be Any Stars in My Crown?" "My Faith Has Found a Resting Place," "Sunshine in My Soul," "More About Jesus," and this hymn, "When We All Get to Heaven."

It came to her as she studied John 14, where Jesus told His disciples, "Let not your heart be troubled; you believe in God, believe also in Me. In My Father's house are many mansions; if it were not so, I would have told you. I go to prepare a place for you."

But this wasn't Eliza's only hymn about heaven. Though now seldom sung, one of her most unique songs is entitled "The Everlasting Hymn," in which she imagines the majesty of worshipping the Lord as we gather around Him in the heavenly places, vibrantly echoing the biblical song of the angels:

> *Holy, holy, holy; / Angel voices singing;*
> *Holy, holy, holy, / Through high heaven ringing.*
> *From that temple, pure and bright, / Bathed in streams of crystal light,*
> *Hear the everlasting hymn, / Holy, holy, holy.*

> *Holy, holy, holy; / Grandest music swelling;*
> *Holy, holy, holy, / All sweet notes excelling.*
> *Those who conquered by His might, / Wearing now their crowns of light,*
> *Join the everlasting hymn, / Holy, holy, holy.*

> *Holy, holy, holy; / Come, let us adore Him;*
> *Holy, holy, holy, / Humbly bow before Him.*
> *Wisdom, glory, love and might, / With the seraphim unite*
> *In the everlasting hymn, / Holy, holy, holy.*

That's what we'll be singing—when we all get to heaven.

---

*See the story behind "I'd Rather Have Jesus."

Near to the Heart of God

Cleland B. McAfee

Cleland B. McAfee

1. There is a place of qui - et rest, Near to the heart of God;
2. There is a place of com - fort sweet, Near to the heart of God;
3. There is a place of full re - lease, Near to the heart of God;

A place where sin can - not mo - lest, Near to the heart of God.
A place where we our Sav - ior meet, Near to the heart of God.
A place where all is joy and peace, Near to the heart of God.

O Je - sus, blest Re - deem - er, Sent from the heart of God,

Hold us, who wait be - fore Thee, Near to the heart of God.

Near to the Heart of God

1903

He will gather the lambs with His arm, and carry them in His bosom . . .
Isaiah 40:11

Park University in Parkville, Missouri, with thirty-eight campuses across the United States, boasts of an enrollment of over 17,000 students. It was begun in 1875, with only seventeen students, by John A. McAfee, and by Colonel George Park, the colorful founder of Parkville, who donated the land.

McAfee had five sons and a daughter who all became involved in the college. The fourth son, Cleland, graduated from what was then Park College; after studying at Union Theological Seminary, he returned to Park as chaplain and choir director. Cleland's daughter, Katharine, later told how her father came to write the great hymn, "Near to the Heart of God":

> My father's father, John A. McAfee, was one of the founders and the first president of Park College in Missouri. In the last years of the past century, his five sons [Lowell, Howard, Lapsley, Cleland, Ernest] and his only daughter [Helen] were all living in Parkville, serving the college. My father was the college preacher and director of the choir, and it was his custom, when communion services came, to write the words and music of a response which his choir could sing and which would fit into the theme of his sermon.
>
> One terrible week, just before a communion Sunday, the two little daughters of my Uncle Howard and Aunt Lucy McAfee died of diphtheria within twenty-four hours of each other. The college family and town were stricken with grief. My father often told us how he sat long and late thinking of what could be said in word and song on the coming Sunday . . .
>
> So he wrote ["Near to the Heart of God"]. The choir learned it at the regular Saturday night rehearsal, and afterward they went to the Howard McAfee's home and sang it as they stood under the sky outside the darkened, quarantined house. It was sung again on Sunday morning at the communion service.

"Near to the Heart of God" was published in October 1903, in *The Choir Leader*.

In later years, Cleland pastored in the Presbyterian denomination, taught at McCormick Theological Seminary in Chicago, and helped direct the Presbyterian foreign missions program. He is the author of a number of textbooks including *The Greatest English Classic: A Study of the King James Version and Its Influence* and *Ministerial Practices: Some Fraternal Suggestions*, published in 1928.

His Eye Is on the Sparrow

Civilla D. Martin

Charles H. Gabriel

1. Why should I feel dis - cour - aged? Why should the shad - ows come? Why should my heart be lone - ly And long for heaven and home When Je - sus is my por - tion? My con - stant friend is He: His eye is on the spar - row, And I know He watch - es me; His eye is on the spar - row, And I know He watch - es me.

2. When - ev - er I am tempt - ed, When - ev - er clouds a - rise, When song gives place to sigh - ing, When hope with - in me dies, I draw the clos - er to Him; From care He sets me free; His eye is on the spar - row, And I know He watch - es me; His eye is on the spar - row, And I know He watch - es me.

His Eye Is on the Sparrow

1905

Are not two sparrows sold for a copper coin? And not one of them falls to the ground apart from your Father's will. Matthew 10:29

ost people have a hobby of some sort to provide a healthy diversion from the rigors of work. Long ago, there was a woodworker in Nazareth who counted bird-watching among His diversions. We can make that assumption because Jesus later referred frequently to birdlife in His sermons, saying things such as:

- "Are not two sparrows sold for a copper coin? And not one of them falls to the ground apart from your Father's will." (Matthew 10:29)
- "Look at the birds of the air, for they neither sow nor reap nor gather into barns; yet your heavenly Father feeds them. Are you not of more value than they?" (Matthew 6:26)
- "Consider the ravens . . ." (Luke 12:24)
- "Do not fear . . . you are of more value than many sparrows." (Luke 12:7)

It was this theme that caused the author of "God Will Take Care of You" to write, a year later, another great hymn on God's care: "His Eye Is on the Sparrow."

Civilla Durfee Martin was a Canadian by birth, born on August 21, 1869, in Nova Scotia. She became a school and music teacher, but when she married Dr. Walter Martin, an evangelist, she gave up teaching to travel with him and assist in his meetings.

This is her account of the writing of this song:

Early in the spring of 1905, my husband and I were sojourning in Elmira, New York. We contracted a deep friendship for a couple by the name of Mr. and Mrs. Doolittle—true saints of God. Mrs. Doolittle had been bedridden for nigh twenty years. Her husband was an incurable cripple who had to propel himself to and from his business in a wheel chair. Despite their afflictions, they lived happy Christian lives, bringing inspiration and comfort to all who knew them. One day while we were visiting with the Doolittles, my husband commented on their bright hopefulness and asked them for the secret of it. Mrs. Doolittle's reply was simple: "His eye is on the sparrow, and I know He watches me." The beauty of this simple expression of boundless faith gripped the hearts and fired the imagination of Dr. Martin and me. The hymn "His Eye Is on the Sparrow" was the outcome of that experience.

The day after writing the song, she mailed it to the famous gospel composer Charles Gabriel, who penned the music.

229

Have Thine Own Way, Lord

Adelaide A. Pollard

George C. Stebbins

1. Have Thine own way, Lord! Have Thine own way!
2. Have Thine own way, Lord! Have Thine own way!
3. Have Thine own way, Lord! Have Thine own way!
4. Have Thine own way, Lord! Have Thine own way!

Thou art the Pot - ter, I am the clay.
Search me and try me, Mas - ter, to - day!
Wound - ed and wea - ry, help me, I pray!
Hold o'er my be - ing ab - so - lute sway!

Mold me and make me af - ter Thy will,
Whit - er than snow, Lord, wash me just now,
Pow - er, all pow - er sure - ly is Thine!
Fill with Thy Spir - it till all shall see,

While I am wait - ing, yield - ed and still.
As in Thy pres - ence hum - bly I bow.
Touch me and heal me, Sav - ior di - vine!
Christ on - ly, al - ways, liv - ing in me!

230

Have Thine Own Way, Lord

1907

As the clay is in the potter's hand, so are you in My hand . . . Jeremiah 18:6

Hope deferred makes the heart sick," says Proverbs 13:12. Yet "*dis*appointments are *His* appointments." God uses setbacks to renew our focus on Him, to strengthen our faith, and to divert us to other opportunities. In this case, a bitter disappointment led to one of our greatest invitational hymns.

Its author, Adelaide Pollard, was born in Iowa during the Civil War. Her parents named her Sarah, but when she was old enough, she changed her name to Adelaide, not liking the name Sarah. After attending the Boston School of Oratory (Emerson College), she moved to Chicago to teach in a girls' school.

While in Chicago and struggling with frail health, she was attracted to the strange ministry of John Alexander Dowie, a Scottish-born faith healer who was drawing international attention. In 1901, Dowie announced he was the Elijah who would precede the Coming of Christ. Purchasing 6,800 acres of land outside Chicago, he began building "Zion City," which, despite a strong start, ended in failure. Adelaide, however, was apparently healed of diabetes through Dowie's ministry.

Afterward, she became very involved in the work of an evangelist named Sanford, who was predicting the imminent return of Christ. In New England, where she had moved to assist Sanford, she felt God was calling her to Africa as a missionary. But, to her intense disappointment, she was unable to raise her financial support. Heartsick, Adelaide, in her forties at the time, attended a prayer meeting. That night an elderly woman prayed, "It doesn't matter what you bring into our lives, Lord. Just have your own way with us."

That phrase rushed into Adelaide's heart, and the verses began shaping in her mind. At home that evening, she read again the story of the potter and the clay in Jeremiah 18. By bedtime she had written out the prayer "Have Thine Own Way."

Adelaide did eventually make it to Africa, but the outbreak of World War I sent her to Scotland and, later, back to America, where she wrote poems, spoke to groups, and ministered freely.

In the middle of December 1934, Adelaide, seventy-two, purchased a ticket at New York's Penn Station. She was heading to Pennsylvania for a speaking engagement. While waiting for the train, she was stricken with a seizure and shortly thereafter died.

I'd Rather Have Jesus

Rhea F. Miller

George Beverly Shea

1. I'd rath-er have Je-sus than sil-ver or gold; I'd rath-er be His than have rich-es un-told; I'd rath-er have Je-sus than hous-es or lands. I'd rath-er be led by His nail-pierced hand.

2. I'd rath-er have Je-sus than men's ap - plause; I'd rath-er be faith-ful to His dear cause; I'd rath-er have Je-sus than world-wide fame. I'd rath-er be true to His ho - ly name.

3. He's fair-er than lil-ies of rar-est bloom; He's sweet-er than hon-ey from out the comb; He's all that my hun-ger-ing spi - rit needs. I'd rath-er have Je-sus and let Him lead.

Than to be the king of a vast do-main Or be held in sin's dread sway.

I'd rath-er have Je-sus than an-y-thing This world af-fords to-day.

232

I'd Rather Have Jesus

1922

For what profit is it to a man if he gains the whole world and loses his own soul?
Matthew 16:26

G eorge Beverly Shea, "America's beloved gospel singer," has traveled with the Billy Graham evangelistic team since 1946. He was born in 1909 in Winchester, Ontario, where his dad served as pastor of the Wesleyan Methodist Church. Bev's mother, the church organist, had a piano that came from England; and, seated in front of its keys, she became a sort of "human alarm clock" for the family. Every weekday morning, striking an E-flat chord, she would sing Eliza Hewitt's old song:

> *Singing I go along life's road, | Praising the Lord, praising the Lord,*
> *Singing I go along life's road, | For Jesus has lifted my load.*

On Sundays, she chose a different selection, Isaac Watts's hymn:

> *Lord, in the morning Thou shalt hear | My voice ascending high;*
> *To Thee will I direct my prayer, | To Thee lift up mine eye.*

When Bev was twenty-one, he began working for the Mutual Insurance Company of New York, assisting medical examiners in obtaining information relating to the applicant's health history. Among those who came into the office was Fred Allen, host of a coast-to-coast radio talent show. Learning that Bev liked to sing, Mr. Allen arranged an audition, and a few weeks later Bev found himself singing "Go Down Moses" to a nationwide audience on the National Broadcasting Company. Though he lost the contest to a yodeler, he received fifteen dollars and a taste of widespread fame.

One Sunday shortly afterward, Bev sat down at his mother's organ to practice for the morning church service. His eyes fell on a clipping she had left for him there, a poem written in 1922 by Mrs. Rhea F. Miller. As Bev read the words, they spoke to him about his own aims and ambitions in life. An appropriate melody came easily, practically composing itself.

When Bev's mother came in from the kitchen, he played and sang it for her. Wrapping both arms around him, she placed a wet cheek against his. In church that morning, Bev sang "I'd Rather Have Jesus" publicly for the first time. It later became a sort of "signature song" expressing his own decisions in life.

> *I'd rather have Jesus than men's applause, | I rather be faithful to His dear cause;*
> *I'd rather have Jesus than worldwide fame, | I'd rather be true to His holy name . . .*

233

Turn Your Eyes Upon Jesus

Helen H. Lemmel

Helen H. Lemmel

1. O soul, are you wea-ry and trou - bled? No light in the
2. Thro' death in - to life ev - er - last - ing He passed, and we
3. His word shall not fail you He prom - ised; Be - lieve Him, and

dark-ness you see? There's light for a look at the Sav - ior, And
fol - low Him there; O - ver us sin no more hath do - min - ion For
all will be well; Then go to a world that is dy - ing, His

life more a - bun - dant and free!
more than con - qu'rors we are!
per - fect sal - va - tion to tell!

Turn your eyes up - on Je - sus,

Look full in His won - der - ful face, And the things of

earth Will grow strange-ly dim In the light of His glo - ry and grace.

Turn Your Eyes Upon Jesus
1922

Let us run with endurance the race set before us, looking unto Jesus, the author and finisher of our faith . . . Hebrews 12:1–2

H elen Howarth Lemmel was born in England in 1863, into the home of a Wesleyan minister who immigrated to America when Helen was a child. She loved music, and her parents provided the best vocal teachers they could find. Eventually Helen returned to Europe to study vocal music in Germany. In time, she married a wealthy European, but he left her when she became blind, and Helen struggled with multiple heartaches during midlife.

At age fifty-five, Helen heard a statement that deeply impressed her: "So then, turn your eyes upon Him, look full into His face and you will find that the things of earth will acquire a strange new dimness."

"I stood still," Helen later said, "and singing in my soul and spirit was the chorus, with not one conscious moment of putting word to word to make rhyme, or note to note to make melody. The verses were written the same week, after the usual manner of composition, but nonetheless dictated by the Holy Spirit."

Pastor Doug Goins of Palo Alto, California, and his parents, Paul and Kathryn Goins, both eighty-two, of Sun City, Arizona, knew Helen in Seattle. "She was advanced in years and almost destitute, but she was an amazing person," said Doug. "She made a great impression on me as a junior high child because of her joy and enthusiasm. Though she was living on government assistance in a sparse bedroom, whenever we'd ask how she was doing, she would reply, 'I'm doing well in the things that count.'"

One day the Goinses invited her to supper. "We had never entertained a blind person before," recalled Kathryn, "and it was interesting. Despite her infirmities, she was full of life. I remember how amused we were when, following supper, she said, 'Now if you will lead me to the bathroom, I'll sit on the throne and reign.'

"But she was always composing hymns," said Kathryn. "She had no way of writing them down, so she would call my husband at all hours and he'd rush down and record them before she forgot the words."

Helen had a small plastic keyboard by her bed. There she would play, sing, and cry. "One day God is going to bless me with a great heavenly keyboard," she'd say. "I can hardly wait!"

Helen Lemmel, who wrote nearly five hundred hymns during her lifetime, died in Seattle in 1961, thirteen days before her ninety-eighth birthday.

He Lives

Alfred H. Ackley

Alfred H. Ackley

1. I serve a ris-en Sav-ior. He's in the world to-day.
2. In all the world a-round me I see His lov-ing care;
3. Re-joice, re-joice, O Chris-tian. lift up your voice and sing.

I know that He is liv-ing; what-ev-er men may say.
And tho' my heart grows wea-ry I nev-er will de-spair.
E-ter-nal hal-le-lu-jahs to Je-sus Christ the King.

I see His hand of mer-cy. I hear His voice of cheer,
I know that He is lead-ing thro' all the storm-y blast.
The hope of all who seek Him, the help of all who find.

And just the time I need Him. He's al-ways near.
The day of His ap-pear-ing will come at last.
None oth-er is so lov-ing, So good and kind.

He Lives

1933

He is not here; for He is risen, as He said. Matthew 28:6

W hy should I worship a dead Jew?" That question—and a dreadful sermon—inspired this hymn.

Alfred Henry Ackley was born in Pennsylvania in 1887.* He showed great promise as a child, and his musician-father personally tutored him before sending him to New York City to study music. From there, it was on to the Royal Academy of Music in London. Alfred then returned to the States to attend Westminster Seminary in Maryland, and he was ordained into the Presbyterian ministry in 1914. After pastoring a church in his home state of Pennsylvania, Alfred was called to a congregation in California.

It was there in 1932 that Alfred met a Jewish man to whom he began witnessing. But the man resisted the Christian faith, saying, "Why should I worship a dead Jew?"

That statement played on Alfred's mind as he prepared his Easter Sunday message. Rising early to prepare for the day, Alfred flipped on the radio as he shaved and was astonished to hear a famous liberal preacher in New York say, "Good morning—it's Easter! You know, folks, it really doesn't make any difference to me if Christ be risen or not. As far as I am concerned, His body could be as dust in some Palestinian tomb. The main thing is, His truth goes marching on!"

Alfred wanted to fling the radio across the room. "It's a lie!" he exclaimed. His wife rushed into the bathroom, asking, "Why are you shouting so early in the morning?"

"Didn't you hear what that good-for-nothing preacher said?" Alfred replied.

That morning Ackley preached with great vigor on the reality of Christ's resurrection, and he did the same at the evening service. But later that night, he was still exercised over his friend's question and the morning's radio sermon. "Listen here, Alfred Ackley," his wife said at last. "It's time you did that which you can do best. Why don't you write a song about it and then maybe you'll feel better?"

Alfred went to his study, opened the Bible, and reread the resurrection account from Mark's gospel. A thrill went through him, and he began writing the words to "He Lives." A few minutes later, he was at the piano putting it to music, not dreaming it would become one of the church's most triumphant Easter hymns.

---

*Alfred's older brother, Bentley, was also a renowned gospel songwriter who traveled with the Billy Sunday/Homer Rodeheaver evangelistic team as pianist. Bentley later became a composer and editor with the Rodeheaver Publishing Company, writing more than 3,000 hymns and gospel songs.

O That I Had a Thousand Voices

Johann Mentzer

Johann B. König

1. O that I had a thou-sand voic-es And with a thou-sand
2. O all you pow'rs that God im-plant-ed, A-rise and si-lence
3. You for-est leaves so green and ten-der, That dance for joy in
4. All crea-tures that have breath and mo-tion, That throng the earth, the

tongues could tell Of Him in Whom the earth re-joic-es,
keep no more; Put forth the strength that God has grant-ed,
sum-mer air. You mead-ow grass-es bright and slen-der,
sea, the sky, Now join with me my heart's de-vo-tion,

Who does all things wise-ly and well! My grate-ful
Your no-blest work is to a-dore. O soul and
You flow'rs so won-drous sweet so fair, You live to
Help me to raise His prais-es high. My ut-most

heart would then be free To tell what God has done for me.
bod-y, join to raise With heart-felt joy our Mak-er's praise!
show God's praise a-lone. With me now make His glo-ry known.
pow'rs can ne'er a-right De-clare the won-ders of God's might.

O That I Had a Thousand Voices

1704

Behold, bless the LORD, all you servants of the LORD, who by night stand in the house of the LORD! Lift up your hands in the sanctuary, and bless the LORD.
Psalm 134:1–2

salm 134, one of the shortest chapters in the Bible, instructs those who serve the Lord by night to bless Him, to lift up their hands in the sanctuary and bless the Lord. Sometimes our highest praise occurs during the darkest hours.

Johann Mentzer was pastor in the small village of Kemnitz, located in the middle of the forests of eastern Germany, near the Polish and Czech borders. He began his ministry there in 1696 and became a trusted friend and mentor to the young count, Nicholas Ludwig von Zinzendorf, who was born in 1700 and frequently visited his grandmother in nearby Berthelsdorf.

Most of Mentzer's parishioners, however, were poor serfs whose hard work primarily benefited their wealthy masters. Mentzer's heart went out to his people, toiling in poverty and trouble, and he often counseled them to praise the Lord whatever the circumstances.

One evening Johann was returning from a Bible study in a nearby village. The night was dark, but as he approached his church, he grew alarmed at a frightening red glow in the sky. Hurrying onward, he found his own home, the church parsonage, ablaze. It had been set afire during his absence.

As he later inspected the ashes and ruins, he was disturbed and downhearted. Just then a serf tapped him on the shoulder and asked, "So, pastor, are you still in the mood for praise and thanksgiving?" Johann offered a silent prayer for grace, and at that moment his whole attitude changed. It seemed to him that his praise to God should be louder than the sound of the tongues of flame that had just consumed his own home. The next day he composed this hymn: "O that I had a thousand voices / And with a thousand tongues could tell / Of Him in whom the earth rejoices / Who does all things wisely and well."

Years later, Charles Wesley, undoubtedly inspired by this hymn, wrote his more famous "O for a Thousand Tongues to Sing."

If you're facing difficulty right now, try praise and thanksgiving.

We're Marching to Zion

Isaac Watts   Robert Lowry

1. Come, we that love the Lord, And let our joys be known.
2. Let those re - fuse to sing Who nev - er knew our God;
3. Then let our songs a - bound, And ev - 'ry tear be dry.

Join in a song with sweet ac - cord, Join in a song with sweet ac - cord,
But chil - dren of the heav'n - ly King, But chil - dren of the heav'n - ly King,
We're march - ing thro' Im - man - uel's ground, We're march - ing thro' Im - man - uel's ground.

And thus sur - round the throne, And thus sur - round the throne,
May speak their joys a - broad, May speak their joys a - broad.
To fair - er worlds on high, To fair - er worlds on high.

We're march - ing to Zi - on, Beau - ti - ful, beau - ti - ful Zi - on. We're

march - ing up - ward to Zi - on, The beau - ti - ful cit - y of God.

We're Marching to Zion

1707

Out of Zion, the perfection of beauty, God will shine forth. Psalm 50:2

On the night of November 30, 1940, German planes bombed Southampton, England, and destroyed the Above Bar Congregational Church. The pastor and caretaker were able to rescue the church records, but all else was destroyed—except for a bust of Isaac Watts, the "Father of English Hymnody."

The destruction of those old buildings was a blow to Christian history, for within the walls of the Above Bar Church the hymns of young Isaac Watts were first sung.

Watts was born in Southampton on July 17, 1674, the oldest of nine children. He was a brilliant lad who started learning Latin at age four and Greek and Hebrew soon after. It's said that even before he could speak plainly, he would cry out, "A book! A book! Buy a book!" whenever anyone would give him money.

Isaac advanced so quickly in school that a local physician offered to finance his education at a major university. As members of Above Bar Congregational Church, however, the Watts were committed "Dissenters," Christians who didn't believe in joining the State Church. Dissenters opted instead for establishing independent congregations where they could worship without conforming to government regulations. As such, they were bitterly persecuted, and Isaac's father had even spent time in prison for his beliefs. Nor were dissenters allowed to attend the state universities. So at sixteen, Isaac enrolled instead in an independent academy in London and graduated with honors.

Returning home, Isaac spent two more years living with his parents and attending Above Bar Congregational Church. One day, discontented with the quality of the singing at the church, he wrote a hymn for the church to sing. This was a new and radical innovation, for at that time only the Psalms of David were sung in English churches.

Nonetheless, Above Bar Congregational Church gamely tried the young man's hymn and liked it so much they asked for another. For two and a half years, Isaac churned out hymns for that little congregation. Those two post-college years at home became the "Golden Years" of Watts's hymn writing.

How remarkable that some of the greatest hymns ever sung in the English language—such as "We're Marching to Zion"—should be produced by the "Father of Hymnody" who was only twenty years of age.

The old church building may be gone now, but the hymns first sung there will never die.

Be Still, My Soul

Katharina A. von Schlegel

Jean Sibelius

1. Be still, my soul; the Lord is on thy side. Bear pa-tient-ly the cross of grief or pain; Leave to thy God to or-der and pro-vide. In ev-'ry change He faith-ful will re-main. Be still, my soul; Thy best, Thy heaven-ly Friend Thro' thorn-y ways leads to a joy-ful end.

2. Be still, my soul; Thy God doth un-der-take To guide the fu-ture as He has the past. Thy hope, Thy con-fi-dence let noth-ing shake; All now mys-te-rious shall be bright at last. Be still, my soul; the waves and winds still know His voice Who ruled them while He dwelt be-low.

3. Be still, my soul! The hour is hast'ning on When we shall be for-ev-er with the Lord, When dis-ap-point-ment, grief, and fear are gone, Sor-row for-got, love's pur-est joys re-stored. Be still, my soul; when change and tears are past, All safe and bless-ed we shall meet at last.

Be Still, My Soul

1752

Truly my soul silently waits for God; from Him comes my salvation. Psalm 62:1

Little is known about Katharina von Schlegel, the German author of this poem. Her words, joined with the haunting strains of FINLANDIA by Sibelius, have made this a classic hymn. It was widely sung during World War II when it comforted an entire nation. Virgil J. Bachman of Our Saviour Lutheran Church in Port Huron, Michigan, is a good example. Writing in his church newsletter, he said:

I had probably sung "Be Still, My Soul" many times before, but it was not until I sang it in a small stucco church in a tiny village in France during World War II that [it] became part of my life.

The war in Europe was going badly. The news from the front was disheartening. We had suffered reverses. We were edgy, confused, and discouraged. It was at this crucial time that some Chaplain arranged a service in this quaint church somewhere in France. It seemed the roof of that little village church actually opened up as we weary, dirty, GIs blended our voices under the leadership of that Chaplain and the church's old pump organ.

Halfway through the service it happened. Softly the organ began and we sang, "Be still my soul, the Lord is on thy side." How badly it was needed. It was as though the Lord was speaking to me in a very personal way. "Bear patiently the cross of grief or pain"—the cross of war with its hardships, misery, separation and pain.

As we began the second stanza, "Be still my soul, Thy God doth undertake to guide the future as he hath the past," God seemed to whisper, "Don't give up, I'm still in command, yes, even here. I'll guide the future as I have the past."

The thoughts of dead and missing friends came as through a choked-up throat I sang, "Be still my soul, though dearest friends depart. . . ." Soothing, personal assurance [came] at that moment and in that spot. With renewed spirit I was able to sing the final stanza, "Be still my soul, when change and tears are past, all safe and blessed we shall meet at last."

Peace! Either here or in eternity.

As we left that little church, the peace I felt among the horrors of war was nothing but a gift of the Holy Spirit. God did spare me and allow me to return to my loved ones and His service and still preserves me.

Faith of Our Fathers

Frederick W. Faber

Henri F. Hemy

1. Faith of our fathers, liv - ing still In spite of dun-geon,
2. Our fa-thers, chained in pris - ons dark, Were still in heart and
3. Faith of our fa - thers, we will love Both friend and foe in

fire and sword! O how our hearts beat high with joy
con - science free. How sweet would be their chil - dren's fate
all our strife; And preach Thee, too, as love knows how,

When-e'er we hear that glo - rious word! Faith of our fa - thers!
If they, like them could die for thee! Faith of our fa - thers!
By kind - ly words and vir - tuous life. Faith of our fa - thers!

Ho - ly faith! We will be true to Thee till death!
Ho - ly faith! We will be true to Thee till death!
Ho - ly faith! We will be true to Thee till death!

Faith of Our Fathers

1849

Now faith is the substance of things hoped for, the evidence of things not seen. For by it the elders obtained a good testimony. Hebrews 11:1–2

Frederick William Faber was raised in an Anglican parsonage in Calverley, Yorkshire, England; but both his parents died when he was young. When he moved to Oxford University as a young man, he came under the influence of the great Roman Catholic, John Henry Newman, author of "Lead, Kindly Light." Following graduation, Faber entered the Anglican ministry, but his soul was troubled. He was drawn to the historic, reverent liturgy of the Catholic faith. On Sunday night, November 16, 1845, he announced to his congregation that he intended to leave the Church of England and be ordained as a Roman Catholic.

For the remainder of his short life—Faber died at fifty-nine—he endeavored to provide a body of hymns for English Catholics to sing. Perhaps his most enduring is "Faith of Our Fathers."

What most Protestants don't know is that Faber wrote this song to remind the Catholic Church of its martyrs during the days of the Protestant King Henry VIII and Queen Elizabeth I. "Good Queen Bess," for example, used fines, gallows, gibbets, racks, and whips against those who said Mass, honored the pope, or harbored a priest. Often in the middle of the night, thugs would burst into Catholic homes and drag them away to be scourged, fined, or seared with glowing irons. The dungeons were choked with victims.

Nicholas Owen was such a victim. Probably a builder by trade, Owen designed countless hiding places for endangered Catholics. He hid them in secret rooms, between the walls, and under the floors. He hid them in stone fences and in underground passages. He designed nooks and crannies that looked like anything but hiding places.

When Nicholas was at last betrayed, he was dragged to the Tower of London and his arms were fixed to iron rings. There he hung for hours, his body dangling. Weights added to his feet increased the suffering. The tortures continued until March 2, 1606, when "his bowels broke in a terrible way" and he passed to his reward.

It was for these Catholic heroes, martyred at the hands of so-called "Protestant" monarchs, that "Faith of Our Fathers" was originally written. Now, of course, this great hymn reminds us all of the noble sacrifices made by those in every branch of the Christian family who have passed on their faith to us "in spite of dungeon, fire and sword."

O How I Love Jesus

Frederick Whitfield

American Melody

1. There is a name I love to hear, I love to sing its worth;
2. It tells me of a Sav-ior's love, Who died to set me free;
3. It tells me what my Fa-ther hath, In store for ev-'ry day;
4. It tells of One whose lov-ing heart, Can feel my deep-est woe;

It sounds like mu - sic in my ear, The sweet-est Name on earth.
It tells me of His pre-cious blood, The sin - ner's per-fect plea.
And tho' I tread a dark-some path, Yields sun - shine all the way.
Who in each sor - row bears a part, That none can bear be - low.

O how I love Je - sus, O how I love Je - sus,

O how I love Je - sus; Be - cause He first loved me.

O How I Love Jesus

1855

We love Him because He first loved us. 1 John 4:19

Frederick Whitfield was born on a cold January day in 1829, in tiny Threapwood, England, population about 250. He attended college in Dublin, Ireland, and devoted his life to pastoral ministry in the Church of England. His greatest legacy is this hymn about the name of Jesus, written when he was a student. Generations of Christians have loved "There Is a Name I Love to Hear" with its peppy refrain: "O how I love Jesus, / O how I love Jesus, / O how I love Jesus, / because He first loved me."

You might be interested to know that while Whitfield wrote the *verses* to this hymn, he didn't compose its famous chorus.

Both the simple words and the nimble tune of "O How I Love Jesus" are American inventions of unknown origin. They floated around like orphans, attaching themselves to various hymns in the nineteenth century. One hymnologist found forty-two occurrences of this chorus in early songbooks. Even such stately hymns as "Amazing Grace" and "Alas! And Did My Savior Bleed" were occasionally sung to this lighthearted melody, with "O How I Love Jesus" used as the refrain.

But when "O How I Love Jesus" was finally wedded to Whitfield's "There Is a Name I Love to Hear," it was a marriage made in heaven. We've been singing it ever since. Some of Whitfield's original verses have fallen by the wayside, which is too bad; every verse tells us what the Name of Jesus can do in our lives:

It tells me what my Father hath | In store for every day,
And though I tread a darksome path, | Yields sunshine all the way.

It tells of One whose loving heart | Can feel my deepest woe;
Who in each sorrow bears a part | That none can bear below.

It bids my trembling heart rejoice; | It dries each rising tear.
It tells me, in a "still small voice," | To trust and never fear.

This Name shall shed its fragrance still | Along this thorny road,
Shall sweetly smooth the rugged hill | That leads me up to God.

And there with all the blood-bought throng, | From sin and sorrow free,
I'll sing the new eternal song | Of Jesus' love for me.

Little Brown Church in the Vale

William S. Pitts   William S. Pitts

1. There's a church in the val-ley by the wild-wood, No love-li-er
2. There close by the side of that loved one, To the trees where the
3. How sweet on a clear Sab-bath morn-ing, To list to the
4. From the church in the val-ley by the wild-wood, When day fades a-

spot in the dale; No place is so dear to my child-hood
wild flow-ers bloom; Where the fare-well hymn will be chant-ed,
clear ring-ing bell; Its tones so sweet-ly are call-ing,
way in-to night. I would fain from this spot of my child-hood,

No spot is so dear To my child-hood

Fine

As the lit-tle brown church In the vale.
I shall rest by her side in the tomb. Oh, come, come, come, come
Oh, come to the church In the vale.
Wing my way to the man-sions of light.

As the lit-tle brown church in the vale.

D.S. al Fine

Come to the church in the wild-wood, Oh, come to the church in the vale;

Little Brown Church in the Vale

1857

Remember the Sabbath day, to keep it holy. Exodus 20:8

*T*he Little Brown Church in the Vale sits in a beautiful park alongside Highway 218 in the town of Bradford, near Nashua, in northern Iowa. But it wasn't there when the song was written.

A New York native named William Pitts, about twenty-seven, was traveling by stagecoach from his home in Wisconsin to Fredericksburg, Iowa, to see his girlfriend. It was a bright afternoon in 1857. When the stagecoach made a pit stop in Bradford, Pitts took a stroll among the trees to stretch his legs. The gently sloping hills formed a slight valley, and the Cedar River flowed peacefully by. That grove of trees, it seemed to Pitts, would be the perfect setting for a church.

Unable to erase the scene from his mind, Pitts returned home and composed the words and music to "Little Brown Church in the Vale." Nothing came of his song, however, and he filed it away.

Five years later, Pitts, now married to his sweetheart, relocated to Iowa to be near his elderly in-laws and to teach music at Bradford Academy. Imagine his surprise when he saw a church building sitting in the very spot he had previously envisioned it. Christians in the community, growing tired of meeting in abandoned stores, had determined to build a church. The Civil War was raging and times were hard, but by 1862, the building was up. It had to be painted using the cheapest color—which was brown.

When Pitts saw the little brown church in the vale, he rushed home and found "Little Brown Church in the Vale," packed among his papers. He sang his hymn at the building's dedication in 1864. Soon afterward, he sold his manuscript to a publisher in Chicago for twenty-five dollars. He used the money to enroll in Rush Medical College, and William spent the rest of his life as the town physician in Fredericksburg, Iowa, about fourteen miles from Bradford.

Today the Little Brown Church boasts a membership of about one hundred, but it's best known for the hundreds of weddings and thousands of tourists who flock there each year to see the church in the valley by the wildwood, the little brown church in the vale.

Almost Persuaded

Philip B. Bliss

Philip B. Bliss

1. "Al-most per-suad-ed" now to be - lieve;
2. "Al-most per-suad-ed," come, come to - day;
3. "Al-most per-suad-ed," har - vest is past!

"Al - most per - suad - ed" Christ to re - ceive:
"Al - most per - suad - ed," turn not a - way:
"Al - most per - suad - ed," doom comes at last!

Seems now some soul to say, "Go, Spir - it, go Thy way;
Je - sus in - vites you here, An - gels are lin - gering near,
"Al - most" can - not a - vail, "Al - most" is but to fail!

Some more con - ven - ient day On Thee I'll call."
Prayers rise from hearts so dear, O wan - derer, come.
Sad, sad, that bit - ter wail, "Al - most," but lost!

Almost Persuaded

1871

Then Agrippa said to Paul, "You almost persuade me to become a Christian."
Acts 26:28

o one in the history of gospel music is more revered than Philip P. Bliss, a gifted young musician who died tragically at age thirty-five in a train disaster. Interestingly, just a year before his death, this hymn—which he wrote—had a profound influence in his decision to give himself to full-time gospel ministry.

Philip, his wife, Lucy, and their two small children lived in Chicago, where Philip worked for a publishing company, writing sacred and secular songs. He was considered a rising star on the American music scene. As time allowed, he also volunteered as a soloist and song leader in evangelist meetings.

One day he was assisting a preacher named Rev. Brundage. During the sermon, the evangelist quoted Acts 26:28 and declared, "He who is almost persuaded is almost saved, and to be almost saved is to be entirely lost!" Struck by those words, Philip penned this hymn, "Almost Persuaded."

Shortly afterward, Philip received a letter from evangelist D. L. Moody, urging him to "sing the gospel" by becoming a full-time evangelistic song leader. As they prayed over the decision, Philip and Lucy were understandably cautious, for it would mean the end of a stable, regular income. It would cost Bliss's career in secular music and entail a nomadic lifestyle of itinerate evangelism. "I am willing," Lucy wrote, "that Mr. Bliss should do anything that we can be sure is the Lord's will, and I can trust the Lord to provide for us, but I don't want him to take such a step simply on Mr. Moody's will."

Shortly afterward, evangelist Daniel Whittle requested Philip's help with evangelistic rallies in Waukegan, Illinois. The meetings started slowly, but on March 26, 1871, as Philip sang his new hymn, "Almost Persuaded," an unusual power swept over the crowd. Lucy wrote, "In different parts of the house, sinners arose as he sang, presenting themselves for prayer, and souls that night rejoiced in Christ. Our hearts were very full, and a great responsibility was upon us."

The next day Philip made a formal commitment to the Lord to leave all secular concerns and engage himself in full-time ministry. In the year left to him, Philip Bliss exerted a lasting influence on gospel music, singing multitudes into the Kingdom and writing many of the hymns we love today.

Nobody Knows the Trouble I've Seen

African-American Spiritual

African-American Spiritual

No-bo-dy knows the trou-ble I've seen; No-bo-dy knows but Je-sus.

No-bo-dy knows the trou-ble I've seen; Glo-ry hal-le-lu-jah.

1. Some - times I'm up; some - times I'm down; Oh yes, Lord.
2. Al - though You see me goin' a - long, Oh yes, Lord,
3. What makes old Sa - tan hate me so? Oh yes, Lord;

Some - times I'm al - most to the ground; Oh yes, Lord.
I have my trou - bles here be - low; Oh yes, Lord.
He got me once and let me go; Oh yes, Lord

Nobody Knows the Trouble I've Seen

1872

Let not your heart be troubled; you believe in God, believe also in Me. John 14:1

Fisk University in Nashville, Tennessee, opened its doors in 1866, at the close of the Civil War. It was one of the schools established for liberated slaves by the American Missionary Association. As students and professors arrived on campus, they found themselves living in abandoned Union Army hospital barracks built on the site of old slave pens.

Among the arriving professors was a New York Yankee, a white man named White. As music instructor, George White taught his students classical cantatas and patriotic songs, but he was particularly intrigued by the old plantation melodies and slave songs he overheard in the dorms and among the students between classes. White had trouble coaxing his students to sing him those songs; it seemed a particularly private type of hand-me-down music. There were no written scores or words—just plaintive strains passed voice to voice between the generations.

Within a few years, the old buildings at Fisk started rotting. The university found itself in crisis, without even money to buy food for its four hundred students. Regretfully, the Missionary Association decided to close the school. When White approached the trustees suggesting a series of fund-raising concerts, the board refused (they called his scheme "a wild goose chase"). White decided to try it anyway. "I'm depending on God, not you," he told the board.

Selecting nine students (most of them former slaves), White and his wife sold their jewelry and personal belongings to finance the first tour. On October 6, 1871, the singers boarded a train in Nashville for the Midwest. It was a hard trip, and at times the young people had to relinquish their seats to white folks. Other times they were evicted from trains or hotels. Sometimes the little group, braving threats, insults, obscenities, and indignities, sang in nearly empty halls and churches.

At the National Council of Congregational Churches meeting in Oberlin, Ohio, some of the delegates protested giving time to the "colored students from Fisk University." The problem was the pressing nature of denominational business. Their slate was full, and the delegates didn't want interruptions in their business sessions. But George White wouldn't be denied, and finally the Fisk students sang one song during a recess as the delegates were milling around in little groups and leaving the building.

What happened next changed the course of American music.

Continued in the next story . . .

253

Swing Low, Sweet Chariot

African-American Spiritual African-American Spiritual

Swing low, sweet char - i - ot, Com - in' for to car - ry me home;

Swing low, sweet char - i - ot, Com - in' for to car - ry me home.

1. I looked o - ver Jor - dan and what did I see, Com - in' for to car - ry me home?
2. If you get there be - fore I do, Com - in' for to car - ry me home,

A band of an - gels com - in' af - ter me; Com - in' for to car - ry me home.
Just tell my friends I'm com - in' home too; Com - in' for to car - ry me home.

Swing Low, Sweet Chariot
1872

The chariots of God are twenty thousand, even thousands of thousands; the Lord is among them . . . Psalm 68:17

I t had been a gray, overcast day in Oberlin, Ohio. Delegates to the National Council of Congregational Churches were weary from the dismal weather and long business sessions. When the meeting recessed, singers from Fisk University filed quietly into the choir loft. Suddenly the clouds parted and sunshine streamed through the windows. Delegates stopped talking, and every face turned toward the music. "Steal away, steal away, steal away to Jesus," came the song in beautiful, brooding harmony. After a moment of stunned silence, the convention burst into wild applause and cries for more.

Among the delegates was Henry Ward Beecher, a noted pastor from Brooklyn who immediately begged the group to cancel its tour and come directly to his church in New York. Unable to do that, director George White offered the group for a December concert.

Knowing the importance of this engagement, White agonized about naming his group; and in Columbus, Ohio, after spending much of the night in prayer, he found the answer. They would be the Jubilee Singers, the biblical year of Jubilee in Leviticus 25 being a time of liberation for slaves.

On December 27, 1871, the Jubilee Singers sang at Plymouth Church in Brooklyn. Rev. Beecher, deeply moved, stood and said, "Ladies and gentlemen, I'm going to do what I want every person in this house to do." He turned his pockets inside out, giving all the money to the Jubilee Singers. That night the offering was $1,300! Newspapers picked up the story, and soon the Jubilee Singers had engagements around the world.

In their concerts, the section that most stirred their audiences was their "spirituals"—those soulful plantation songs born of slavery and full of yearning.

In 1872, gospel music publisher Biglow & Main hired a musician to meet the Jubilee Singers and record these timeless, authorless songs on paper. Later that year, a little volume was published under the title *Jubilee Songs: Complete. As Sung by the Jubilee Singers of Fisk University.* It was a milestone for both gospel and popular music; it introduced the "Negro spiritual" to America and to the world. Among the favorites were "Nobody Knows the Trouble I've Seen" and "Swing Low, Sweet Chariot."

Thanks to the Jubilee Singers, Fisk University is still training young people today—and still sending out its Jubilee Singers to churches and concert halls across America and around the world.

Whiter Than Snow

James Nicholson

William G. Fischer

1. Lord Je - sus, I long to be per - fect - ly whole; I
2. Lord Je - sus, look down from Thy throne in the skies And
3. Lord Je - sus, be - fore You I pa - tient - ly wait; Come

want Thee for - ev - er to live in my soul. Break down ev - ery
help me to make a com - plete sac - ri - fice. I give up my-
now and with - in me a new heart cre - ate. To those who have

i - dol, cast out ev - ery foe. Now wash me and I shall be
self and what - ev - er I know, Now wash me and I shall be
sought Thee, Thou nev - er saidst, "No." Now wash me and I shall be

whit - er than snow. Whit - er than snow, Yes, whit - er than

snow, Now wash me and I shall be Whit - er than snow.

Whiter Than Snow

1872

Wash me, and I shall be whiter than snow. Psalm 51:7

James Nicholson, author of "Whiter Than Snow," was a dedicated Christian who lived in Washington, D.C., where he worked for the post office. Born in Ireland in the 1820s, James had immigrated to America in the 1850s, originally settling in Philadelphia, where he became active in the Wharton Street Methodist Episcopal Church as a Sunday school and evangelistic worker. In 1871, he moved to Washington to assume his new duties with the post office, and the next year he published this hymn.

"Whiter Than Snow" is based on Psalm 51:7, the prayer of repentance offered by King David after his sin with Bathsheba: "Wash me, and I shall be whiter than snow." It originally had six stanzas, all of them beginning, "Dear Jesus . . ." An unknown editor later altered the words to "Lord Jesus." "Whiter Than Snow" was first published in 1872 by the Methodist Episcopal Book Room in Philadelphia, in a sixteen-page pamphlet entitled *Joyful Songs No. 4.*

Philadelphia musician William Gustavus Fischer composed the music to this hymn. He learned to read music while attending singing classes at a German-speaking church in Philadelphia. When he started his life's occupation as a bookbinder, he still spent his evenings pursuing music. He was eventually hired to teach music at a Philadelphia college, and late in life he entered the piano business.

Fischer was best known as a popular song leader for revival meetings. In 1875, he led the one-thousand-voice choir at the D. L. Moody/Ira Sankey Campaign in the great tabernacle at Thirteenth and Market Streets in Philadelphia. He composed more than two hundred hymn tunes, including this one. He also composed the melody for "I Love to Tell the Story."

The splendor of snowfall is only one of the pictures used in Scripture to illustrate God's forgiveness of sin. Micah 7:19 says God casts our sins into the ocean. Psalm 103 says He removes them as far from us as east from west. According to Isaiah 38:17, God casts them behind His back. Colossians 2:14 says they are wiped out like erased handwriting. If you're suffering pangs of guilt and regret, needing a fresh experience of God's forgiveness, try singing this old hymn with new sincerity:

Break down every idol, cast out every foe,
Now wash me, and I shall be whiter than snow.

To God Be the Glory

Fanny J. Crosby

William H. Doane

1. To God be the glo-ry, great things He hath done. So loved He the world that He gave us His Son, Who yield-ed His life, an a-tone-ment for sin, And o-pened the life-gate, that all may go in. Praise the Lord, praise the Lord, Let the earth hear His voice! Praise the Lord, praise the Lord, Let the peo-ple re-joice! O come to the Fa-ther thru Je-sus the Son, And give Him the glo-ry, great things He hath done.

To God Be the Glory

1875

Be exalted, O God, above the heavens, and Your glory above all the earth.
Psalm 108:5

O ccasionally a hymn drops into the furrows of history to be buried and forgotten awhile, only to later spring to life for future generations. That's what happened with Fanny Crosby's "To God Be the Glory." It first appeared in *Brightest and Best*, a little volume of hymns published in 1875 by William Doane and Robert Lowry. This small hymnal proved to be a treasure trove, introducing such classics as "Christ Arose!," "All the Way My Savior Leads Me," "Savior, More Than Life to Me," "I Am Thine, O Lord," "Rescue the Perishing," "Jesus, Keep Me Near the Cross," and this one—"Praise for Redemption" (as it was originally called).

As it turned out, "Praise for Redemption" wasn't much of a hit. It wasn't widely sung nor included in many hymnals; it just lay hidden for eighty years.

In 1954, Billy Graham was planning an evangelistic crusade at London's Harringay Arena. As Cliff Barrows, music director for the Graham team, was compiling hymns for the *Greater London Crusade Song Book*, Rev. Frank Colquhoun, a prolific British preacher at Norwich Cathedral and a great lover of hymns, approached him. Colquhoun gave Barrows a copy of "Praise for Redemption," with its exuberant chorus: "Praise the Lord! Praise the Lord! Let the earth hear His voice!" Though unfamiliar with the hymn, Barrows decided to use it anyway.

Meanwhile problems were mounting for Graham. The British Press was critical of the young evangelist, and an Anglican bishop predicted he would return to America with "his tail between his legs." Funds were short, forcing the Graham team to take pay cuts. A member of Parliament threatened a challenge in the House of Commons, accusing Graham of interfering in British politics under the guise of religion. Friends in high places were advising Graham to cancel or postpone the meetings. Graham, shaken, dropped to his knees repeatedly, beseeching help from heaven.

As it turned out, Harringay Arena was packed for three months, and the crusade sparked a sense of revival across Great Britain. "To God Be the Glory" seemed a fitting theme. Fanny Crosby's old hymn was sung almost every night in Harringay, launching it into worldwide popularity as one of Christianity's favorite hymns.

I Am Thine, O Lord

Fanny J. Crosby

William H. Doane

1. I am Thine O Lord; I have heard Thy voice, And it told Thy
2. Con - se - crate me now to Thy ser - vice Lord, By the power of
3. O the pure de - light of a sin - gle hour That be - fore Thy
4. There are depths of love that I can - not know 'Til I cross the

love to me. But I long to rise in the arms of faith,
grace di - vine; Let my soul look up with a stead-fast hope,
throne I spend, When I kneel in prayer, and with Thee my God,
nar - row sea; There are heights of joy that I may not reach

And be clos - er drawn to Thee.
And my will be lost in Thine. Draw me near - er, near - er bless-ed Lord,
I com - mune as friend with friend!
'Til I rest in peace with Thee.

To the cross where Thou hast died. Draw me near - er, near - er,

near - er bless - ed Lord, To Thy pre - cious bleed - ing side.

I Am Thine, O Lord

1875

Let us draw near with a true heart in full assurance of faith. Hebrews 10:22

She's called the "Queen of American Hymn Writers," and the "Mother of Congregational Singing in America." During her ninety-five years, Fanny Crosby wrote more than eight thousand hymns. In addition, she was one of the three most prominent evangelical leaders in America during the last part of the 1800s, the others being D. L. Moody and Ira Sankey. She was one of America's most popular preachers and lecturers; in many cases lines of people would circle the block where she was scheduled to speak, hoping to get a seat.

When she traveled, it was usually by train; and she was fiercely independent, insisting on traveling alone, despite her blindness, until she was up in her eighties. Fanny lived in the rundown tenements of lower Manhattan so she'd be nearer her beloved Rescue Missions where she worked with the homeless and addicted.

But to me, the most remarkable thing about Fanny Crosby was her phenomenal memory. After her eyes were blinded in infancy, her grandmother Eunice took a special interest in teaching her Bible verses. Later a woman named Mrs. Hawley, the Crosbys' landlady, took over the job, committed to helping Fanny memorize the entire Bible! Every week the child was given a certain number of chapters to learn, and Mrs. Hawley drilled them into her during their review sessions together. Fanny learned by heart all of Genesis, Exodus, Leviticus, Numbers, and Deuteronomy, plus the four Gospels, most of the Psalms, all of Proverbs, and many portions of the rest of the Bible.

From the fountainhead of these Scriptures flowed her hymns.

Ira Sankey, in his autobiography, gives us the story behind this particular hymn: "Fanny Crosby was visiting Mr. W. H. Doane, in his home in Cincinnati, Ohio. They were talking together about the nearness of God, as the sun was setting and evening shadows were gathering around them. The subject so impressed the well-known hymn-writer, that before retiring she had written the words to this hymn, which has become one of the most useful she has ever written. The music by Mr. Doane so well fitted the words that the hymn has become a special favorite wherever the gospel hymns are known."

It was first published in 1875, in the little hidden treasure of hymns called *Brightest and Best*. Underneath the hymn was this Scripture quotation: "Let us draw near with a true heart" (Hebrews 10:22).

Beulah Land

Edgar P. Stites

John R. Sweney

1. I've reached the land of joy di - vine, And all its beau - ty now is mine,
2. The Sav - iour comes and walks with me, And sweet com - mu - nion here have we;
3. A sweet per - fume up - on the breeze, Is borne from ev - er ver - nal trees,
4. The zeph - yrs seem to float to me, Sweet sounds of heav - en's mel - o - dy,

Here shines un - dimmed one bliss - ful day, For all my night has passed a - way.
He gent - ly leads me with His hand, For this is heav - en's bor - der - land.
And flow'rs that nev - er fad - ing grow Where streams of life for - ev - er flow.
As an - gels, with the white-robed throng, Join in the sweet re - demp - tion song.

O Beu - lah Land, sweet Beu - lah Land, As on thy high - est mount I stand,

I look a - way a - cross the sea, Where man - sions are pre - pared for me,

And view the shin - ing glo - ry shore, My heav'n, my home for - ev - er more!

Beulah Land

1876

You shall be called Hephzibah, and your land Beulah; for the LORD delights in you . . . Isaiah 62:4

T he author of this hymn, Edgar Stites, was a descendant of John Howland, who came to America on the *Mayflower*. He was born in Cape May, New Jersey, in March of 1836, and was born again in Philadelphia during the Revival of 1857. He served Union Forces during the Civil War by feeding the troops that passed through Philadelphia.

After the war Edgar became a riverboat pilot on the Delaware River and a Methodist preacher. He also served a stint as home missionary to South Dakota. For more than sixty years, he was a member of the First Methodist Episcopal Church of Cape May, New Jersey. In 1870, he joined a number of other ministers and laymen in founding the Ocean Grove Camp Meeting Association. Today Ocean Grove is a full-fledged town as well as Christian community and conference center.

It was in Ocean Grove that "Beulah Land" was first sung.

The word *Beulah* is an Old Testament term that occurs only in Isaiah 62:4: "You shall no longer be termed Forsaken, nor shall your land be Desolate; but you shall be called Hephzibah, and your land Beulah; for the LORD delights in you, and your land shall be married." *Beulah* comes from a Hebrew word meaning "to marry." The idea is a land that is loved, that is as delightful to the Lord as a beautiful bride. As such, it has come to represent heaven.

"It was in 1876 that I wrote 'Beulah Land,'" Edgar Stites said. "I could write only two verses and the chorus, when I was overcome and fell on my face. That was one Sunday. On the following Sunday I wrote the third and fourth verses, and again I was so influenced by emotion that I could only pray and weep. The first time it was sung was at the regular Monday morning meeting of Methodists in Philadelphia. Bishop McCabe sang it to the assembled ministers. Since then it is known wherever religious people congregate. I have never received a cent for my songs. Perhaps that is why they have had such a wide popularity. I could not do work for the Master and receive pay for it."

Immortal, Invisible, God Only Wise

Walter Chalmers Smith

Welsh Hymn Melody

1. Im - mor - tal, in - vis - i - ble, God on - ly wise,
2. Un - rest - ing, un - hast - ing, and si - lent as light;
3. To all, life Thou giv - est, to both great and small;
4. Great Fa - ther of glo - ry, pure Fa - ther of light;

In light in - ac - ces - si - ble hid from our eyes;
Nor want - ing, nor wast - ing, Thou rul - est in might.
In all life Thou liv - est, the true life of all;
Thine an - gels a - dore Thee, all veil - ing their sight;

Most bless - ed, most glo - rious, the An - cient of Days;
Thy jus - tice, like moun - tains, high soar - ing a - bove
We blos - som and flour - ish as leaves on the tree,
All praise we would ren - der: O help us to see

Al - might - y, vic - to - rious, Thy great name we praise.
Thy clouds, which are foun - tains of good - ness and love.
And with - er and per - ish, but naught chang - eth Thee.
'Tis on - ly the splen - dor of light hid - eth Thee.

Immortal, Invisible, God Only Wise
1876

Now to the King eternal, immortal, invisible, to God who alone is wise, be honor and glory forever and ever. Amen. 1 Timothy 1:17

*T*he city of Edinburgh, Scotland, with its Royal Mile and rugged hilltop castle, has produced some of Christianity's greatest hymnists: George Matheson ("O Love That Wilt Not Let Me Go"), Horatius Bonar ("I Heard the Voice of Jesus Say"), Elizabeth Celphane ("Beneath the Cross of Jesus"), and William MacKay ("Revive Us Again"), to name a few. And who but the sturdy Scotch Presbyterians could produce such a powerful hymn on the sovereign, eternal power of God as "Immortal, Invisible, God Only Wise"?

The author, Walter Chalmers Smith, was born in Aberdeen on December 5, 1824. After attending grammar school at the University of Aberdeen, he enrolled in New College, Edinburgh, and was ordained as a minister in the Free Church of Scotland in 1850. He pastored churches in several places, including the lovely Scottish village of Milnathort from 1853 to 1858.

In 1874, he became pastor of the Free High Church (Presbyterian) of Edinburgh, a charge he kept until his retirement in 1894.* Two years into his pastorate, he published a collection of hymns titled *Hymns of Christ and the Christian Life.* It was here that "Immortal, Invisible, God Only Wise" was introduced to the world.

Walter Smith was blessed with two other honors. In 1893, he was elected Moderator of the Free Church of Scotland. And in 1902, a collection of his poetry was published. His poems reflect his Scottish nature and remind us of Robert Burns. A number of them had appeared in various publications over the years, published under the pseudonyms "Orwell" and "Herman Knott." One of his best-known poems, "Glenaradale," begins:

> *There is no fire of the crackling boughs | On the hearth of our fathers,*
> *There is no lowing of brown-eyed cows | On the green meadows,*
> *Nor do the maidens whisper vows | In the still gloaming,*
> *Glenaradale.*

"Immortal, Invisible, God Only Wise" was based on 1 Timothy 1:17. It was originally published in six stanzas. When the hymn was republished in 1884, Smith made a few alterations. Today's version uses Smith's first three stanzas, and the fourth stanza is pieced together from lines in the now-discarded verses.

The powerful melody is called St. Denio based on a Welsh folk song.

---

*The beautiful building of Edinburgh's Free High Church was vacated by its members in 1934, and now serves as the library for the University of Edinburgh. It is obvious to anyone who enters the library that it was originally a church.

Softly and Tenderly

Will L. Thompson

Will L. Thompson

1. Soft - ly and ten - der - ly Je - sus is call - ing, Call - ing for
2. Why should we tar - ry when Je - sus is plead - ing, Plead - ing for
3. O for the won - der - ful love He has prom - ised, Prom - ised for

you and for me. See, on the por - tals He's wait - ing and watch - ing,
you and for me? Why should we lin - ger and heed not His mer - cies,
you and for me! Though we have sinned, He has mer - cy and par - don,

Watch - ing for you and for me. Come home, come home,
Mer - cies for you and for me? Come home, come home,
Par - don for you and for me.

Ye who are wea - ry, come home; Ear - nest - ly,

ten - der - ly Je - sus is call - ing, Call - ing, "O sin - ner, come home!"

Softly and Tenderly

1880

When Jesus heard it, He said to them, ". . . I did not come to call the righteous, but sinners, to repentance." Mark 2:17

T he author of this hymn, Will Lamartine Thompson, was born on November 7, 1847, in East Liverpool, Ohio, a small town on the Ohio River across from Kentucky. His father was a local merchant and a member of the Ohio state legislature. Will attended Mt. Union College in nearby Alliance, Ohio. His musical abilities took him on to the Boston Conservatory of Music and to Leipzig, Germany, to study with the greats.

Will was interested in writing secular and patriotic songs, but when he traveled to Cleveland to sell his music manuscripts, he was offered only twenty-five dollars. Feeling slighted, Will rolled up his music, returned to East Liverpool, and prayed about what to do next.

When his father sent him to New York on business, Will took his songs to a printer, intent on publishing and selling them himself. "My Home on the Old Ohio" and "Gathering Shells from the Sea" were hits, and Will soon became known as the "Bard of Ohio." He became a millionaire.

The young man credited the Lord with his success, and, wanting to return thanks, he dedicated himself to writing Christian songs—and Christian songs only. He established Will L. Thompson & Co. with offices in East Liverpool and Chicago, and his quartet numbers sold two million copies.

In 1880, this hymn, "Softly and Tenderly," appeared in a book entitled *Sparkling Gems, Nos. 1 and 2 Combined*, published by Thompson & Co.

Despite his success and wealth, Will was known as a simple and sincere man. He felt concerned that while famous musicians traveled to the great cities to perform before large crowds, people in the rural areas and small towns seldom had anyone to come and minister to them in like fashion. So he loaded an upright piano on his two-horse wagon and drove into the country to sing and play his own songs in small churches throughout the Midwest.

In the late 1890s, he paid a visit to evangelist D. L. Moody, who was very ill and near death. Most visitors had been turned away, but when Moody heard that Thompson was downstairs, he called for him. "Will," he said, "I would rather have written 'Softly and Tenderly Jesus Is Calling,' than anything I have been able to do in my whole life."

The Lily of the Valley

Charles W. Fry

William S. Mays

1. I have found a friend in Je-sus, He's ev-'ry-thing to me, He's the
2. He all my grief has tak-en and all my sor-rows borne, In temp-
3. He will nev-er, nev-er leave me nor yet for-sake me here, While I

fair-est of ten thou-sand to my soul; The Lil-y of the Val-ley, in
ta-tion He's my strong and might-y tow'r; I have all for Him for-sak-en and
live by faith and do His bless-ed will; A wall of fire a-bout me, I've

Lil-y of the Val-ley, the

Fine

Him a-lone I see All I need to cleanse and make me ful-ly whole.
all my i-dols torn From my heart, and now He keeps me by His pow'r.
noth-ing now to fear, From His man-na He my hun-gry soul shall fill.

Bright and Morn-ing Star, He's the fair-est of ten thou-sand to my soul.

In sor-row He's my com-fort, in trou-ble He's my stay, He
Though all the world for-sake me and Sa-tan tempt me sore, Through
Then sweep-ing up to glo-ry I'll see His bless-ed face, Where

D.S. al Fine

tells me ev-'ry care on Him to roll; He's the
Je-sus I shall safe-ly reach the goal; He's the
riv-ers of de-light shall ev-er roll; He's the

Hal - le - lu - jah!

268

The Lily of the Valley

1881

I am the rose of Sharon, and the lily of the valleys. Song of Solomon 2:1

As Christianity flourished during England's Victorian Era, great concern emerged for the orphans, the poor, the homeless, and the great masses battered by the rising Industrial Revolution. One man determined to make a difference.

William Booth, born in Nottingham in 1829, became a Christian as a teenager and instantly began winning others to Christ. He moved to London to open a pawnbroker's shop, but soon left his business to travel around as a Methodist evangelist. By 1865, his ministry was primarily focused among the poor of London's East End. Some evenings he stumbled home, haggard with fatigue, his clothes torn, and bloody bandages swathing his head where a stone had struck him.

In 1878, Booth began calling his ministry "The Salvation Army," and something about that name captured people's imagination. Men, women, and children saw their conversion as leaving their old lives behind to enlist in a new army—the Lord's army. The movement spread throughout England and around the world.

That very year, 1878, a group of Salvation Army workers sought to establish a ministry in Salisbury, about ninety miles west of London. They were treated badly, bricks and eggs flying in their direction whenever they tried to preach on the streets.

There lived in Salisbury a local builder and amateur musician named Charles Fry, an active layman in the Methodist Church. Seeing the abuse hurled at the Salvation Army workers, Charles offered, along with his three strapping sons—musicians all— to serve as bodyguards.

The next day the four Frys showed up bearing their weapons—two cornets, a trombone, and a small tuba. Between fighting off hooligans, the four drew crowds for the preachers with their music. Thus was born the first of the now-famous Salvation Army Brass Bands.

In 1881, Charles Fry wrote "The Lily of the Valley." It was published that year in the December 29th issue of the Salvation Army magazine, *War Cry*.

The next August, Charles passed away. Another verse he had written was inscribed on his grave:

> *The former things are past, and ended is the strife,*
> *I'm safe home at last! I live an endless life!*

There Shall Be Showers of Blessing

Daniel W. Whittle

James McGranahan

1. There shall be show-ers of bless-ing: This is the prom-ise of love;
2. There shall be show-ers of bless-ing: Pre-cious re-viv-ing a-gain;
3. There shall be show-ers of bless-ing: Send them up-on us, O Lord;
4. There shall be show-ers of bless-ing: O, that to-day they might fall,

There shall be sea-sons re-fresh-ing, Sent from the Sav-ior a-bove.
O-ver the hills and the val-leys, Sound of a-bun-dance of rain.
Grant to us now a re-fresh-ing, Come, and now hon-or Thy Word.
Now as to God we're con-fess-ing, Now, as on Je-sus we call!

Show - ers of bless - ing, Show-ers of bless-ing we need:
Show - ers, show-ers of bless - ing,

Mer-cy drops 'round us are fall - ing, But for the show-ers we plead.

There Shall Be Showers of Blessing

1883

I will cause showers to come down in their season; there shall be showers of blessing. Ezekiel 34:26

There Shall Be Showers of Blessing" by Major Daniel Whittle is one of those songs that, if learned in childhood, is never forgotten. Based on Ezekiel 34:26, it uplifts us with the happy assurance of God's unceasing blessing on our lives, even during our worst days.

When Howard Rutledge's plane was shot down over Vietnam, he parachuted into a little village and was immediately attacked and imprisoned. For the next seven years he endured brutal treatment. His food was little more than a bowl of pig fat. He was frequently cold, alone, and often tortured. How did he keep his sanity?

In his book *In the Presence of Mine Enemies*, Rutledge wrote, "I wanted to talk about God and Christ and the church. But in Heartbreak [his concentration camp], there was no pastor, no Sunday school teacher, no Bible, no hymnbook . . . I had completely neglected the spiritual dimension of my life. It took prison to show me how empty life is without God, and so I had to go back in my memory to those Sunday school days in Tulsa, Oklahoma. If I couldn't have a Bible and hymnbook, I would try to rebuild them in my mind.

"I tried desperately to recall . . . gospel choruses from childhood, and hymns we sang in church. The first three dozen songs were relatively easy. Every day I'd try to recall another verse or a new song. One night there was a huge thunderstorm—it was the season of the monsoon rains—and a bolt of lightning knocked out the lights and plunged the entire prison into darkness. I had been going over hymn tunes in my mind and stopped to lie down and sleep when the rains began to fall. The darkened prison echoed with wave after wave of water. Suddenly, I was humming my thirty-seventh song, one I had entirely forgotten since childhood.

> *Showers of blessing, showers of blessing we need!*
> *Mercy drops round us are falling, but for the showers we plead.*

"The enemy knew that the best way to break a man's resistance was to crush his spirit in a lonely cell," Howard wrote. "In other words, some of our POWs after solitary confinement lay down in a fetal position and died. All this talk of Scripture and hymns may seem boring to some, but it was the way we conquered our enemy and overcame the power of death around us."*

---

*Howard and Phyllis Rutledge with Mel and Lyla White, *In the Presence of Mine Enemies* (Old Tappan, NJ: Fleming H. Revell Co., 1973), excerpts taken from chapter 5.

Jesus, I Come

William T. Sleeper

George C. Stebbins

1. Out of my bond-age, sor-row, and night, Je-sus, I come; Je-sus I come.
2. Out of my shame-ful fail-ure and loss, Je-sus, I come; Je-sus, I come.
3. Out of un-rest and ar-ro-gant pride, Je-sus, I come; Je-sus, I come.
4. Out of the fear and dread of the tomb, Je-sus, I come; Je-sus I come.

In - to Thy free - dom, glad-ness, and light, Je-sus, I come to Thee.
In - to the glo - rious gain of Thy cross, Je-sus, I come to Thee.
In - to Thy bless - ed will to a - bide, Je-sus, I come to Thee.
In - to the joy and light of Thy home, Je-sus, I come to Thee.

Out of my sick-ness, in - to Thy health, Out of my want and in - to Thy wealth.
Out of earth's sor - rows in - to Thy balm, Out of life's storms and in - to Thy calm.
Out of my - self to dwell in Thy love, Out of de - spair to rap-tures a - bove,
Out of the depths of ru - in un - told, In - to the peace-ful, shel-ter-ing fold,

Out of my sin and in - to Thy - self, Je-sus, I come to Thee.
Out of dis-tress to ju - bi - lant psalm, Je-sus, I come to Thee.
Up - ward I rise on wings like a dove, Je-sus, I come to Thee.
Ev - er Thy glo-rious face to be - hold, Je-sus, I come to Thee.

272

Jesus, I Come

1887

I will exalt you, O LORD, for you lifted me out of the depths . . . Psalm 30:1 NIV

One of the best histories of the gospel song era is George Stebbins's autobiography, *Reminiscences and Gospel Hymn Stories.* Stebbins was born in the mid-1800s in New York and showed early musical prowess. At age twenty-three, he moved to Chicago, where he worked in churches and became acquainted with some of the "greats" of gospel music, such as Sankey and Bliss. In the late 1870s, D. L. Moody got hold of him, sending him into a lifetime of music evangelism.

Stebbins's first impressions of Moody are fascinating. Major Daniel Whittle had invited him to Northfield, Massachusetts, to meet Moody. That Sunday, Moody preached at the village church, asking Stebbins to lead the singing. Stebbins, a bit nervous, sat at the little organ in front of the pulpit.

As he played the organ and led the congregation, he was discomposed by a terrible wheezing noise. He described it as "a discordant sound I kept hearing during the singing, which I at first thought was caused by something wrong with the organ. I determined to ascertain if my suspicions were well founded, so when there was an interval between verses, I listened to see if there might be one of the notes of the organ sounding when it ought to be silent, and found the discords were not from that source.

"I was not long in doubt, however, for I soon heard the voice of Mr. Moody singing away as heartily as you please, with no more idea of tune or time than a child. I then learned for the first time that he was one of the unfortunates who have no sense of pitch or harmony."

Stebbins went on to work for years alongside Moody, in the process composing several of our favorite hymn tunes. Included among them are the invitation hymns "Have Thine Own Way, Lord," "Jesus Is Tenderly Calling You Home," "What Will Ye Do with Jesus?" and this one, "Jesus, I Come."

Stebbins's friend, William Sleeper, a New England home missionary and pastor, wrote the words to "Jesus, I Come." The two had previously collaborated on the hymn "Ye Must Be Born Again." Sleeper developed the words to "Jesus, I Come" and sent them to Stebbins, who put them to music. It first appeared in 1887 in *Gospel Hymns, No. 5.* with this Bible verse as a subtitle: "Deliver me, O my God" (Psalm 71:4).

He Hideth My Soul

Fanny J. Crosby

William J. Kirkpatrick

1. A won - der - ful Sav - ior is Je - sus my Lord, A
2. When clothed in His bright - ness trans - port - ed I rise To

won - der - ful Sav - ior to me; He hid - eth my soul in the
meet Him in clouds of the sky, His per - fect sal - va - tion, His

cleft of the rock, Where riv - ers of pleas - ure I see.
won - der - ful love, I'll shout with the mil - lions on high.

He hid - eth my soul in the cleft of the rock That shad - ows a

dry, thirst - y land. He hid - eth my life in the depths of His love,

And cov - ers me there with His hand, And cov - ers me there with His hand.

He Hideth My Soul

So it shall be, while My glory passes by, that I will put you in the cleft of the rock, and will cover you with My hand while I pass by. Exodus 33:22

Bouncing back—that is a quality to be cultivated because life is full of struggles. How do we become resilient? Unsinkable? Joyful amid the blows and burdens of life? This hymn tells us:

> *A wonderful Savior is Jesus my Lord, He taketh my burden away;*
> *He holdeth me up, and I shall not be moved, He giveth me strength as my day.*

This hymn by Fanny Crosby explains the author's life. During her ninety-five years, Fanny faced three incredible hardships. The first was her blindness, caused by a careless doctor when she was only six weeks of age.

The second was a less-than-ideal marriage. Fanny was teaching at the New York Institution for the Blind when a young musician named Alexander Van Alstyne joined the faculty. Fanny later recalled, "After hearing several of my poems, he became deeply interested in my work; and I after listening to his sweet strains of music became interested in him. Thus we soon grew to be very much concerned for each other . . . Love met love, and all the world was changed. We were no longer blind, for the light of love showed us where the lilies bloomed." The two were married on March 5, 1858. No one knows what happened, but years later the two drifted apart and in the end occupied separate addresses.

Fanny's deepest blow was the loss of her child. To this day, no one knows if it was a boy or a girl. Fanny seldom spoke of the infant. The child's death seems to have devastated her, and she privately bore the sadness all her life.

Yet all who knew Fanny Crosby spoke of her energy, her zest for life, her joy. One biographer said, "Even in extreme old age, she would tire out people twenty or thirty years her junior."

She said, "How long am I going to travel and lecture? Always! There is nothing that could induce me to abandon my work. It means nothing to be eighty-four years of age because I am still young! What is the use of growing old? People grow old because they are not cheerful, and cheerfulness is one of the greatest accomplishments in the world!"

Fanny Crosby lived out her song every day of her life: "He hideth my soul in the depths of His love, and covers me there with His hand."

No, Not One!

Johnson Oatman, Jr.

George C. Hugg

1. There's not a friend like the low-ly Je-sus, No, not one! No, not one!
2. No friend like Him is so high and ho-ly, No, not one! No, not one!
3. There's not an hour that He is not near us, No, not one! No, not one!
4. Did ev-er saint find this Friend for-sake Him? No, not one! No, not one!
5. Was e'er a gift like the Sav-ior giv-en? No, not one! No, not one!

None else could heal all our soul's dis-eas-es, No, not one! No, not one!
And yet no friend is so meek and low-ly, No, not one! No, not one!
No night so dark but His love can cheer us, No, not one! No, not one!
Or sin-ner find that He would not take Him? No, not one! No, not one!
Will He re-fuse us a home in heav-en? No, not one! No, not one!

Je-sus knows all a-bout our strug-gles, He will guide 'til the day is done;

There's not a friend like the low-ly Je-sus, No, not one! No, not one!

No, Not One!

<u>1895</u>

For He Himself has said, "I will never leave you nor forsake you." Hebrews 13:5

My keenest memories of this hymn involve a story my father, John Morgan, told about two churches across the road from one another in our native Tennessee mountains. The congregations had originally been one, but a split had occurred and bad feelings lingered. One evening a passerby paused between the churches to listen to their music. One of the churches was singing "Will There Be Any Stars in My Crown?" From across the road came the reply: "No, Not One! No, Not One!"

Johnson Oatman, the author of "No, Not One!" was born to Christian parents near Medford, New Jersey, on April 21, 1856. He was a child during the Civil War, and after the war he joined his father in the mercantile business. He also stood beside his father in church, for both men had good voices and enjoyed singing.

Johnson was ordained a Methodist minister as a young man, but spent most of his life working in the business world rather than pastoring. After his father's death, he moved to Mount Holly, New Jersey, where he sold insurance.

In 1892, when he was in his midthirties, Johnson began writing gospel songs. The next year failing health forced him to retire from business, and he began devoting himself to full-time songwriting.

Some sources say that he wrote 3,000 hymns; other sources put the number at 5,000. The usually reliable 1992 edition of *Handbook to the Baptist Hymnal* claims that Oatman wrote more than 7,000 texts. He was usually only paid a dollar or so per song, but he became one of the most important gospel songwriters of the turn of the century.

This song, "No, Not One!," emphasizes friendship with Christ. The Gospels call Jesus the "Friend of Sinners" (Matthew 11:19). In John 15, He told His disciples, "Greater love has no one than this, than to lay down one's life for his friends. You are My friends . . . I have called you friends" (vv. 13, 15). Jesus is a friend who "sticks closer than a brother" (Proverbs 18:24). If you're feeling lonely today, could you ever find a better, closer, wiser, stronger friend?

No, not one.*

---

*Incidentally, those who complain that today's praise and worship music is too repetitious should notice that in singing Oatman's hymn, we repeat the phrase "No, Not One" thirty times!

Open My Eyes That I May See

Clara H. Scott   Clara H. Scott

1. O-pen my eyes that I may see Glimps-es of truth Thou hast for me;
2. O-pen my ears that I may hear Voic-es of truth Thou send-est clear;
3. O-pen my mouth and let me bear Glad-ly the warm truth ev-ery-where.
4. O-pen my mind that I may read More of Thy love in word and deed.

Place in my hands the won-der-ful key That shall un-clasp and set me free.
And while the wave-notes fall on my ear, Ev-ery-thing false will dis-ap-pear.
O-pen my heart and let me pre-pare Love with Thy chil-dren thus to share.
What shall I fear while yet Thou dost lead? On-ly for light from Thee I plead.

Si-lent-ly now I wait for Thee, Read-y, my God, Thy will to see.

O-pen my eyes, il-lu-mine me, Spir-it di-vine!
O-pen my ears, il-lu-mine me, Spir-it di-vine!
O-pen my heart, il-lu-mine me, Spir-it di-vine!
O-pen my mind, il-lu-mine me, Spir-it di-vine!

Open My Eyes That I May See

1895

The LORD opens the eyes of the blind; the LORD raises those who are bowed down; the LORD loves the righteous. Psalm 146:8

Next time you sit down to read your Bible, try pausing a moment, asking God to bless your time in His Word. Two great biblical prayers teach this. The first is in 1 Samuel 3:9, where the boy Samuel was taught to pray, "Speak, Lord, for Your servant hears." That simple prayer has inspired a number of hymns, such as Frances Havergal's tender "Master, Speak! Thy Servant Heareth!"

> *Thy Master, speak! Thy servant heareth,*
> *Waiting for Thy gracious word,*
> *Longing for Thy voice that cheereth;*
> *Master! let it now be heard.**

The other biblical prayer is Psalm 119:18: "Open my eyes, that I may see wondrous things from Your law." This verse inspired Clara Scott to compose both the words and the music to "Open My Eyes That I May See" in 1895.

Clara was born in 1841, just outside Chicago. She was drawn toward music at an early age, having the privilege of attending the first musical institute of Chicago, conducted by the famous music publisher C. M. Cady.

Three years later, she became the music teacher of an all-girls' school in Iowa. In 1861, she married Henry Clay Scott and began writing songs. Some of her work came to the attention of Horatio Palmer, author of "Yield Not to Temptation." With his encouragement, she started writing in earnest, and Palmer published a number of her songs in his collections.

In 1882, she published *The Royal Anthem Book*, which holds the distinction of being the first volume of anthems ever published by a woman. In 1895, "Open My Eyes That I May See" was published and became her best-known hymn. The next year she published a book called *Truth in Song for Lovers of Truth*.

The next year, 1897, began with the excitement of another book on the way, Clara's *Short Anthems*. But that summer, as she was visiting in the Mississippi River town of Dubuque, Iowa, she climbed into a horse-drawn carriage. Something spooked the horse, sending it careening down the street at breakneck speed. Clara was thrown from the runaway buggy and killed. She was fifty-five.

---

*There is also a glorious old German hymn by Anna Sophia of Hessen-Darmstadt, published in 1658, titled "Speak, O Lord, Thy Servant Heareth." The final stanza says: "Precious Jesus, I beseech Thee, / May Thy Words take root in me. / May this gift from heav'n enrich me, / That I may bear fruit for Thee."

Will the Circle Be Unbroken?

Ada Ruth Habershon

Charles H. Gabriel

1. There are loved ones in the glo-ry, Whose dear forms you of-ten miss;
2. In the joy-ous days of child-hood, Oft they told of won-drous love,
3. You re-mem-ber songs of heav-en Which you sang with child-ish voice
4. You can pic-ture hap-py ga-th'rings Round the fire-side long a-go,

When you close your earth-ly sto-ry, Will you join them in their bliss?
Point-ed to the dy-ing Sav-ior Now they dwell with Him a-bove.
Do you love the hymns they taught you, Or are songs of earth your choice?
And you think of tear-ful part-ings, When they left you here be-low:

Will the cir-cle be un-bro-ken, By and by, Lord, by and by?

In a bet-ter home a-wait-ing, In the sky, in the sky?

Will the Circle Be Unbroken?

1908

And the heavens will praise Your wonders, O LORD; Your faithfulness also in the assembly of the saints. Psalm 89:5

ne of my choice possessions is a little black-and-white photograph taken when I was a toddler in the early 1950s. It is a picture of my father's family, standing by a Christmas tree. My dad is beside his mother, surrounded by his six brothers and sisters. I'm a tiny fellow being held in my Uncle George's arms.

I look at the picture wistfully now, for my dad, my grandmother, and all my uncles and aunts are gone; I think of that picture whenever I hear this song because it poses a poignant question. As one of the verses puts it:

> *One by one their seats were emptied,*
> *One by one they went away;*
> *Here the circle has been broken—*
> *Will it be complete one day?*

Many people consider this an Appalachian folk hymn because the Carter Family, the founding family of country music, popularized it. A. P. Carter wrote the bluegrass version sometime between 1931 and 1939, and the Carter Family's version became so well known that he is sometimes credited with composing the song.

The words, however, were actually written by a brilliant London Bible teacher named Ada Ruth Habershon, the youngest daughter of a godly doctor, S. O. Habershon. Ada was a precocious child and a tender Christian, and even as a teen she was an avid Bible student. When D. L. Moody and Ira Sankey toured England in 1884, they were so impressed with Ada, then twenty-three, they invited her to visit America and teach the Bible at Moody's Conference Center in Northfield, Massachusetts. Her lectures on the Old Testament were later published, along with a number of other books, some of which are still in print. They include *Study of the Types, Study of the Miracles, Study of the Parables, Study of the Tabernacle,* and *Types in the Old Testament.*

In 1901, when Ada was forty and suffering from an illness, she began writing poetry. Four years later, when the powerful evangelistic team of R. A. Torrey and Charles M. Alexander visited England, Alexander asked her to write some gospel songs. Within a year, she had sent him two hundred!

Ada Habershon never married, and she passed away in 1918, at the age of fifty-seven. But her books continue to be studied to this day, and her hymns are still sung around the world.

281

Rise Up, O Men of God

William P. Merrill

William H. Walter

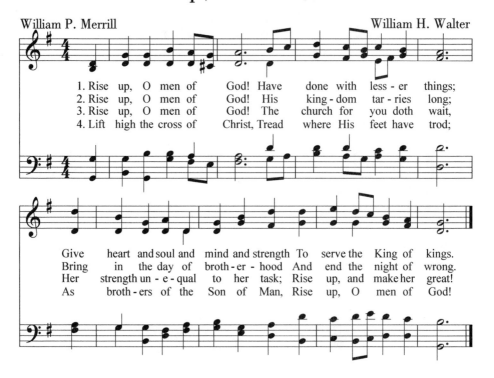

1. Rise up, O men of God! Have done with less-er things;
2. Rise up, O men of God! His king-dom tar-ries long;
3. Rise up, O men of God! The church for you doth wait,
4. Lift high the cross of Christ, Tread where His feet have trod;

Give heart and soul and mind and strength To serve the King of kings.
Bring in the day of broth-er-hood And end the night of wrong.
Her strength un-e-qual to her task; Rise up, and make her great!
As broth-ers of the Son of Man, Rise up, O men of God!

Rise Up, O Men of God
1911

Who will rise up for me against the evildoers? Who will stand up for me against the workers of iniquity? Psalm 94:16

This hymn was written somewhere on Lake Michigan, on a steamship heading toward Chicago. Its author was William Merrill, who was nearing the end of his pastorate in Chicago before moving east to assume the leadership of New York's famous Brick Church.

Merrill had come to Christ at age eleven. As a young man, he attended Rutgers College and Union Theological Seminary and was ordained into the Presbyterian ministry in 1890. He pastored churches in Philadelphia, then in Chicago.

In 1911, he became pastor of the Brick Presbyterian Church, where he remained until his retirement in 1938.* He wrote ten books and several hymns, the best known of which was "Rise Up, O Men of God."

He once explained how the hymn was written. While pastoring in Chicago, he was associated with a Presbyterian publication known as the *Continent*. Its editor, Nolan R. Best, approached him, suggesting the need for a strong hymn challenging men to rise up for Christ, especially in light of the Brotherhood Movement within the Presbyterian Church. Shortly afterward, Merrill read an article by Gerald Stanley Lee entitled "The Church of Strong Men."

"I was on one of the Lake Michigan steamers going back to Chicago for a Sunday at my own church," Merrill later wrote, "when suddenly this hymn came up, almost without conscious thought or effort." It first appeared in the *Continent* on February 16, 1911, and the next year was published in *The Pilgrim Hymnal*.

William Merrill was also instrumental in starting the Church Peace Union, now known as the Carnegie Council on Ethics and International Affairs. In 1914, the steel magnate, Andrew Carnegie, wanted to establish an organization seeking to end war forever. They planned to gather on August 1, 1914, on the shore of Lake Constance in southern Germany. But when Germany invaded Belgium, trains carrying delegates were halted and turned back and other delegates were arrested by German authorities. The arrival of the First World War crushed Carnegie's dreams of banning war; but the Church Peace Union continued its work, and William Merrill served as its first president. Today on Manhattan's Upper East Side, two adjoining townhouses, named for William Merrill, serve as headquarters for the Carnegie Council's popular public speaker series.

---

*Other famous pastor/hymnists of Brick Church include Henry Van Dyke ("Joyful, Joyful, We Adore Thee") and Maltbie Babcock ("This Is My Father's World").

Love Lifted Me

James Rowe

Howard E. Smith

1. I was sink-ing deep in sin, Far from the peace-ful shore, Ver-y deep-ly
2. All my heart to Him I give; Ev-er to Him I'll cling, In His bless-ed
3. Souls in dan-ger, look a-bove; Je-sus com-plete-ly saves. He will lift you

stained with-in, Sink-ing to rise no more. But the Mas-ter of the sea
pres-ence live, Ev-er His prais-es sing. Love so might-y and so true
by His love Out of the an-gry waves. He's the Mas-ter of the sea,

Heard my de-spair-ing cry, From the wa-ters lift-ed me-Now safe am I.
Mer-its my soul's best songs; Faith-ful, lov-ing ser-vice, too, To Him be-longs.
Bil-lows His will o-bey. He your Sav-ior wants to be, Be saved to-day.

Love lift-ed me! Love lift-ed me! When noth-ing
e-ven me, e-ven me,

else could help, Love lift-ed me;. Love lift-ed me.

Love Lifted Me
1912

My hands also I will lift up to Your commandments, which I love, and I will meditate on Your statutes. Psalm 119:48

*T*he two huddled together, working line by line, bar by bar, composing this hymn in tandem. The words were jotted down by James Rowe, and the music was hammered out at the piano by his friend, Howard E. Smith, whose hands were so twisted from arthritis that his friends wondered how he could play the piano at all. But there they were, James pacing back and forth while Howard banged away the melody. When they finished, the world had "Love Lifted Me."

James Rowe was a New Year's baby, born in Devonshire, England, on the first day of 1865. His father, John Rowe, was a copper miner. As a young man, James went to work for the Irish government, but when he was in his midtwenties, he decided to immigrate to the United States. He settled down in Albany, New York, got married, and found a job with the railroad. He later became superintendent of the Hudson River Humane Society in Albany before eventually becoming a full-time writer. He composed hymns and edited music journals for several publishers. His last years were spent in Wells, Vermont, where he supported himself by writing messages for greeting card publishers, working alongside his daughter, who was an artist.

During his lifetime, James claimed to have written more than 19,000 song texts. James Rowe and Howard Smith created "Love Lifted Me" in Saugatuck, Connecticut, in 1912, and sold the copyright to Charles Tillman, who transferred it to Robert Coleman in 1915 for one hundred dollars.

Several of James's other hymns are well-known, including "I Choose Jesus," "I Would Be Like Jesus," and "Sweeter as the Days Go By." Among his lesser-known songs is one entitled "God Holds the Future in His Hands":

Dread not the things that are ahead,
The burdens great, the sinking sands,
The thorns that o'er the path are spread,
God holds the future in His hands.

God holds the future in His hands
And every heart He understands.
On Him depend, He is your Friend,
He holds the future in His hands.

Since Jesus Came into My Heart

Rufus H. McDaniel

Charles H. Gabriel

1. What a won-der-ful change in my life has been wrought, Since Je-sus came
2. I have ceased from my wan-d'ring and go-ing a-stray, Since Je-sus came
3. I'm pos-sessed of a hope that is stead-fast and sure, Since Je-sus came
4. I shall go there to dwell in that Cit-y, I know, Since Je-sus came

in-to my heart! I have light in my soul, For which long I have sought,
in-to my heart; And my sins, which were man-y, are all washed a-way,
in-to my heart; And no dark clouds of doubt now my path-way ob-scure,
in-to my heart; And I'm hap-py, so hap-py, as on-ward I go,

Since Je-sus came in-to my heart. Since Je-sus came in-to my
Since Je-sus came in, came

heart, Since Je-sus came in-to my heart, Floods of joy o'er my
in-to my heart, Since Je-sus came in, came in-to my heart,

soul Like the sea bil-lows roll, Since Je-sus came in-to my heart.

Since Jesus Came into My Heart

1914

Let not your heart be troubled; you believe in God, believe also in Me. John 14:1

Rufus McDaniel, born in rural Ohio in 1850, was licensed to preach when he was only nineteen. He was soon afterward ordained into the Christian Church and married. His blessings were tripled by the births of Clarence, Minnie, and Herschel. Clarence, the firstborn, followed in his father's footsteps and became a minister in the Christian denomination. The daughter, Minnie, married an Ohio boy and lived nearby in Dayton. It was Herschel who broke his dad's heart by his untimely death in 1913.

After Rufus had buried his son, he realized anew that joy and contentment cannot be based on human affection or external gift. They flow from an endless relationship with our Lord Jesus Christ. Out of that experience, he wrote "Since Jesus Came into My Heart."

Rufus went on to pastor churches in southern Ohio for many years before retiring to Dayton to be near his daughter. He wrote more than a hundred hymns, but this is the only one that has endured. It, too, would have been lost to us but for the great evangelist Billy Sunday, who counted it among his favorites.

This notice appeared among the obituaries in the *Dayton Daily News* on February 13, 1940:

Rev. McDaniel, Noted Writer of Hymns, Dies.

The Rev. Rufus H. McDaniel, 90, retired Congregational Christian minister, died at 9 a.m. Tuesday at the home of the daughter, Mrs. Frank R. Liesenhoff . . . He had been ailing for some time, but had been seriously ill about one week. The Rev. McDaniel, who celebrated his ninetieth birthday on Jan. 29, composed and published more than one hundred hymns that have been used by all denominations, yet he received nothing in the way of cash remuneration. He was the guest on Ken Randolph's program over WHIO the day after he had celebrated his eighty-ninth birthday, and sang "Since Jesus Came Into My Heart," a hymn he wrote many years ago and which is now one of the best known of its type in evangelistic circles.

Living for Jesus

Thomas O. Chisholm

C. Harold Lowden

1. Liv-ing for Je - sus, a life that is true.
2. Liv-ing for Je - sus Who died in my place,
3. Liv-ing for Je - sus, wher - ev - er I am.
4. Liv-ing for Je - sus, through earth's lit - tle while,

Striv - ing to please Him in all that I do.
Bear - ing on Cal - v'ry, my sin and dis - grace.
Do - ing each du - ty in His ho - ly name.
My dear - est trea - sure, the light of His smile.

Yield - ing al - le - giance, glad heart - ed and free.
Such love con - strains me, to an - swer His call,
Will - ing to suf - fer af - flic - tion or loss.
Seek - ing the lost ones, He died to re - deem.

This is the path - way of bless - ing for me.
Fol - low His lead - ing and give Him my all.
Deem - ing each tri - al a part of my cross.
Bring - ing the wea - ry to find rest in Him.

Living for Jesus

1917

And I give them eternal life, and they shall never perish; neither shall anyone snatch them out of My hand. John 10:28

In the 1950s, a frail figure would be seen on the boardwalks of Ocean Park, New Jersey. Though modest and shy, he was warmly greeted as he ducked in and out of shops and cafés. Behind his back people would whisper. "See that man? He's the author of 'Great Is Thy Faithfulness,' 'Living for Jesus,' and 'O to Be Like Thee.'"

His name was Thomas Obadiah Chisholm, and he had settled into the Methodist Home for the Aged in Ocean Park to enjoy his sunset years.

Thomas was born in 1866, in a log cabin in Franklin, Kentucky. His education was sparse, yet at age sixteen he began teaching in the same one-room schoolhouse he had attended as a child. Four years later, the local newspaper, the *Franklin Advocate*, offered him a job.

When Thomas was twenty-seven, the founder and president of Asbury College, Dr. H. C. Morrison, came to Franklin to preach. During that revival, Thomas found Christ as his Savior, and Dr. Morrison soon asked him to become office editor and business manager for the *Pentecostal Herald*, headquartered in Louisville.

In 1903, Thomas applied for ordination in the Methodist church and accepted the pastorate of a church in Scottsville, Kentucky. He labored there a single year before his health collapsed, forcing him to move to Winona Lake, Indiana, where his family had property. There he supported himself by selling insurance.

Thomas wrote poems for personal therapy, some of which were published and came to the attention of pastor/musician C. Harold Lowden of New Jersey. One day in 1915, Lowden composed a song for the children in his church. He called it the "Sunshine Song" and used it during a Children's Day service. Two years later, as Lowden prepared to publish a songbook, he wanted to use his tune but felt the words were lacking. He contacted Thomas, asking him to compose new words.

"[Thomas] returned it to me," Lowden later wrote, "saying he didn't have the slightest idea as to the method used in writing words to music. Immediately, I sent the material back to him, telling him I believed God led me to select him."

Since Thomas couldn't read music, he asked his daughter to hum the melody over and over until he understood it enough to compose suitable words. Thus was born "Living for Jesus." It was published in Lowden's collection of hymns, *Uplifting Songs*, in 1917.

Jesus Is All the World to Me

Will L. Thompson

Will L. Thompson

1. Je-sus is all the world to me, My life, my joy, my all;
2. Je-sus is all the world to me, My Friend in tri-als sore;
3. Je-sus is all the world to me, And true to Him I'll be;
4. Je-sus is all the world to me, I want no bet-ter friend;

He is my strength from day to day, With-out Him I would fall;
I go to Him for bless-ings, and He gives them o'er and o'er.
Oh, how could I this Friend de-ny, When He's so true to me?
I trust Him now, I'll trust Him when life's fleet-ing days shall end.

When I am sad, to Him I go, No oth-er one can cheer me so;
He sends the sun-shine and the rain, He sends the har-vest's gold-en grain;
Fol-low-ing Him I know I'm right, He watch-es o'er me day and night;
Beau-ti-ful life with such a Friend, Beau-ti-ful life that has no end;

When I am sad, He makes me glad, He's my Friend.
Sun-shine and rain, har-vest of grain, He's my Friend.
Fol-low-ing Him, by day and night, He's my Friend.
E-ter-nal life, e-ter-nal joy, He's my Friend.

Jesus Is All the World to Me

1904

There is one God, the Father, of whom are all things, and we for Him; and one Lord Jesus Christ, through whom are all things, and through whom we live.
1 Corinthians 8:6

Y ou can take the boy out of the town, but you can't take the town out of the boy. Will L. Thompson grew up in East Liverpool, Ohio, in the mid-1800s. A few hours away by horseback were the grimy steel mills of Pittsburgh, Pennsylvania, but East Liverpool was known for a happier trade—its pottery. Will's parents, Josiah and Sarah Thompson, were local entrepreneurs who had helped transform the area into a pottery manufacturing region.

Will showed early signs of his dad's entrepreneurial spirit, and, being from a financially comfortable family, he was also able to devote time to his other passion—music. By age sixteen, he had already published two songs, "Liverpool Schottische" and "Darling Minnie Gray."

After musical training in Boston and Germany, Will tried to sell his music to major publishers. When they didn't offer him enough money, he published them himself. He printed copies of his most popular song, "Gathering Shells by the Sea," and sent them to minstrel organizations throughout the country. Soon "Gathering Shells" was one of America's most popular songs, just behind Stephen Foster's "Old Folks at Home" in popularity.

With his earnings, Will established his own music publishing business in Chicago, Will L. Thompson & Co. Having arrived at financial success, Will decided to devote himself exclusively to Christian music. He wrote the great invitational hymn "Softly and Tenderly," the rousing gospel song "There's a Great Day Coming," and this beautiful hymn, "Jesus Is All the World to Me."

Despite being wealthy, famous, widely traveled, and in great demand, Will never wanted to leave his hometown. He opened a music business in East Liverpool.* He became a prominent land developer and owned property throughout the town. He was a generous philanthropist, heavily supporting the local YMCA and the Emmanuel Presbyterian Church. He served as the first president of the local library. He also donated acreage for a park that bears his name to this day, stipulating that no alcoholic beverages be allowed in the park and no sports permitted there on Sundays.

He regularly hitched up his two-horse wagon on which he placed a portable piano, and he traveled throughout the area singing his hymns in churches and public squares.

Will Thompson died in 1909, but in 2002, the grateful citizens of East Liverpool inducted him into the Lou Holtz/Upper Ohio Valley Hall of Fame.

---

*The store Thompson built still stands at the corner of Fourth and Washington Streets and now houses the Pottery City Galleries Antique Mall.

In My Heart There Rings a Melody

Elton M. Roth

Elton M. Roth

1. I have a song that Je-sus gave me, It was sent from heav'n a-bove; There nev-er was a sweet-er mel-o-dy, 'Tis a mel-o-dy of love.

2. I love the Christ who died on Cal-v'ry, For He washed my sins a-way; He put with-in my heart a mel-o-dy, And I know it's there to stay.

3. 'Twill be my end-less theme in glo-ry, With the an-gels I will sing; 'Twill be a song with glo-rious har-mo-ny, When the courts of heav-en ring.

In my heart there rings a mel-o-dy, There rings a mel-o-dy with heav-en's har-mo-ny; In my heart there rings a mel-o-dy, There rings a mel-o-dy of love.

In My Heart There Rings a Melody

1923

Let the word of Christ dwell in you richly in all wisdom, teaching and admonishing one another in psalms and hymns and spiritual songs, singing with grace in your hearts to the Lord. Colossians 3:16

T he great evidence of being "Spirit-filled" is singing, according to Ephesians 5:18–19: "Be filled with the Spirit, speaking to one another in psalms and hymns and spiritual songs, singing and making melody in your heart to the Lord." That is the theme of this happy little gospel chorus with its irresistible melody. It has been a favorite for many years around the world.

Its author, Elton Menno Roth, was born during the Thanksgiving season of 1891. He led his first church choir when he was only fourteen. After attending Moody Bible Institute and Fort Wayne Bible School in his native state of Indiana, he studied music in Europe.

Roth became a singing evangelist and song leader for evangelistic meetings. In the 1930s, he formed a popular singing group called the Ecclesia Choir that performed across the country. He was also a noted instructor of music at a number of Christian schools and colleges. Los Angeles became his home in his latter years, and he passed away there at age sixty on the last day of 1951.

"I Have a Song That Jesus Gave Me" was one of the first of the one hundred or so hymns written by Elton Roth. He composed this hymn in 1923 while conducting evangelistic meetings in Texas. "One hot summer afternoon," he wrote, "I took a little walk to the cotton mill just outside of town. On my way back through the burning streets . . . I became weary with the oppressive heat, and paused at a church on the corner. The door being open, I went in.

"There were no people in the pews, no minister in the pulpit. Everything was quiet, with a lingering of the sacred presence. I walked up and down the aisle and began singing, 'In My Heart There Rings a Melody,' then hurried into the pastor's study to find some paper. I drew a staff and sketched the melody, remaining there for an hour or more to finish the song, both words and music. That evening I introduced it by having over two hundred boys and girls sing it at the open-air meeting, after which the audience joined in the singing. I was thrilled as it seemed my whole being was transformed by the song."

Jesus Is the Sweetest Name I Know

Lela B. Long

Lela B. Long

1. There have been names that I have loved to hear, But nev-er has there
2. There is no name in earth or heav'n a - bove, That we should give such
3. And some day I shall see Him face to face To thank and praise Him

been a name so dear To this heart of mine as the name di - vine, The
hon - or and such love As the bless-ed name; let us all ac-claim That
for His won-drous grace Which He gave to me when He made me free; The

pre - cious, pre-cious name of Je - sus.
won - drous, glo-rious name of Je - sus. Je - sus is the sweet-est name I
bless - ed Son of God called Je - sus.

know, And He's just the same as His love-ly name, And that's the rea-son

why I love Him so; O Je-sus is the sweet-est name I know.

Jesus Is the Sweetest Name I Know

1924

Repent, and let every one of you be baptized in the name of Jesus Christ for the remission of sins; and you shall receive the gift of the Holy Spirit. Acts 2:38

W e're indebted to gospel songwriter and historian Al Smith for the story of this hymn by Lela B. Long. Smith collected it firsthand from Dr. P. W. Philpot, who told him:

"While I was pastor of Moody Church in Chicago, I received a frantic phone call about two o'clock in the morning from the Stephens Hotel. The voice on the line pleaded with me to come, for a young lady was very ill and very disturbed. At the hotel I found a very sick young lady who from outward appearances did not have long to live. I spent some time talking with her and was eventually able to lead her to the Lord. As I left, her family thanked me and assured me they would keep me informed as to her progress. Late the next day, having not heard from them and anxious to know how she was, I phoned the hotel and was informed that they had checked out and were en route to California, which was their home. For the remaining years of my stay in Chicago, I did not again receive any communication from them. I then moved to California where I became pastor of the Church of the Open Door in Los Angeles.

"One Sunday afternoon after the service, who should come to see me but the three people I had met at the hotel in Chicago those many years before. They told me that their leaving Chicago had been so sudden they had forgotten to advise me. That past week they had seen a church ad in the paper and had come to thank me for my help and to apologize for not advising me sooner of what had transpired. The young lady especially thanked me for leading her to Christ and testified to the fact that her life had been wonderfully changed and that now she was using a special talent the Lord had given her in music, for Him. The talent was writing gospel songs. With that she handed me a manuscript of a new song saying, 'I have written this especially for you in remembrance of the day that you introduced me to the most wonderful person I have ever known.' As I opened the manuscript I saw a beautifully written song she had titled, 'Jesus Is the Sweetest Name I Know.'"*

*Condensed from Alfred B. Smith's *Treasury of Hymn Histories.*

I'll Fly Away

I'll Fly Away

1932

Therefore you now have sorrow; but I will see you again and your heart will rejoice, and your joy no one will take from you. John 16:22

I *could* tell you this old Southern hymn was written by a sacred soul on his knees with Psalm 90 open before him: "The days of our lives are seventy years; and if by reason of strength they are eighty years, yet their boast is only labor and sorrow; for it is soon cut off, and we fly away."

The truth, however, is a little plainer.

Albert E. Brumley was born on a cotton farm near Spiro, Oklahoma, in 1905. The medium of radio was gaining popularity as he grew up, and one of the most requested songs was a sad ballad called "If I Had the Wings of an Angel," which said:

> *Now if I had the wings of an angel,*
> *Over these prison walls I would fly,*
> *I'd fly to the arms of my poor darling,*
> *And there I'd be willing to die.*

One hot Oklahoma day Albert was in the fields, picking cotton and singing this song. The thought of flying away suddenly seemed quite appealing to him, and he began composing "I'll Fly Away" on the spot. "I was dreaming of flying away from that cotton field when I wrote 'I'll Fly Away,'" he later said. The middle verse of Albert's song echoes the old prison ballad when it says:

> *When the shadows of this life have grown, I'll fly away;*
> *Like a bird from prison bars has flown, I'll fly away.*

Of course, "I'll Fly Away" is about far more than escaping cotton fields. It expressed Brumley's personal hope of eternal life through Jesus Christ. It was one of a number of gospel songs he wrote during those days, but all of them were stashed away in drawers and boxes, unpublished.

Two years later, Albert married Goldie Schell, whom he met while teaching a singing school in Powell, Missouri. With her encouragement, Albert mailed "I'll Fly Away" to the Hartford Music Company. It was published in 1932, and shortly afterward, Albert was hired by Hartford for $12.50 a month. He spent thirty-four years writing for the Hartford and Stamps/Baxter companies before forming the Albert E. Brumley & Sons Music Company. In all, Albert wrote over eight hundred songs and became one of the most respected names in the development of twentieth-century Southern gospel music.

Wherever He Leads, I'll Go

B. B. McKinney   B. B. McKinney

1. "Take up Thy cross and fol-low Me," I heard my Mas-ter say; "I
2. He drew me clos-er to His side, I sought His will to know, And
3. It may be through the shad-ows dim, Or o'er the storm-y sea, I
4. My heart, my life, my all I bring To Christ who loves me so; He

gave my life to ran-som Thee, Sur-ren-der your all to-day." Wher-
in that will I now a-bide; Wher-ev-er He leads, I'll go.
take my cross and fol-low Him Wher-ev-er He lead-eth me.
is my Mas-ter, Lord, and King, Wher-ev-er He leads I'll go.

ev-er He leads, I'll go, Wher-ev-er He leads, I'll go, I'll

fol-low my Christ who loves me so; Wher-ev-er He leads, I'll go.

Words & Music: B. B. McKinney. © Copyright 1936. Published by Broadman Press. Used by permission.

Wherever He Leads, I'll Go

1936

Then he said to them all: "If anyone would come after me, he must deny himself and take up his cross daily and follow me." Luke 9:23 (NIV)

The twentieth century produced no greater hymnist than Baylus Benjamin McKinney, who wrote such classics as "Breathe on Me," "Have Faith in God," "Send a Great Revival," "Satisfied with Jesus," "Lord, Lay Some Soul Upon My Heart," "Let Others See Jesus in You," and "The Nail-Scarred Hand."

McKinney was born in Heflin, Louisiana, during the summer of 1886. He attended Southwestern Baptist Theological Seminary, and after further training in music, he returned to the seminary as a member of the music faculty. When the Great Depression sent the seminary into financial crisis, McKinney resigned to serve as assistant pastor of the Travis Avenue Baptist Church in Fort Worth.

In 1935, McKinney was named music editor for the Baptist Sunday School Board of the Southern Baptist Convention. In January of the following year, he traveled to Clanton, Alabama, to participate in the Alabama Sunday School Convention, where he led the music. The featured speaker at the meetings was his good friend, R. S. Jones, missionary to Brazil. Late one afternoon as the two men had supper together, Jones told McKinney that the doctors were forbidding him from returning to Brazil. His health wouldn't allow it.

McKinney's heart went out to his friend, and he asked if Jones had any idea what he'd do now. "I don't know," said Jones, "but wherever He leads I'll go." It was a sentence that lingered in McKinney's mind. Returning to his hotel, McKinney sat down and wrote the words and music of this hymn before leaving for the convention session that night. After Jones had preached, McKinney told the audience of their earlier conversation, and handing a copy of the music to the organist, he sang it as a solo for the first time.

> *Wherever He leads, I'll go,*
> *Wherever He leads I'll go;*
> *I'll follow my Christ who loves me so;*
> *Wherever He leads I'll go.*

For the next several years, McKinney traveled widely among Southern Baptists, promoting the ministry of Christian music and leading singing in churches and conventions. On Sunday, September 7, 1952, McKinney left a conference in Ridgecrest, North Carolina, heading for Gatlinburg, Tennessee. Near Bryson City, North Carolina, he was killed in a car wreck.

He left behind a wife, two sons, several brothers, and a legacy of hundreds of hymns.

Heaven Came Down

John W. Peterson

John W. Peterson

1. O what a won-der-ful, won-der-ful day, Day I will nev-er for-
get; Af-ter I'd wan-dered in dark-ness a-way, Je-sus, my
Sav-ior I met. O what a ten-der, com-pas-sion-ate friend,
He met the need of my heart; Shad-ows dis-pel-ling, with
joy I am tell-ing, He made all the dark-ness de-part!

2. Born of the Spir-it with life from a-bove In-to God's fam-ily di-
vine, Jus-ti-fied ful-ly thro' Cal-va-ry's love, O what a
stand-ing is mine! And the trans-ac-tion so quick-ly was made,
When as a sin-ner I came, Took of the of-fer, of
grace He did prof-fer, He saved me, O praise His dear name!

3. Now I've a hope that will sure-ly en-dure Af-ter the pass-ing of
time; I have a fu-ture in heav-en for sure, There in those
man-sions sub-lime. And it's be-cause of that won-der-ful day
When at the cross I be-lieved; Rich-es e-ter-nal and
bless-ings su-per-nal, From His pre-cious hand I re-ceived.

Heaven Came Down

1961

The heavens declare His righteousness, and all the peoples see His glory.
Psalm 97:6

As a teenager, John W. Peterson dreamed of being a singer and soloist. He often sang on local radio programs and in churches. "Only in singing did I feel competent and confident," he wrote. "Here was at least one place where I could excel. I knew it, and I made the most of it."

One summer John got a job in a factory, earning fifteen cents an hour at a machine making canvas for wheat binders. The machines were so noisy he sang at the top of his lungs, hours on end, making up melodies and imagining he was on stage.

John realized too late that he was ruining his voice. "I put such a terrific strain on my faltering voice," he wrote, "through overuse and inexperience that I damaged it beyond repair. When I realized fully what had happened, that my voice would never again be beautiful, I suffered such an emotional shock that it took months before I recovered."

Looking back now, John is grateful. "If that had not happened, I might never have developed as a writer," he wrote. "With my voice damaged, I turned more and more to writing, and that talent was allowed to emerge and develop. What at first seemed a tragedy was used for good, and the course of my life began to take shape."

Today John W. Peterson is called the "Dean of Modern Hymn Writers." He's the author of such favorites as "So Send I You," "It Took a Miracle," "Surely Goodness and Mercy," "Jesus Led Me All the Way," "No One Understands Like Jesus," and "I Believe in Miracles."

"Heaven Came Down," one of John's most popular compositions, was written during the summer of 1961. He was ministering at Montrose Bible Conference Grounds in Montrose, Pennsylvania. During one of the sessions, an opportunity was given for people to share a word of testimony. A man known as "Old Jim" rose to his feet and told of how he had come to Christ. "It seemed like Heaven came down and glory filled my soul," he said.

"Right away I sensed that it would be a fine title for a song," John wrote, "so I wrote it down and later in the week completed the song. It became a favorite almost immediately."*

CHORUS:

Heaven came down and glory filled my soul (filled my soul),
When at the cross the Savior made me whole (made me whole);
My sins were washed away and my night turned to day,
Heaven came down and glory filled my soul (filled my soul)!

---

*Adapted from *The Miracle Goes On* by John W. Peterson with Richard Engquist (Grand Rapids: Zondervan, 1976), 71–72.

Alphabetical by Title

Alphabetical by Author/Songwriter

Grant, Robert
 O Worship the King, 170–71

Habershon, Ada Ruth
 Will the Circle Be Unbroken?, 280–81
Hall, Elvina M.
 Jesus Paid It All, 72–73
Hanby, Benjamin R.
 Who Is He in Yonder Stall?, 50–51
Handel, George Frideric
 Hallelujah Chorus, 12–13
Hankey, A. Katherine
 I Love to Tell the Story, 92–93
Havergal, Frances R.
 Take My Life and Let It Be, 206–7
Hawks, Annie S.
 I Need Thee Every Hour, 198–99
Heber, Reginald
 Holy, Holy, Holy! Lord God Almighty,
  168–69
Hewitt, Eliza E.
 When We All Get to Heaven, 224–25
Hoffman, Elisha A.
 Are You Washed in the Blood?, 104–5
 Leaning on the Everlasting Arms,
  214–15
Holland, Josiah G.
 There's a Song in the Air, 54–55
Hopkins, John H., Jr.
 We Three Kings of Orient Are, 38–39
Howe, Julia Ward
 Battle Hymn of the Republic, 130–31

Jones, Lewis E.
 There Is Power in the Blood, 78–79

Ken, Thomas
 Praise God, from Whom All Blessings
  Flow, 110–11
Key, Francis Scott
 The Star-Spangled Banner, 126–27

Lemmel, Helen H.
 Turn Your Eyes Upon Jesus, 234–35
Long, Lela B.
 Jesus Is the Sweetest Name I Know,
  294–95
Longfellow, Henry Wadsworth
 I Heard the Bells on Christmas Day,
  46–47
Lowry, Robert
 Christ Arose!, 98–99

I Need Thee Every Hour, 198–99
Nothing but the Blood, 102–3
Shall We Gather at the River?, 188–89
Luther, Martin
 A Mighty Fortress Is Our God, 142–43
 From Heaven Above to Earth I Come,
  2–3
Lyte, Henry F.
 Abide with Me, 178–79

Martin, Civilla D.
 His Eye Is on the Sparrow, 228–29
McAfee, Cleland B.
 Near to the Heart of God, 226–27
McDaniel, Rufus H.
 Since Jesus Came into My Heart,
  286–87
McKinney, B. B.
 Wherever He Leads, I'll Go, 298–99
Mentzer, Johann
 O That I Had a Thousand Voices,
  238–39
Merrill, William P.
 Rise Up, O Men of God, 282–83
Mieir, Audrey
 His Name Is Wonderful, 84–85
Miles, C. Austin
 In the Garden, 80–81
Miller, Rhea F.
 I'd Rather Have Jesus, 232–33
Mohr, Joseph
 Silent Night, 20–21
Montgomery, James
 Angels, from the Realms of Glory,
  18–19
Morgan, Robert J.
 Jesus Christ Is Born Today!, 60–61
Mote, Edward
 The Solid Rock, 172–73

Neale, John M.
 Good King Wenceslas, 32–33
 O Come, O Come, Emmanuel, 30–31
Neander, Joachim
 Praise Ye the Lord, the Almighty,
  148–49
Newell, William R.
 At Calvary, 76–77
Newton, John
 Amazing Grace, 162–63

First Line of Hymn